THE RUSSIAN REVOLUTIONARY EMIGRES,
1825–1870

THE JOHNS HOPKINS UNIVERSITY STUDIES IN HISTORICAL
AND POLITICAL SCIENCE   104TH SERIES (1986)

THE RUSSIAN REVOLUTIONARY EMIGRES 1825–1870

Martin A. Miller

THE JOHNS HOPKINS UNIVERSITY PRESS

Baltimore and London

*This book has been brought to publication with
the generous assistance of the Andrew W. Mellon Foundation.*

The Johns Hopkins University Press
701 West 40th Street
Baltimore, Maryland 21211
The Johns Hopkins Press Ltd., London

The poem on page vii is from Ezra Pound, *Personae.* Copyright 1926 by
Ezra Pound. Reprinted by permission of New Directions Publishing
Corporation (New York) and Faber and Faber Ltd. (England).

The paper used in this publication meets the minimum requirements of
American National Standard for Information Sciences—Permanence of
Paper for Printed Library Materials, ANSI Z39.48-1984.

LIBRARY OF CONGRESS CATALOGING-IN-PUBLICATION DATA

Miller, Martin A. (Martin Alan), 1938–
The Russian revolutionary émigrés, 1825–1870.
(The Johns Hopkins University studies in historical
and political science ; 104th ser., 2)
Bibliography: p.
Includes index.
1. Russians—Foreign countries—Political activity.   2. Soviet Union—
Politics and government—19th century.   I. Title.   II. Series.
DK215.M53   1986   947'.07   86-2715
ISBN 0-8018-3303-5 (alk. paper)

To Ylana, Joshua, and Zina

I have seen the dawn mist
Move in the yellow grain
I have seen the daubed purple sunset;
You may kill me, but I do not accede,
You may ignore me, you may keep me in exile,
You may assail me with negations,
or you may keep me awhile, well hidden;
But I am after you and before you,
And above all, I do not accede.

EZRA POUND, "From Chebar"

Contents

Acknowledgments

This study could not have been completed without the splendid cooperation of a number of archivists and librarians who helped me locate some very difficult source materials. In particular, I wish to thank the staffs of the Lenin Library, the Central State Archive of the October Revolution, and the Central State Archive for Literature and Art, who were extremely generous with their busy schedules during my stay in Moscow. I am also grateful to the staffs of the Hoover Institution, Columbia University's Butler Library, and Duke University's Perkins Library. The collections of nineteenth-century Russian émigré journals and newspapers at the Collindale branch of the British Libraries in London and at the Bibliothèque Documentation Internationale Contemporaine on the Nanterre campus of the University of Paris richly supplement the collections in the Soviet Union. The Archives Nationales also should be mentioned, especially for the material on the Russian émigrés in the Paris police files. My thanks to the cooperative staffs of these institutions as well for facilitating my work there.

Earlier drafts of this book were read by Leopold Haimson, Jonathan Sanders, Victor Ripp, and Ylana Miller. In addition, Henry Tom, Senior Social Sciences Editor at Hopkins, gave the entire manuscript a careful and critical reading which raised many vital issues. The revisions I made as a result of these readings have unquestionably improved this book. I am indebted to each of these individuals for their help; needless to say, none of them is responsible for any problems which remain. Finally, for an expert job of typing the manuscript, I wish to express my gratitude to Thelma Kithcart and Dorothy Sapp at Duke.

Financial support for this study was indispensable. I am especially grateful to the National Endowment for the Humanities and the Duke University Research Council for their aid. A grant from the International Research and Exchanges Board made my trip to the Soviet Union possible.

Much of this book was written at the W. Averill Harriman Institute for Advanced Study of the Soviet Union, Columbia University, during several extended visits to New York as a visiting Senior Fellow. I wish to thank my colleagues for their stimulating discussions about my work, and the staff of the Institute for assistance that facilitated my research and writing.

I have utilized the Library of Congress Slavic transliteration system, with exceptions for names already familiar in English (such as Nicholas I and Dostoevsky). Regarding dating, since most of the materials cited in this study were written in Western Europe, I have used the Gregorian calendar for these; however, for the materials produced within the Russian Empire, I have retained the Julian calendar dates, which were twelve days behind the Gregorian calendar during the nineteenth century.

I

THE FIRST GENERATION

In all of Europe, I, with my Russian
anguish, was the only free man.

DOSTOEVSKY

The World of Emigration
in Nineteenth-Century Europe

Emigration as a Problem of Historical Investigation

The presence of émigrés from Russia in the capitals of Western Europe has been a source of continual fascination for over a century. Vivid representations of these escapees from tsarist oppression in the years prior to World War I have appeared in literature, in journalistic reportage, and in political discussions in every country in which they resided. The Russian revolutionary émigré has furnished the world with a special prototype—the fiercely committed intellectual who lives abroad for the express purpose of preparing himself for the revolution he seeks at home. The fanatics in the novels of Dostoevsky and Conrad left indelible impressions on many minds, echoes of which can be found in numerous empathic contemporary accounts such as the following:

We recognize at once a man for whom the outside world scarcely exists, the dreamer who sees not forms, but problems, the inveterate bookworm who daily escapes only by miracles from the snares that carts and omnibuses lay for his absent mindedness. . . . His life is an exposition of principles or a perpetual discussion, and all the time we spend with him he is theorizing, comparing dates and events, describing a skeleton Russia wherein there seems to be neither men, women, nor children, but only an abstract population of problems.[1]

Initial efforts by Europeans to try to comprehend the motivation and mentality of these uninvited political guests began, for the most part, in the 1860s, when the word *nihilism* was used as a comprehensive descriptive term for all Russian émigrés who were at odds with the Russian autocracy.[2] During the 1870s, when the revolutionary movement in Russia was gathering momentum and the numbers of Russian political exiles increased markedly in the cities of Western Europe, the imagery of the Russian emigration assumed almost mythic proportions. Europeans observed with great attention the spread of closed communities of these émigrés, who insisted upon speaking their own language, living in their own neighborhoods, meeting at specially designated cafés and restaurants, and operating their own publications intended for use in the homeland left behind. Abroad, the émigrés refused the possibilities of assimilation and, instead, as a recent commentator has put it, reestablished "the same cadres of militant activism" they had been forced to abandon in Russia.[3] The response of the European governments to this new political subculture varied, but their concern over the émigrés was evident. In France and England, police agents were assigned to watch the activities of the Russian émigrés closely.[4] In addition, pressure from the Russian government to extradite the émigrés was a constant threat.

The importance of the emigration and its continuity as a force for change in Russian history was recognized by Russian revolutionaries at this time. Prior to the arrival of Lenin in Europe, Russian émigrés were already at work on the adaption of Marxist theory for use as a strategy for the transformation of Russia. Moreover, the émigrés were conscious of the foundation for revolutionary activity which had been solidified by an earlier generation of Russian émigrés. According to one source writing about this period,

By necessity, all work which arose in connection with social democracy was concentrated at first on the intelligentsia, and the intelligentsia first and foremost, was abroad, studying in advanced foreign schools. Here in the 1880s, in Geneva and in Zurich, small circles gathered around Plekhanov, Akselrod and Zasulich, just as they had grouped about Bakunin and Lavrov in the 1870s. In this way, young people gradually became imbued with the ideas of contemporary socialism and from that point, upon returning to the homeland, they began to disseminate these ideas little by little among Russian student youth.[5]

Few would dispute the fact that the major theorists of revolutionary populism were émigrés—Bakunin, Herzen, and Lavrov were all abroad when they formulated their concepts of an agrarian socialist revolution in Russia involving an aroused and disaffected peasantry. Similarly, it is understood that Russian Marxism was forged abroad by émigrés from Plekhanov through Lenin and Trotsky, just as Russian anarchism was developed by Bakunin and Kropotkin during their émigré years. What has not been fully appreciated, however, is the overall context in which this work was done. The Russian emigration throughout the nineteenth century took on a life of its own. It emerged as a kind of society-in-exile, a second Russia abroad. The emigration became the repository of the dreams of thousands of people who believed that a day would some-day dawn when the tsarist autocracy would be abolished and re-placed by a more humane system of rule. It also became the focus of a violent battle between state and society for control of the political destiny of Russia. As the Russian émigré communities expanded and grew more committed to the eventual destruction of the tsarist regime, the Russian government took the unprecedented step of creating a foreign branch of the political police. From the offices of the Okhrana headquarters in Paris, Russian agents infiltrated émi-gré meetings, gathered reams of information on their tactics and plans, and sent back reports to the central government in St. Petersburg.

The Russian emigration was a distinct phenomenon that pro-foundly influenced developments at home. It acted as a testing ground, as an experimental laboratory for new ideas and strategies for radical change in Russia which could not possibly be developed within the restrictive borders of the empire. Especially during the second half of the nineteenth century, the emigration became an alternative for many Russians committed to social and political change. For these people, there had previously been only two choices: they could renounce radical political solutions in order to compromise with the regime and resume a legal life, or they could face capture and life in Siberian exile after the hardships of an underground existence. There was now a new possibility—to flee abroad and continue to work there for the revolutionary future. This book is an inquiry into the origins of this alternative, the formation of the Russian emigration.

The materials used in this study are largely archival sources from the Soviet Union and primary published sources, many of which have not been previously studied in this framework.[6] Chronologically, the book deals with the period between 1825, when Nikolai Turgenev was declared the first "émigré" by an act of the Russian government, and 1870, the year of Alexander Herzen's death and the eve of the emergence of the populist revolutionary movement which significantly altered the composition, numbers, and guiding ideas of the Russian emigration. Methodologically, this book is based on a series of biographical chapters on the pioneering émigrés—the first two generations of Russians abroad—who are analyzed within the overall context of a social movement in formation.

Before moving on to a discussion of the early Russian émigré communities in Western Europe, it will be useful first to examine the word *émigré* in a broader historical context. Some questions come immediately to mind. What is the difference between an émigré and an immigrant? When does the individual cease to be the former and begin to assume the status of the latter? How is the émigré distinguished from the refugee, the expatriate, the exile, or the so-called *internal émigré,* a term which was popularized (if not actually invented) by Trotsky during the 1920s? These terms are not mutually synonymous, although they generally have been used that way rather carelessly. The primary thread which runs through all these terms is the notion of an individual's (or group's) separation from his (its) country of national origin. This separation may be one or more of four kinds: physical, legal, ideological, or psychological. Furthermore, the separation may be either voluntary or compulsory, and it may be as much a question of self-protection as an act of government.

The term *refugee* implies a legal category of people who have been forced to abandon their homeland against their will for a variety of reasons. These include natural disasters, political or religious persecution, and economic poverty. Villagers who are caught in war zones and are forced to move to another country are considered refugees. Refugees include persons displaced during World War II and the masses of poor people from Eastern Europe who sought refuge in England or America.[7] The word itself (*réfugié*) seems to have originated in 1685 to describe the French Huguenots seeking asylum in England after the Revocation of the Edict of Nantes. Refugees are considered helpless and in need; efforts are usually made to resettle them. If these efforts are successful, the refugee becomes an immigrant, that is, a member of an uprooted social group whose expressed purpose is to become absorbed into the framework of a new homeland. It is not the length of time one resides abroad that determines this distinction, but rather the host country's legal definitions on the one hand, and the intent or perception of the individual or group on the other. Many writers, such as Nabokov, have lived outside their native land for decades, but have never considered themselves immigrants and have never truly assimilated.

An *expatriate* is the opposite of the refugee. He is abroad entirely by his own choice, and generally does not belong to a large exile constituency. He tends to be an isolated, apolitical intellectual. The classic expatriate is the individual writer or artist who, like James Joyce, has forsaken his homeland in order to pursue his craft and his life style in a manner judged more satisfying and freer, or at least less constraining, than his former way of life. He ordinarily has no desire to return home, though—and this is crucial—legally he may do so if he wishes.

The *exile*, by contrast, cannot return home, though he may devote his entire life to this end. He has been driven from his homeland for political or ideological (national, religious, racial, etc.) reasons, and refuses to resettle anywhere permanently.

All of these categories have varying relationships to the host society. The refugee-cum-immigrant respects the host society and willingly adopts its language and values during the transition. The expatriate tolerates the host culture but need not be dependent upon it for nourishment. The exile avoids the host society as completely as possible. His mission is to work to alter conditions in his homeland so that he may return without compromising his convictions.

The term *émigré* is a specific subcategory of the exile grouping. *Internal émigré* is applied almost exclusively to certain individuals in the Soviet Union who strongly disagree with the existing regime but who have chosen to remain. (In some cases, they have no choice.) They are, therefore, isolated—or, to use my earlier phrase —separated by the regime from their homeland while physically still within its boundaries. Despite strict limitations on their actions, they are permitted to function *as though* conditions were normal. The internal émigré is "a man who has taught himself to behave as if he had already crossed a frontier while refusing to leave his house."[8] Similarly, *émigré* as a political term has a specificity that refers to two revolutionary dates: 1789 and 1917. In the earlier instance, the émigrés were Royalists who fled France in the wake of the collapse of the Old Regime, particularly during the Jacobin Terror.[9] In the second case, the classification refers to a longer time period punctuated on either side by 1917. Before the revolution, Russian émigrés were primarily antitsarist radical *intelligenty,* whereas in the postrevolutionary era, emigration from Russia has been composed of a variety of anti-Bolshevik groupings, from monarchist to anarchist in ideology. The factor of ideology is perhaps the most significant one in both of these groups in defining the nature of the separation of the individual émigré from his homeland.

In addition, the term *émigré* has been used to refer to the political exiles of other revolutionary upheavals. The Poles who fled their homeland after the victory of Russian troops in 1831 were followed by émigrés who appeared in European countries as part of resistance movements opposed to regimes in their native lands, especially in the aftermath of the revolutionary events of 1848.[10]

The émigrés have always been in a precarious position, wherever they have decided to settle. They are deprived of any legal protection, have no claims to the civic rights accorded members of their host society, and find access to employment extremely difficult. They are defenseless and unable to make demands on their own behalf because they have been outlawed by their country of origin and refuse to be assimilated into the society in which they live. In short, émigrés are stateless and without citizenship anywhere. Moreover, because of their political commitments, which remain their primary concern, they are regarded with great suspicion by European government officials, who frequently see them as a potential threat to the stability of their own regimes. In an age when nation-states were demanding political loyalty as a defining feature of citizenship, no social group was more suspect than the émigrés, who were becoming fiercely committed to ideologies that challenged the legitimacy of those governments. Thus, even in countries where they were permitted to live, they were under constant surveillance by local police.[11]

The psychology and sociology of the émigré remain to be conceptualized by social scientists, but a few characteristics of the émigré mentality seem to be generally agreed upon in the existing literature. As a result of the physical transition and resettlement process, a number of problems inevitably arise, albeit at different levels of intensity and awareness in each individual case. Insecurities, anxieties, and frustrations emerge in the transition process as the émigré realizes the finality of his decision to abandon his homeland and confronts for the first time the difficulties of coping with the social, cultural, economic, and political forces in the new society. Familiarity with the new language, a network of waiting comrades, and a strong sense of purpose all help to mute these anxieties, but the change nevertheless affects the migrating émigré in many ways, as we shall see shortly in the case of the Russian emigration.[12]

For any émigré, the shift from homeland to foreign land involves a challenge to his relationship to political authority, economic system, social structure, and cultural values. In most cases, these involvements, commitments, and familiarities are disrupted. Once abroad, the émigré must either find a way to continue his former pursuits and uphold his values or face the inevitability of assimilation and acculturation. Isolation from the culture and politics of the homeland may result in estrangment, alienation, and dysfunctionalism if the émigré does not learn to fuse important aspects of his former world with the new culture and politics of his host society and government. In some instances, when host society influences are overwhelming or the individual is particularly vulnerable, a recasting of goals and strategies takes place. The émigré's chief political objective is to utilize the resources of his host society as a vehicle toward the realization of his goal of working for the reconstruction of his homeland and its transformation into a new order to which he can return. The degree to which the theories developed in emigration are compatible with the forces of change at work in the homeland is one of the important indicators of the survival and perhaps the success of the émigrés. One of the great trends in the Russian emigration during the nineteenth century was the continual effort to bring together theory abroad and reality at home.

A significant reflection of the ability of the émigré to function meaningfully abroad can be seen in the effort to establish an institutional structure to carry out the tactics of radical change similar to what was left behind. Russian émigrés, for example, found that they had to set up (or re-create) a revolutionary organization that resembled the formal structure of their underground existence in tsarist Russia. Ultimately, a "colony" of radical émigrés developed, with individuals forming into groups professing similar goals. In some cases, these activities and organizations were based on Western models more than they were on prior Russian ones, and in other instances, a combination of the two emerged. The émigrés generally were not seeking to reevaluate their fundamental loyalties and commitments but were looking for new and freer means to realize already formulated goals. The colony had to resist efforts that threatened to disturb or disrupt its unity and vitality. A social substructure was therefore created abroad which eased the pain of loss and the terror of the unfamiliarity of the new milieu within which the new organizational activities were set in motion.

Language is of the utmost importance to the émigré. It is the medium of communication for ideals, strategy, and tactics. Because of the importance of language, ideology achieved a transcendent significance for émigrés in the nineteenth century. Language permitted the émigré to continue his revolutionary work abroad and gave him both an identity and a career. Revolutionary journalism, as we know, became the most prevalent form of expression for the émigrés at this time. Utilizing the written word to aid the revolutionary cause while abroad was a way of overcoming what one writer on this subject has called "emigration as a state of suspension."

Emigration itself was difficult to sustain, and in many cases led to repatriation (the "renegades" of the Russian emigration such as Kelsiev and, later, Tikhomirov, for example) or assimilation as immigrants. Through language and ideology, many émigrés were able to hold on to what frequently had become obsolete political beliefs, while others formulated notions that were in advance of their time. At some point, however, the choice of returning to Russia or assimilating abroad had to be confronted by every émigré.[13]

The Beginnings of the Emigré Communities in Western Europe

The history of exile and emigration has yet to be written, but the evidence indicates that there is a great deal of material to analyze. Exile has existed as long as recorded history. According to one authority, the first known exile occurred two thousand years ago when, as Sinuhe wrote in a document describing his situation, "I tore myself by force from the soil upon which I stood."[14] In the ancient world, ostracism and banishment were common; Ovid's well-known exile remains one of the most familiar instances from this era. The names of prominent exiles in history, especially those who made their lasting contributions while abroad, is indeed a long and distinguished list. Dante, Machiavelli, Erasmus, Grotius, Voltaire, and Rousseau are among the most significant prior to the nineteenth century.[15] During the nineteenth century, Etienne Cabet, Louis Kossuth, Giuseppi Mazzini, Karl Marx, and Alexander Herzen all achieved fame as political figures in Western Europe away from their homelands, and established the networks and modes of operation for later generations of émigrés.

The nineteenth century was *the* century of exile and emigration until it was surpassed by the events of the twentieth century. Not only were there increasing numbers of individual exiles, but there were also groups and organizations of exiles completely dedicated to the transformation of their homelands. They were, as a recent historian has put it, committed to "a continuation of war by other means."[16] Earlier examples of exiled groups include the Marian exiles, the Puritans, the Huguenots, the Royalists from Cromwellian England, and the aristocratic exiles from revolutionary France in the 1790s, but it was not until the nineteenth century that nationalist and socialist emigrations developed with permanent organizations designed to resist and transform the existing governments in their homelands. The reason for this development at this time was, primarily, the conjuncture of events involving the formation or redefinition of nation-states and multinational empires. Increased emphasis was being placed on *national* characteristics of peoples and countries. At this historical moment, émigrés in the modern sense came into existence as transnational or revolutionary nationalist figures, exiled from their homelands and compelled to survive in the context of an alien nationality. This sense of national consciousness abroad leaps from the pages of every émigré memoirist in this period. Each nationality abroad portrayed the surrounding world in terms of nationalist stereotypes which, had they been within their own borders, would have been the source of irreparable division. Abroad, facing similar experiences of discomfort, alienation, and sometimes harassment, they learned to transcend their own nationality identities to a degree. Without this process, international movements of socialists, for example, would have been impossible. Still, it is important to keep in mind that the emigrations remained largely separate groups organized along nationality lines, committed to their individual causes and to visions of a desired future reconciliation in their respective homelands.

The first large modern emigration originated in Italy. The unsuccesful revolutions in Naples (1820), Piedmont (1821), and the Central Provinces (1831) sent the first wave of Italian émigrés to London, which, in the course of the century, was to become one of the major centers for political exiles. Many of these Italians returned to their homeland to fight in the 1848 revolutions, only to flee into exile once again after the defeats of the following year. The treatment of the Italians in London varies with the account, but there was a certain fascination in educated society with these persecuted figures from abroad who were romanticized to some extent by wealthy English families sympathetic to the goals of national independence. Balls, parties, and dinners were given in their honor, and certain Whig institutions such as Holland House and Lansdowne House were known to be especially hospitable to the Italian émigrés. The family of William Henry Ashurst is frequently cited as an example of this hospitality and sympathy for the Italian cause, largely because their most illustrious guest and friend among the émigrés they welcomed was Mazzini.[17]

Moreover, Mazzini provided the model for all future revolutionary émigré organizations with his Young Italy group, which he formed in exile in 1831. The international body based on this organization was established in Bern by Mazzini three years later under the name of Young Europe. Delegations from several countries in Europe were invited to join in the growing world-wide structure for radical and nationalist transformation. Mazzini moved to London in 1837 and continued his work there. We shall note Mazzini's specific influence upon Alexander Herzen shortly, but it is hardly an exaggeration to state that, particularly in the years prior to 1848, no one within the emerging émigré communities in Western Europe surpassed Mazzini's stature.[18]

Another important exile community during the period prior to the 1848 revolutions was the German emigration. In addition to the currents of national independence which so animated the Italian émigrés, the Germans developed more radical socialist themes and were more closely in touch with the growing working-class protest movements in Switzerland and France. German émigré organizations can be traced to the early 1830s, when the German People's Union and the Mazzini-oriented Young Germany were established. In 1834, Theodor Schuster, a German émigré in Paris, formed the League of Outlaws, which has been called "the first international organization of social revolutionaries."[19] During the 1840s, many German émigrés moved to London, where émigrés from other countries, including Russia, were later to congregate. There they organized new groups under the leadership of Karl Schapper, Wilhelm Weitling, and others. Once in London, the Germans began to cooperate with the Chartist movement and eventually created the foundation for the socialist international organizations that developed later. At this time also, it should be noted, the German Workers' League was organized in Brussels by Wilhelm Wolff; he established contact there with another German émigré, Karl Marx, who together with Friedrich Engels had recently set up the Communist League in Brussels.[20]

Of all the exile nationality groups abroad at this time, the largest and most active by far was the Polish emigration. Beginning with the 1830 uprising against the Russians, Poles fled in increasing numbers to Paris, Brussels, and London, where they set up networks and organizations that were to act as models for the Russian émigrés who arrived later. Estimates from official data show that there were between 8,000 and 10,000 Poles abroad in the years of "the great emigration."[21] The Polish émigrés were divided into many factions, with varying notions of nationalism and socialism in militant competition. Although this factionalism was true for all of the émigré communities, the problem was magnified in the case of the Poles because of their vast numbers. Among the most important groups, the Polish Democratic Society, formed in 1832, was the largest of the early organizations of émigré Poles. Three years later, a more radical group was formed, the Polish People, led by Stanislaw Worcell, who later was to become a close friend of Alexander Herzen's. Another important figure in the Polish emigration was the romantic poet Adam Mickiewicz, who also befriended Herzen. The Polish émigrés functioned at their zenith in the period between 1830 and 1848. After the 1848 revolution and through the revolt in Poland in 1863, the Polish emigration declined in numbers and influence, according to a leading historian of this movement.[22] It is of interest for comparative purposes to keep in mind that the Polish and Russian emigrations moved at counterpoint in the 1850s and 1860s. At the historical moment when the Polish emigration was in decline and losing its influence, the Russian emigration was just starting its ascent, which would continue throughout the century and climax in 1917, when the émigrés returned home to witness the problems and prospects of their ultimate dream—a revolutionary society.

The period following the defeat of the 1848 revolutions was a watershed not only for the governments of Europe but for the émigré communities as well. For the émigrés, the despair over these failures culminated when Louis Napoleon seized control of France and established the Second Empire. Their mood was perhaps best expressed by Proudhon, who was at the time already in the Sainte-Pelagie prison: "On December 2, 1851, a great outrage was committed, in circumstances that left an indelible stain on the morality of our nation."[23] A significant change took place among the revolutionary exiles of Europe in the wake of Louis Napoleon's coup d'état. At first there was confusion, demoralization, and disorientation. "Socialists, communists, Jacobins, and Red Republicans were reduced to the status of journalists without newspapers, speakers without rostrums, politicians without parties, and patriots without a country."[24] This situation quickly changed, however, as new forms of radical thought and action evolved. As governments reconsolidated their authority, radical émigrés were forced to migrate en masse once more, this time to London, which had already become the new center of émigré politics. The émigrés refused to renounce their causes, but did change their strategy significantly. The nationalism of the pre-1848 era was replaced by a new internationalism, just as the republicanism of that earlier period, defined by Mazzini and Ledru-Rollin, had been overtaken by new and more radical notions of proletarian and socialist societies of the future. While the émigrés established new organizations dedicated to the destruction of the existing order, governments on the Continent increased their police forces and their methods of surveillance of the activities of the émigrés in London. Often, reports of invasions by émigré forces which appeared in smuggled pamphlets and leaflets were believed literally by government officials.[25]

The first major organization set up by the émigrés after the 1848 debacle was the Central Democratic European Committee, lauched by Mazzini in the summer of 1850. He managed to obtain the support of several important émigrés, including Ledru-Rollin of France, Albert Darasz of Poland, and the German Arnold Ruge, but efforts to convince Herzen to join and represent Russia failed. Herzen's critique of this effort is significant as a reflection of the problems facing the émigrés in general and of those facing Herzen in particular. He was quite clear-sighted in his refusal to accept Mazzini's invitation. "I tremble for Mazzini," he wrote to a German friend at the time; "one more step and he will be, not ahead, as he always has been, but behind." Herzen described the new organization as devoid of profundity, unity, and necessity. In an especially insightful passage, he wrote: "The aspect of the movement that the Committee represented, that is, the reestablishment of oppressed nationalities, was not strong enough in 1850 to give life to an open organization. The existence of such a committee only showed the tolerance of English legislation." He also objected to the alternative of setting up a secret society along Mazzini's lines. The risk was great, Herzen argued, that such an organization would degenerate into "a revolutionary bureaucracy." By this he meant that the group would become dominated by the formalism of meetings, protocols, votes, resolutions, and manifestoes, "just as our chancellery bureaucracy does." Herzen decided to remain apart from this effort organized by people he respected but considered "incomplete revolutionaries." His reply to Mazzini ended with this personal proclamation: "From the age of 13 to the age of 38, I served only one idea, I had only one flag: war against all authority, against all slavery in the name of absolute independence of the individual. I will continue this little partisan war, like a real Cossack, *auf eigene Faust,* as the Germans say, attached to the great revolutionary army, but without enlisting myself on the rolls—until it is completely reorganized, that is, revolutionized."[26]

Herzen's response, however accurate it may have been in its critical analysis, was not typical of the émigrés in London at that time. Mazzini and Ledru-Rollin did manage to publish a statement of principles and, for a short time, a newspaper in which they proclaimed their dedication to the tenets of republicanism (universal suffrage, progressive taxation, free association, abolition of royalty, etc.), but as Herzen had predicted, support for their enterprise was too weak for the organization to survive. The Central Committee disappeared in 1853, by which time it had already been surpassed by a rival and more socialist group, the Commune revolutionnaire. The Commune, formed in 1852 by Felix Pyat and a number of other French exiles in London, took its name from the Paris Commune of the 1790s and considered itself the heir of the Jacobin revolutionary tradition. The Commune publicly condemned the more moderate ideas held by Mazzini and Ledru-Rollin after being attacked by Mazzini in print.[27]

In addition to the Commune, the other major émigré groups in the early 1850s which commanded the allegiance of the almost 4,400 émigrés from all countries in London were the Deutsche Arbeiterbildungsverein, led by Karl Schapper and Heinrich Bauer; the National Charter Association of Great Britain, under the leadership of Ernest Jones; and the Lud Polski-Gromada Rewolucyjna of the Polish socialists. These four organizations combined forces to form the International Committee at St. Martin's Hall in London on 27 February 1855 in what was the largest gathering of revolutionary émigrés ever to take place in Europe. Mazzini refused to participate, but Herzen came and gave one of the many speeches on the agenda of the meeting.[28] Hopes ran high among the émigrés of

Europe as, a year later, the International Committee was transformed into the International Association, a more permanent body composed of members from all countries representing working-class socialist constituents. The attacks on Mazzini continued as the new organization attempted to forge its own distinctive ideology in dealing with the major problems of the age. Mazzini was by now clearly identified with the discredited notions of nationalism and bourgeois republicanism, which were being superseded by strategies and tactics oriented around the theories of class conflict and a proletarian social revolution.[29] During the next several years, these ideas were developed further, attracting more adherents among the émigrés, the working class, and socialist intellectuals as well. The main result of these currents was the formation of the International Workingmen's Association in 1864, which under the leadership of the German exile Karl Marx inaugurated another chapter in the history of Europe's radical émigré communities.

Herzen among the Emigrés

Alexander Herzen, an aristocrat whose name is synonymous with the development of Russian socialism, arrived in Western Europe on the eve of the outbreak of revolution in France in 1848. Herzen's role abroad, where he spent the most creative years of his life, was so overwhelming that he has come to be seen as the epitome of the entire Russian emigration during the nineteenth century. In the world of emigration, Herzen assumed a multidimensional role among the exiles of Europe. This role was appreciated in particular by later Russian émigrés, who worked in the same cities and for many of the same causes that Herzen had proclaimed as so necessary decades before. Plekhanov, who as an émigré conceptualized for the first time the fusion of Russian radicalism and European Marxism, spoke most knowingly of Herzen when he wrote that Herzen could never have achieved what he did had it not been for the "free conditions of West-European life" and the "rich supply of impressions that he received in the West."[30] Herzen's role was formed gradually during his years abroad, not suddenly upon his arrival. Once he did come to a coherent formulation, it was both specific and complex. He became, in the words of one of the most perceptive commentators on Herzen's career, "the first and as yet unsurpassed mediator between democratic Europe and the Russian intelligentsia."[31]

Herzen achieved this significance because of his unusual personal gifts and because he arrived in Western Europe at a critical moment in the separate but interacting histories of Russia and Europe. Herzen left Russia voluntarily, but the circumstances of his life made it imperative that he abandon his homeland if he was to continue to think, write, and act in the manner he had chosen. As is well known from the many studies of his pre-émigré career, Herzen had, on unsubstantiated charges, been exiled to Viatka, near the Urals, during his student years, had begun writing articles critical of the autocratic regime under Nicholas I, and had, since his childhood, looked to the West as a source of inspiration in studying the kind of political and social change he believed to be necessary in his own country.[32]

Herzen's first years abroad were shattering, disruptive, stimulating beyond even his own wildest dreams, and also depressing in a way he had not anticipated. He arrived in Paris as the revolution broke out, and made his initial contacts with friends and comrades as well as opponents and enemies in the context of this upheaval. He had come from a country where critical thought and action were severely restricted, and found himself suddenly thrust into a world where boundaries of all kinds were being broken down and redefined. Thus, not only was he experiencing the impact of the historic difference between "backward" Russia with its enserfed peasantry, entrenched aristocracy, and exclusive autocracy, and the "modern" West with its political pluralism, industrialized capitalist economy, and rich culture which set standards of quality and excellence for the rest of the world; he was also encountering the cracking apart of a historical paradigm that had dominated Europe and Russia since the defeat of Napoleon. The conservative structure of traditional Europe, fashioned out of the Congress of Vienna in 1814 and watched over by the Holy Alliance, had undergone many challenges in the ensuing decades. It was not until the outbreak of revolutions across the continent of Europe in 1848, however, that the extent to which the Old Order and its values had been undermined by the opposition currents of the preceding years was fully realized.

Herzen's involvement with the revolution in France is told in great detail in his own memoir and has been discussed by the historians who have written about him. There is no doubt that the revolution left him profoundly disturbed about Europe, Russia, and his own future. Because the revolution was defeated—and because of the particularly violent way in which it was—Herzen left Paris for Switzerland and Italy. He knew only that he could not return to Russia, and that fact, combined with the revolutionary failure in France, forced him to begin to evaluate his entire system of values and convictions. He has left a lengthy record of this process of self-discovery and self-redefinition in his many writings from this period.[33]

During the years of his wandering from France to Switzerland and Italy before finally settling in London, Herzen met some of the most prominent members of the European exile community. These included Mazzini, Felice Orsini (who later gained notoriety in 1858 when he attempted to assassinate Napoleon III), Aurelio Saffi (a member of the ruling Triumvirate in revolutionary Rome during 1848 and later a literature professor at Oxford), and Garibaldi among the Italians, Proudhon, Victor Hugo, Louis Blanc, and Ledru-Rollin among the French, as well as Arnold Ruge and Georg Herwegh from Germany, Louis Kossuth from Hungary, Worcell and Edmund Chojecki (Charles Edmond) from Poland, and numerous others who are described in depth in Herzen's memoir.[34] Herzen mentions in passing that he also met three Russian émigrés in this period—Michael Bakunin, Nikolai Sazonov, and Ivan Golovin—but he has little to say about them, for reasons we shall examine shortly. In his own individualistic and somewhat removed manner, Herzen was, for the moment, at one with the cosmopolitan and internationalist mood, movement, and emerging vocabulary being generated among the exiles. These émigrés, "colonies of compatriots in an alien land," were seeking to transcend their national differences by inventing a new international nationality of humanity. This sense of a new and higher kind of national identity oriented around a radical vision of the future order was symbolized by the expressions often used in the letters the émigrés wrote to each other. Hugo, for example, addressed Herzen as "Dear Fellow Citizen" because of their shared desire for a society based on "the unity of humanity" rather than the divisive aspects of contemporary governments.[35] In a sense, Herzen played a role among the émigrés at this time not unlike that of Alexander I at the Congress of Vienna. He brought the reality of Russia to the consciousness of Europe by his presence, his involvement, and his activities. He became, through his writings and his wide-ranging contacts among the émigrés of Europe, a participant on the "general staff of the European revolution," and the "representative of Russian democracy" abroad.[36]

As Herzen compared and contrasted Russia and the West in his writings, which were, to a large extent, reflections of the struggle he was undergoing to establish a role and a new identity as an émigré, he observed with a penetrating eye the exiles around him whose difficult situation so resembled his own. No one has expressed the anguish and the significance of emigration as eloquently as Herzen did. After leaving Paris, Herzen went to Geneva, "the old haven of refuge for the persecuted." "Switzerland," he wrote, "was at this time the meeting place in which the survivors from European political movements gathered together from all parts. Representatives of all the unsuccessful revolutions were shifting about between Geneva and Basle, crowds of militiamen were crossing the Rhine, others were descending the St. Gothard or coming from beyond the Jura."[37] As for the émigrés themselves, he was painfully aware of the influence of the circumstances of their lives. Exile, he wrote,

checks development and draws men away from the activities of life into the domain of fantasy. Leaving their native land with concealed anger, with the continual thought of going back to it once more on the morrow, men do not move forwards but are continually thrown back upon the past; hope prevents them from settling down to any permanent work; irritation and trivial but exasperated disputes prevent their escaping from the familiar circle of questions, thoughts and memories which make up an oppressive, binding tradition. . . . All emigres, cut off from the living environment to which they belonged, shut their eyes to avoid seeing bitter truths, and grow more and more acclimatized to a closed, fantastic circle consisting of inert memories and hopes than can never be realized.[38]

Herzen's portraits of individual émigrés reacting to these stresses and strains are both scathingly critical[39] and uncritically admiring.[40] He was also aware of the difficulties these émigrés placed upon the governments that accepted them. In Geneva, for instance, exiles streamed in because the government was under the control of James Fazy, who had for years been involved with radical causes in Switzerland. The émigrés, Herzen wrote, "tormented Fazy and poisoned his existence. . . . The passions loosed during revolutionary movements had not been appeased by failure and, having no other outlet, expressed themselves in an obstinate restiveness of spirit. These men had a mortal longing to speak just when they should have held their tongues, retired into the background, effaced themselves and concentrated their forces." Instead, out of necessity and desperation, they produced inflammatory pam-

phlets, held public meetings, and "frightened the foolish governments with impending insurrections."[41] Herzen knew about this
firsthand. He himself had been expelled from Nice less than a
month after the demonstration of 19–20 May 1851, which terrified
local government officials blamed on radical exiles.[42]

The émigrés, according to Herzen, could not immediately find
a way to direct their energies into effective paths of action. They
became "absorbed in wrangling among themselves, in personal disputes, in melancholy self-deception, and, consumed by unbridled
vanity, they kept dwelling on their unexpected days of triumph" in
"the revolution of the past." They then broke into small groups
dominated less by principles than by petty hostilities. As they retreated more and more into their own exclusive camps and became
more obsessed with the glories and the mistakes of the past, they
began to express themselves—to dress and to act—in a distinct
manner that, according to Herzen, created "a new class, the class of
refugees."[43] Although Herzen himself did not express all these traits
and moods, he did undergo a period in which his personal life overwhelmed his political concerns. This was the time he considered his
greatest tragedy—the loss of his mother and son at sea, and the
discovery of his wife's affair with his friend Herwegh.[44]

Herzen came to London in the summer of 1852 to begin what
became the first stable period of his émigré years. Many of the
émigrés whom he had seen and known on the Continent also had
come to London around the same time. He still saw many of the
problems that had riddled the émigré communities in Italy and
Switzerland in the aftermath of 1848. "Meeting the same men, the
same groups, in five or six months, in two or three years, one becomes frightened: the same arguments are still going on, the same
personalities and recriminations; only the furrows drawn by poverty
and privation are deeper; jackets and overcoats are shabbier; there
are more grey hairs, and they are all older together and bonier and
more gloomy . . . and still the same things are being said over and
over again."[45] He also admitted his own state of confusion. Thinking
at first that he would stay in London only briefly, "little by little I
began to perceive that I had absolutely nowhere to go and no reason
to go anywhere."[46] He reestablished contact with his émigré comrades from the Continent—Mazzini, Ledru-Rollin, Kossuth, and
others. Now, however, he began to ask himself, "Are not these men
becoming the sorrowful representatives of the past, around whom
another life and different questions are boiling up?"[47] After meeting

with Worcell, whom he continued to respect, he nevertheless wondered, "How could he imagine that England would incite Poland to rise, that France of Napoleon III would provoke a revolution? How could he build hopes on the Europe which had allowed Russia into Hungary and the French into Rome? Did not the very presence of Mazzini and Kossuth in London loudly remind one of the decline of Europe?"[48] The absurdities of this fading mode of existence struck Herzen as well. He noted that Ledru-Rollin and Kossuth, who had friends and a general cause in common, had lived in London for over three years before meeting personally because it could not be decided to their satisfaction which of them should visit the other according to the dictates of émigré protocol!

Herzen was determined not to become part of this ossifying generation. He therefore began to turn his attention more directly to his homeland as he made plans to set up an émigré printing press in London. He was aided in this process of reestablishing his identity as a Russian in an émigré context by the curious manner in which he was treated in his new milieu. The English regarded Herzen with both more respect and greater distance than he was accustomed to experiencing since his departure from Russia. He made a great and lasting impression on some English radical figures, particularly W. J. Linton and Ernest Jones, who helped him gain entrée into the world of British publishing. Linton wrote in his memoir that Herzen "was short of stature, stoutly built, in his last days inclined to corpulence, with a grand head, long chestnut hair and beard, small, luminous eyes, and rather ruddy complexion. Suave in his manner, courteous, but with an intense power of irony, witty, choice as well as ready in speech, clear, concise and impressive, he was a subtle and profound thinker, with all the passionate nature of the 'barbarian,' yet generous and humane."[49]

During the 1850s, Herzen reached the height of his fame. His home became a visiting site for streams of people from Russia, from Western Europe and from London. This is how Herzen's home was described by one of his comrades:

The visitor to London generally informed Trübner [Herzen's London publisher] of his desire to have the honor of making Herzen's acquaintance. Trübner would give him the address and offer to write a note. In answer to this note, Herzen would arrange a meeting, either at his place or at that of the visitor, if the latter for some reason did not want to be seen in Herzen's house. Such cases were very frequent. . . . People did not use their real names in Herzen's house,

or used them very rarely. Whoever did not wish to conceal his visits
gave his own name; with those who were uncertain or asked that their
names not be given out, we either changed them (which, incidentally,
happened rarely) or dealt with indiscreet questions by saying that we
didn't remember, didn't know, it was a difficult name, etc. And in fact
it was hard to remember all those who came to worship, there were so
many of them. They flashed by, one after the other; they came in,
trembling with reverence, heard every word of Herzen and engraved
it in their memory; they gave him information, either orally or in the
form of prepared notes; they expressed their sympathy to him and the
sympathy of their acquaintances; they thanked him for the benefits
conferred upon Russia by his unmasking and for the fear which the
Bell inspired in everything dishonest and unclean; then they took
their leave and disappeared. Whom did I not see at Herzen's in my
time! There were governors, generals, merchants, litterateurs, ladies,
old men and old women—there were students. A whole panorama of
some kind passed before one's eyes, really a cascade—and all this
without taking into account those whom he saw *tête à tête*. Many a
time, standing at the fireplace in his study in Fulham, I laughed inside
to hear some retired captain, who had travelled to London expressly
to see Herzen from some backwater like Simbirsk or Vologda, declare
his sympathy, explain that he was not a reactionary.[50]

With the death of Nicholas I in 1855, the arrival of his close
friend Nicholas Ogarev, and the creation of his Russian Free Press,
Herzen achieved an international reputation. He still believed he
was acting in concert with progressive opponents of reactionary
regimes everywhere, but now he had found an appropriate instru-
ment through which to act on his principles. He had become, as he
said, Russia's "free, uncensored voice," which only an émigré could
raise and transmit.[51]

Herzen's influence not only coincided with, but was integrally
related to, the decidedly changed atmosphere under the new regime in Russia, that of Alexander II. For the first time, a commitment to abolish serfdom was made publicly and the process of how
to work out the least disruptive manner of emancipation was set in
motion. Hopes for change were aroused on many levels throughout
Russian society, and the demand for an open discussion of the issues
intensified. Nowhere, at least in the Russian language, was the
problem of peasant emancipation and a variety of associated problems as freely discussed as they were in Herzen's émigré press,
particularly in his newspaper, *Kolokol* (The Bell). We shall return to
an analysis of this publication in our treatment of the émigré press in

general, but suffice it to say at this point that Herzen's place and authority in the wide-ranging currents of reform that swirled during the late 1850s and early 1860s were solidified through the prestige of his *Kolokol*. Herzen found himself in indirect contact with his country through the vast number of letters he received for his paper, and through the large number of visitors who came to his door with information about the hidden and horrible events that lay behind the official shadows of the autocracy. As a prominent writer of the time put it, not only was Herzen's paper "read in Russia by people of all social grades, from the Winter Palace to the smallest police official," but Herzen was the person "who gave the chief impulse to political and social radicalism in Russia."[52]

The Original Portrait of the Early Russian Emigrés

Our knowledge of the origins of the Russian emigration beyond Herzen, however, remains both limited and distorted. It is limited because the subject has not been investigated sufficiently. Much of what we know about the early émigrés comes from E. H. Carr's engaging but rather melodramatic portraits of Herzen and his entourage in *The Romantic Exiles,* or from Franco Venturi's monumental history of revolutionary populism, *Roots of Revolution,* which includes discussions of individual Russian radicals abroad but not of the emigration as a phenomenon of the revolutionary movement. In addition, we have for too long accepted, virtually uncritically, the perception and interpretation of the early emigration as presented by two of its original chroniclers—the literary critic Pavel Annenkov and Herzen himself—who probably without conscious intention seriously distorted the entire subject in their writings.

Annenkov's elegant and insightful memoir is unquestionably a monument to the highest achievements of this literary genre. Herzen's is even more so, because to elegance and insight must be added its ringing evocation of passionate commitment and its vast scope. The two writers knew each other quite well, were born in the same year (1812), came from the same aristocratic background, and created similar portraits of the emigration's beginnings; for both of them, that historical moment occurred when Herzen arrived in Western Europe in 1847.

Curiously, Annenkov says that when he arrived in Paris late in the spring of 1846, he "found a whole Russian colony already established there," although he concludes that "no such thing as a Russian political emigration was even thought of yet."[53] He names Bakunin and Sazonov as the colony's "outstanding members." He also mentions "the well-known Golovin" as the man who became the first Russian political émigré when he refused the tsar's request to return to Russia in 1843. Somehow, though, he managed to completely ignore the career of Nikolai Turgenev, who had been abroad since 1824 and was in fact the first émigré from Russia in the nineteenth century.

A good example of Annenkov's attitudes toward this generation of Russian émigrés can be seen in his description of Golovin. Golovin, Annenkov writes,

had received an official recall to Russia because of a trifling little book which he had published in French in Paris without permission. The book, an essay in political economy, was something even less than a textbook—it was a simple set of extracts from student notebooks, and not altogether coherent extracts at that, but in any case quite innocuous. I would venture to say that I have never in my life met a writer less worthy of attention than this Golovin, who simultaneously played the stock market and a role in the opposition, wormed his way into the Jockey Club, into the world of libertines, and into democratic consiliabula—a brazen and childishly craven man. Despite the recall, he remained in Paris and became, before anybody else, a Russian political emigre, and at that, on a very special principle—out of fear; he was haunted by terrors of all possible kinds, which were simply unthinkable in connection with him.[54]

Of greater interest is Annenkov's description of the Paris to which Herzen came and the impact the city had on him and other émigrés. Paris, in the fall of 1847, was on the eve of a revolutionary transformation that was to influence Herzen as much as the social and cultural forces of the city had affected him immediately upon his arrival. It was a city of political development and power, a city in which opposition movements were being spawned more quickly than they could be assimilated by a constituency of followers. "One could not resist feeling drawn to this activity," Annenkov writes. For Russians, their peculiar situation made them more vulnerable than other nationalities to the magnetic attraction of the city.

Owing to various aspects of its political life, Paris had a captivating effect on Russians who made their way there always in a more or less secret, stealthy way, since it was officially forbidden in those days to have the word France inscribed in one's passport. The impression

Paris produced on the travelers from the North was something like what ensues upon a sudden windfall; they flung themselves on the city with the passion and enthusiasm of a wayfarer who comes out of a desert wasteland and finds the long-expected fountainhead.[55]

The results of this interaction between traveler and metropolis was the submission of the former to the latter. Russians absorbed the influences around them as they involved themselves in the activities of the new environment, and they underwent what Annenkov calls a process of "external and internal metamorphoses."[56] Annenkov is scornful of the debates, meetings, and writings that animated his countrymen; "there was no other term by which to call this type of concern with European issues such as existed then among Russians than—an amusement." It consisted primarily of "the manufacture of the endless, variegated gold-embroidered fabric of conversations, arguments, conclusions, propositions and counter-propositions" in which "no one had any notion yet of a responsibility to one's own conscience."[57] Herzen, however, joined the searchers for integrated doctrines of socialism and "threw himself into that sparkling sea of daring assumptions, merciless polemics, and high feelings of every sort, and came out of it a new and extremely nervous man. . . . There was not another person who would have reacted against the insubstantiality of the European order of life more mercilessly and who would have at the same time so decisively adjusted himself to it," Annenkov says.[58] Herzen soon formed a circle of admirers around himself, and his house "became a sort of Dionysius' 'ear' where all the noises of Paris, the least movement and perturbation playing over the surface of its streets and intellectual life, were clearly echoed." Gradually the Russian past faded under the onslaught of the new forces. For Herzen's "impressionable wife, with her refined nature and character," the embrace of the new, together with the disintegration of the past, "utterly made her over."[59]

Annenkov could not restrain himself from judging the cruelty of this dilemma. Europe, he believed, ultimately destroyed the Herzens; he was issuing a warning to all émigrés that a similar fate awaited them.

Neither he nor any of his Russian friends thought at all about the possibility of a moment coming when the opportunity of living like an amphibian between two worlds—the Western and Russian worlds— would disappear and one would have to choose between the two spheres, each as powerfully and jealously as the other, although on different bases, claiming rights to possession of the whole man. That moment was not far distant . . . but when it came, there ensued bitter reckonings, painful sacrifices, compulsory and unnatural repudiations which utterly ruined Herzen's life and the lives of many other persons together with him.[60]

In another passage, Annenkov evoked even more powerful images to show how Herzen's genius was shattered by Europe, the implication being that this is the inevitable price one must pay for abandoning one's homeland and pursuing the spurious dreams of Western progress: "Thus, the raging, foaming wave of European life carried that precious nugget [Herzen] thrown into it from some remote, unknown planet—carried it to one side and to another, pounding it to pieces, and, of course, unconcerned about where it could be placed, where made to fit."[61]

Annenkov did not make explicit his distinction between the Russian "colony," which did exist, and the "emigration," which had not as yet been born. Yet it is clear from his memoir that what he had in mind was the boundary between travelers and exiles. The first is a visitor to the West who will return to Russia after satisfying his cultural curiosity and will continue to accept the political status quo in his homeland. The second is a permanent alien abroad who will not—or cannot—return to Russia, who not only refuses to accept the existing tsarist regime but who commits himself to wage war against it from afar. Actually this was the difference between Annenkov and Herzen. At their last meeting together, as Annenkov was preparing to return to Russia, Herzen warned him, "You'll be wretched in Russia." To this Annenkov replied with his own warning: "You may regret staying."[62] They had made their choices, but each was also projecting his own fears upon the other.

The distinction is again revealed in Annenkov's discussion of Bakunin at this time. Annenkov describes Bakunin as "one of the Russian prospectors for political causes," which he now found among the Polish exiles in Paris. "Not a single Russian before him had so boldly cut himself off from his household gods, his former cast of mind, his old remembrances and conceptions in favor of the clandestine religion of the Polish cause." This ability of Bakunin to abandon himself completely to "revolutionary romanticism, where apparitions took precedence over logic," did not convince Annenkov of Bakunin's sincerity.[63] In a letter to Annenkov in October 1847 Bakunin wrote of the chasm between them. Annenkov quoted from the letter to emphasize his point: "I know that you take a somewhat skeptical attitude toward all this; and you, from your own stand-point, are right, and I, also, at times shift to your point of view. But what can one do—there is no changing one's nature. You are a skeptic, I a believer; each of us has his own work cut out for him."[64]

The image of these early Russian émigrés in Annenkov's writings is of a lost generation fanatically committed to illusions of social change which have separated them from Russia irrevocably and doomed them to isolated self-destruction. For a time they live like "amphibians" in both worlds, but ultimately they lose their nationality and, with that, their identity. These émigrés, Annenkov concluded, could never belong to Europe and never return to Russia.

Judging from his extraordinary autobiography, Herzen's own attitudes toward the émigrés he knew during his first years abroad were not far removed from Annenkov's. Nikolai Turgenev and P. V. Dolgorukov are mentioned in passing but are not discussed in any depth. Herzen did devote a small chapter to Nikolai Sazonov, his old friend from Moscow whom he remet in Paris, but it is not a charitable portrait. "Sazonov has passed without leaving a trace," Herzen writes, "and his death has been as unnoticed as the whole of his life." Sazonov was endowed with "conspicuous gifts and conspicuous egoism"; the latter trait led him to seek to dominate his comrades continually. He was, Herzen continues, an idle man who "wasted his immense abilities frittering his life away in all sorts of trivialities abroad." Herzen compared Sazonov to a lost soldier "who is taken prisoner in his first battle and never comes home again." Sazonov surrounded himself "with a retinue of various mediocrities, who listened to him and followed his lead." Once in a conversation in which they had a disagreement over Belinskii, Herzen exclaimed to Sazonov:

But do tell me please: you now, who are not under the censorship, who are so full of faith in yourselves, so full of strength and talent, what have you done? Or what are you doing? Surely you don't imagine that walking from one end of Paris to the other every day to talk over the boundaries of Poland and Russia once more with [some Polish exiles] is doing something? Or that your talks in cafes and at home, where five fools listen to you and understand nothing, while another five understand nothing and talk, is doing something?

Wait a bit, wait a bit, Sazonov said, by now considerably nettled: you forget our situation.

What situation? [Herzen replied.] You have been living here for

years in freedom, in no dire extremity: what more do you want?
Situations are created. Strong men make themselves acknowledged
and force themselves in. Enough of that: one critical article of
Belinsky's is of more value for the younger generation than playing at
being conspirators and statesmen. You are living in a delirium,
walking in your sleep; you're in a perpetual optical illusion with which
you deceive your own eyes.[65]

These are strong words, and they are not tempered by a balanced picture of Sazonov's positive contributions. The only aspect
of Sazonov's political career mentioned by Herzen is his involvement with several French radical newspapers run by Proudhon and
Lamennais in 1849. We are told nothing of Sazonov's political views
except that he exercised poor judgment and continuously quarreled
with his editors.

Herzen also devotes a brief section of his memoir to another
émigré from this period, Ivan Golovin, but the tone is similar to that
of his discussion of Sazonov.[66] He describes Golovin at the time of
their first meeting in 1848 amid the bloody "June Days" in revolutionary Paris as a man "known to me only from his mediocre writings
and from his exceedingly bad reputation as an insolent and quar-
relsome man."[67] Golovin literally forced himself upon Herzen.
"Twice a week he would come to see us, and the moral level of our
home was at once lowered" as quarrels and slander ensued.[68] His
writings, according to Herzen, were an amalgam of rhetoric, liberalism, anecdotes, and platitudes, "with no logic, no definite view, no
coherence. . . . Golovin thought in minced ideas."[69]

There was more. Herzen wrote that Golovin combined all the
hateful qualities of a Russian officer and landowner, "together with a
mass of petty European defects," and without any redeeming traits.
For Herzen, Golovin was the epitome of the lost Russian occupied
by the mindless "amusements" of Western Europe, who is "known
by everybody, and about whom everything is known except two
things: what they live on and what they live for." Herzen explains
that Golovin came to Europe because his superior in state service
was offended by his handwriting, and that he stayed abroad to write
La Russie sous Nicholas, "in which he offended Nicholas most of all
by saying that he made mistakes in spelling."[70] Golovin had no
talent, no curiosity, and no serious occupation. He was a poseur who
"retained the habits of an ill-bred landowner of the middling sort all
his life," living "the nomadic life of the semi-exile and semi-Bohe-
mian." Later, in England, Golovin "unsuccessfully attempted to get

into various political circles, made the acquaintance of everyone in the world and published inconceivable trash."[71]

Herzen had several more contacts with Golovin, but he never changed his opinion. The letters from Golovin which Herzen includes in his memoir reveal less about Golovin than they do about Herzen's relentless effort to discredit him. Perhaps the severity of Herzen's character assassination of Golovin is at least partly related to the fact that he was afraid of being associated with or mistaken for Golovin in certain circles. This, he admits, he could not tolerate: "Europe and the Poles themselves have such a superficial view of Russia, especially in the intervals when she is not beating her neighbors or annexing whole kingdoms in Asia, that I had to work for ten years to escape being confused with the famous Ivan Golovin."[72]

Herzen's contempt for his émigré compatriots was even more savage than Marx's well-known scorn for and suspicion of the Russians he met abroad. Marx was convinced, as Annenkov relates after meeting with him, "that any Russian who came to them should be looked upon first of all as someone sent to spy on them or as some conscienceless deceiver."[73] In a similar vein, at one point during a meeting of workers at which Marx spoke, he pointed to Annenkov and said: "Look here, we have a Russian with us. In his country . . . associations of nonsensical prophets and nonsensical followers are the only things that can be put together and made to work successfully."[74] Marx was merely repeating the common prejudices of European intellectuals about Russians (a view he was, of course, to change drastically later in his life); Herzen, however, had deeper motives behind his attacks on his émigré contemporaries. This is particularly perplexing when one realizes that at the same time that he was so harshly criticizing Russian émigrés he was also formulating a new definition of the Russian emigration in a revolutionary context. In a passage which he published in the original (1851) edition of *Du développement des idées révolutionnaires en Russie* (but which was omitted in subsequent editions), Herzen for the first time conceived of the notion of the emigration as a revolutionary force integrally connected to the emergence of a tsarist opposition movement in Russia. Admittedly influenced by the Italian and Polish exile communities in Paris, the formulation nevertheless deserves more attention than it has received. It reads:

The emigration is the first indication of a revolution which is in preparation. It is astonishing in Russia, where one is not accustomed

to it. And yet in all countries, at the beginning of reforms, when thought is weak and material force is unlimited, the men of strong conviction, of real belief, of true devotion, have found refuge in foreign countries in order to make their voices heard. The banishment, the voluntary exile, have lent their words a superior force and authority; they have proven that their convictions were serious.
. . . Thus, the emigration is the most significant act of opposition which a Russian can engage in at this moment. The government knows this quite well. It has come to realize, with difficulty, that there are people who, summoned to return, have the audacity to remain abroad, the courage to renounce their fatherland and their property.

Who does Herzen have in mind when he speaks of émigrés acting as revolutionaries? Surprisingly, they are the very individuals we have just seen him speak of in such a critical manner. Referring first to Bakunin and Golovin, Herzen says that "both of them gave up assured positions and brilliant careers in Russia." He also explains that proof of the impact that their agitational and publicistic work is having in Russia can be seen in the increasingly more severe measures enacted by the tsar to curtail the émigrés' activities; these include passport restrictions, seizure of private estates, and efforts to obtain extradition of émigrés from Western European countries. Herzen notes that the radical activities of Bakunin and Golovin have "been equally appreciated in France, Germany, and England." Sazonov also is mentioned as active in the cause of realizing democracy in Russia. "The Russian emigration is only a germ, but a germ bearing a great future. The Russian emigration is growing stronger because its opportunity is evident, because it represents not hostility or despair, but love of the Russian people and faith in its future."[75]

Thus, what appears to be a contradiction in Herzen's writings between a negative image of individual émigrés as nonrevolutionaries and a positive image of the emigration as a revolutionary movement of social protest is further complicated by the added contradiction of his portrayal of the same émigrés as nonrevolutionary in his memoir and as revolutionary in Du développement des idées révolutionnaires en Russie. Our task, therefore, is not only to try to understand Herzen in this regard but also to come to a consensus on the political nature of the emigration at mid-century. We must ascertain more clearly the identity of these "amphibians," as Annenkov called them, who had to choose between commitment and country, and who, by living Russia abroad, functioned between two worlds instead of within either one. Further, we need to know whether the process of migration and the impact of resettlement abroad on these early émigrés was as profound and as destructive as Annenkov claimed.

What follows is a series of analytical biographical sketches of the first Russian émigrés which seeks to solve these problems. As the reader will soon see, such an inquiry involves the retrieval of a lost generation, and a reevaluation of the contribution of these original émigrés to the history of Russian opposition movements and social thought.

N. I. Turgenev: The First Political Emigré

Nikolai Ivanovich Turgenev has been more the victim of neglect than of misunderstanding. There is no prerevolutionary scholarship on him, and, aside from several extensive obituaries, the best piece of work on his life before 1917 is Semevskii's biographical essay in the Brockhaus-Efron encyclopedia.[1] After the revolution, two biographies, appeared, though one dealt only with the pre-emigration period of Turgenev's life,[2] and the other, aside from interpretive problems, is too brief to adequately treat his entire career.[3] There have been some specialized articles and chapters of books on specific aspects of Turgenev's thought.[4] Recently, a Soviet historian has assumed the task of rescuing Turgenev from historical oblivion; taken together, her articles represent the equivalent of a monograph on Turgenev, with the concentration being placed on the émigré period of his life.[5]

Turgenev's own writings also are comparatively unknown, even to students of Russian history. He published two books, widely separated in time. The first was a serious analysis of the Russian tax structure and a critique of the serf system which appeared in 1818, when he was only twenty-nine years old.[6] The other, a massive three-volume study written in French and published in Paris in 1847, was divided into an autobiographical volume, a volume devoted to a criticism of the existing political and economic system in Russia, and a third volume concerned with proposals for the future.[7] In addition, Turgenev published a brochure on Russia's response to the 1848 crisis, and many articles on the emancipation problem in Russia during the 1850s and 1860s, including several that Herzen printed in his influential émigré paper *Kolokol*. There is also the voluminous correspondence that Turgenev carried on with individuals as diverse as Russian ministers and American abolitionists.[8]

Indeed, Turgenev's letters are so rich and informative that they must be accorded a high priority as source material in any future study of his life and thought.[9]

Interpretations of Turgenev have undergone some perceptible changes in the century since his death. He was correctly designated as "the first Russian political émigré" as early as 1905, though few historians have noticed this.[10] Turgenev has also generally been considered a liberal in most accounts, a term meant to refer both to his political orientation and to his economic ideas.[11] There has been disagreement however, over two issues of some significance. One concerns Turgenev's awareness of Russian developments during his years abroad, and the other involves the nature of his relationship to the more revolutionary Russian émigrés of his time. In addition, any assessment of Turgenev's political and economic positions would have to stand ultimately on an interpretation of his writings, and here, too, there is no unanimity of opinion among the secondary studies. Some have argued that Turgenev lived an isolated existence abroad and that his views remained frozen in the framework of the 1820s, the period when he was a member of the Decembrist movement.[12] Other students of Turgenev have emphasized his idealization of European democracy, his attachment to aristocratic circles, and the influence of English radicalism on his thinking.[13] All of these interpretations have been challenged by recent scholarship, however, where it is argued that Turgenev had ties to Bakunin, Herzen, and the more revolutionary émigrés, that he gained firsthand knowledge of Russian conditions through his three trips back to Russia at the time of the Emancipation discussions, and that he took a highly critical position on the question of peasant emancipation in his published articles.[14]

Turning to the opinions of Turgenev's contemporaries, we find that Herzen and Bakunin both expressed highly ambivalent attitudes toward him. They had positive things to say about him despite the fact that they considered him far too moderate on most issues. In Bakunin's "Confession" to the tsar, written in 1851 while he was in prison, he described Turgenev as a lonely and isolated man who "lived with his family, far from all political activity and, one might say, from any society." According to Bakunin, Turgenev "wished for nothing so passionately as for forgiveness and permission to return to Russia . . . which he remembered with love and, not infrequently, with tears."[15] In addition, Bakunin claimed that Turgenev "was, after all, not a little frightened by the revolution that was taking place."[16] Yet in a freer context, after his Siberian escape and return to Europe, Bakunin wrote Turgenev this inspired note: "Today I'll be coming to Paris and I must tell you that one of the most ardent of my desires and hopes is to see you, our patriarch, as soon as possible."[17]

Herzen, who seemingly did not consider Turgenev important enough to mention in his autobiography, publicly praised him in an article on Russian émigrés publishing their work abroad: "Each time we encounter the name of Nikolai Ivanovich Turgenev among the ranks of progressive fighters for freedom of the peasants, for judicial freedom, for the freedom of the Russian people in general, it is with a feeling of profound respect."[18]

Perhaps the most accurate contemporary evaluation of Turgenev was the one given by his cousin, the writer Ivan Turgenev. In an obituary article, Ivan Turgenev attempted to describe a complex but consistent personality—a man who combined respect for his government and its ruler with an abiding love for the Russian people and an uncompromising devotion to the amelioration of their condition. He was, Ivan Turgenev wrote, "primarily a political person, a man of the state" (*chelovek po gosudarstvennyi*) whose strength of conviction was expressed in his "love for justice, impartiality, and rational freedom [*razumnaia svoboda*] together with an equal hostility toward oppression and injustice."[19] Beyond this problem of presenting an opposition figure as an individual who was at the same time deeply loyal to the state and the existing regime, Ivan Turgenev expressed one further paradoxical characteristic of his relative: "Despite his many-year sojourn abroad, N. I. Turgenev remained a Russian, a Muscovite. This fundamental Russian essence was expressed in everything—in manners, in all his movements, in all of his habits, in his very pronunciation of French. . . . Exile, permanent resident of France, he was a [Russian] patriot primarily. . . . And thus it is that a completely Russian individual was condemned to live and die abroad. . . . Russia will never forget one of her best sons."[20]

Nikolai Ivanovich Turgenev was born on 11 October 1789 in Simbirsk. He spent his childhood years there before the family moved to Moscow. His father, Ivan Petrovich Turgenev, belonged to a Masonic group and was an associate of N. I. Novikov, for which he was sent to live on a remote estate by order of Catherine II. Death struck Nikolai Turgenev's immediate family with alarming frequency during his early years. Both his parents died when he was in his teens, his older brother (Ivan) died in infancy, another brother (Andrei) died in 1803, and a third (Sergei) in 1827. His remaining brother, Alexander, with whom he conducted one of the century's richest correspondences, died in 1845.[21] Nikolai Turgenev studied at Göttingen University in 1810–11 after attending Moscow University. He concentrated on history, juridical science, political economy, and financial law. After a trip to Paris in 1811, where he witnessed Napoleon at the height of his power, he was recommended to the prominent German reform minister Baron Stein in 1813. In the year that followed, he worked closely with Stein as his assistant in the central administration department, and the association left a life-long positive imprint on Turgenev. His admiration for Stein emerges in numerous instances in his later writings.[22] Turgenev served in the Russian army during the campaigns of 1814–15, then returned to Russia to take up the post of secretary (*shtats-sekretar'*) in the State Senate in 1816.

Under Stein's influence, Turgenev wrote his first book, *Opyt teorii nalogov,* which was published in November 1818.[23] The book is essentially an attack on serfdom, using data on the Russian tax system to argue the case. Turgenev recommended the sale of state estates to peasants and a reformulation of the peasants' financial obligations on these estates which he hoped would serve as a model for the country's private estates to follow. He also favored introducing free trade and lowering all high tariff barriers, together with a lightening of financial burdens on the peasantry. He opposed granting the gentry immunity from taxation. Citing the experiments carried out in Prussia under Stein's plans, he argued that taxation should be based on income and wealth, not on peasant labor. The estate, not the persons working on it, should be the source of taxes. He also proposed the abolition of corporal punishment of peasants. He concluded his book with a statement on the sensitive issue of the kind of politics that might best accompany his economic suggestions. In addition to recommending the extension of the tax base into the wealthier sector of the population, he argued that the success of the taxation system also depended on the forms of administration and government which applied these measures. "[There is] a readiness to pay taxes that is all the more evident in republics, and an aversion toward taxes in despotic governments," he wrote. He then ended his book with these words: "The improvement of the credit system develops directly in conjunction with the improvement of political legislation, particularly with the improvement of popular representation."[24]

In 1819, at the request of the St. Petersburg governor-general, Miloradovich, Turgenev composed a memorandum on serfdom which was to be presented to the tsar. In this 1819 memorandum, titled "Nechto o krepostnom sostoianii v Rossii," Turgenev indicated to the government of Alexander I the necessity of assuming the initiative in bringing about reforms regarding excessively burdensome peasant obligations. Specifically, he proposed contractual limitations on peasant debts and on taxes levied against landowners, opposed the sale of individual peasants apart from their families, and advocated granting the right of petition to peasants in order that they might bring their complaints and suggestions for improvement directly to their landlords. He also recommended reducing private landlords' exclusive rights of possession over their serfs by allowing peasants the right of free movement—a right they had not had since the seventeenth century. Although there is some indication that Alexander I resolved to "do something" about the peasant situation after reading Turgenev's memorandum, none of the memorandum's proposals were acted on until the 1840s.[25]

That same year, 1819, Turgenev joined the Union of Welfare, a secret society concerned with the constitutional reform of the autocracy and with measures to emancipate the peasantry. Turgenev remained with this group (which in 1821, under Nikita Murav'ev, became known as the Northern Society) until his departure from Russia in 1824.[26] He went abroad for reasons of health in 1824, but the following summer received an offer to work under Count Kankrin as director of the department of manufacturing in the Ministry of Finance. Alexander I was already suspicious of Turgenev's "extreme opinions," but he believed him to be "an honest person and that is sufficient for me."[27] Turgenev turned down the position and thus was not in Russia at the time of the uprising of 14 December 1825, which led to the execution and exile of the members of the Northern and Southern societies. Turgenev was nevertheless implicated in the Decembrist movement according to the conclusions reached by a special state commission appointed to bring evidence against the Decembrists. He was ordered back to Russia by imperial decree, and when he refused to return to face trial, he was sentenced to death *in absentia* by the highest judicial tribunal.

The court argued that it had the evidence of twenty-four co-conspirators to prove that Turgenev had been an active participant in an illegal organization dedicated to fomenting uprisings in Russia in order to establish a republican form of government.[28] In addition to the sentence of capital punishment, Turgenev was also deprived of his rank and title. It was this decision that created the new category "political émigré." Turgenev, "the Decembrist without December," thus became the first member of an exile community in Europe that would grow to include increasingly large numbers of opposition figures.

Turgenev lived for a time in London, but was continually hounded by secret agents and efforts by the Russian government to extradite him as a common criminal. He went to Paris in 1831 and made his home on an estate near the French capital for the remainder of his long life. In 1833 he married the daughter of a veteran of the Napoleonic army, with whom he had three children.[29] Financially, he remained secure as he received an income from his family estates in Russia.

In 1833 he began to work in earnest on a large study of Russia, which was completed in 1842 but not published until 1847—La Russie et les Russes; he delayed publication until the death of his brother Alexander, against whom he feared the Russian government might take reprisals. This book was followed by a number of other writings during Turgenev's later years, including his contributions to Herzen's Kolokol (which will be discussed below). After the death of Nicholas I, the new tsar, Alexander II, rescinded the previous sentences against Turgenev, and in 1856 he granted him a conditional amnesty. This led to a series of visits to Russia by Turgenev in 1857, 1859, and 1864. He used these trips not only to see his relatives but also to gather material for further critical studies on the peasant problem and to initiate an emancipation experiment on one of his family estates prior to the 1861 Emancipation Decree.[30] No other émigré of his generation managed to travel between Russia and Europe as Turgenev did in these years. His last published work, "O nravstvennom otnoshenii Rossii k Evrope," was issued in 1869 and he died at his French estate on 29 October 1871, in a world that had changed dramatically since his emigration began almost a half-century before.

The impact of England on Turgenev's ideas is still a matter of dispute among scholars who have examined this problem. Though he lived in England only a short time—between 1826 and 1831— he was there at a critical period in England's history as well as in his own life. He was an admirer of England's government while still a student in Göttingen, but as one scholar has put it, "Turgenev's political views were altered significantly" as a result of his experiences during his years of residence there.[31] Traces of the perceptions of British state and society that he formed at this time were to appear in his writings throughout his career.

England was the country in which Turgenev essentially began his émigré existence. He had no precedent, and no community to aid him in the difficult process of adjustment. He seems to have used his correspondence and diaries to help him absorb and comprehend the world around him. His private opinions of England during his first years there were decidedly critical. To his brother Alexander he wrote: "Here all the advantages are only for the upper classes," whose privileged position is owed largely to their wealth.[32] He noticed that the paths to privilege appeared to be open, but that access to these paths was in practice denied to the majority of the population, whom he described as being in "a horrible situation." Turgenev turned his attention to "the thousands of unemployed workers" and the many more who worked in factories for wages that barely kept them above the level of starvation. The poverty he saw was so widespread and omnipresent that "there are no firm hopes or probabilities for improvement."[33] He informed his brother Alexander that the situation of the workers was even worse in some areas outside London; he noted the city of Manchester in this regard, where Engels was soon to write in detail of such conditions.

To this perception of the class divisions in English society Turgenev added a critique of the country's legal and political systems. The judiciary, despite pretenses to providing justice for all, in fact defended the interests of the wealthy aristocracy. He explained to his brother that lawyers' fees were so extravagant that no member of the lower classes could possibly afford to hire a proper defense in a court. Similarly, he described Parliament as a political organization "composed only of the rich and for the rich." The lower house, which is supposed to represent the nonaristocratic majority, "acts solely according to the House of Lords, and cannot act otherwise [since] the greater part of its members are sent there, directly or indirectly, by the Lords."[34]

At the same time that Turgenev was expressing this critical view of his host society, he had to face additional problems. Not only were there persistent attempts by the Russian embassy in London to extradite him; there was also a coordinated effort by the Russian diplomatic and aristocratic community in London to bar Turgenev from joining English literary and social clubs to which he applied for admission. Under the immediate impact of these difficulties Turgenev asked himself in his diary the classic questions of his generation: "To whom can I be useful? For whom can I work?" Disoriented, he wondered where he could find an outlet for his desire to work for the good of others. Cut off from the problems of the Russian peasants, he asked himself, "Where is the fire of hope" in this land of exile? He could not contain his anxiety over the possibility that he would no longer be able to find significance for his "lost and useless life."[35]

One of the ways in which he resolved this depression was by becoming involved in British utopian socialism. An important role in this reorientation was played by William Thompson, the English economist, industrialist, and disciple of Robert Owen. Through Thompson, Turgenev was introduced to the writings of Jeremy Bentham, Saint-Simon, and Robert Owen. Moreover, Thompson showed Turgenev instances of applied industrial reform in his own factory. From this, Turgenev concluded that the desperate condition of the English working class was directly connected to the nature of the factory system, and that this situation could be alleviated through appropriate industrial reform. This conclusion was more convincingly felt by Turgenev after his visit to the Owenite community in New Lanark, with which he was already familiar as a result of his meeting Allen William, the Quaker and Owenite leader. Turgenev's descriptions of New Lanark in his diary are rhapsodic in praise of Owenite methods of overcoming the excesses of the industrial revolution.[36]

Turgenev also threw himself into the agitated discussions on the proposed Reform Bill, clearly identifying with the radical viewpoint of Jeremy Bentham, James Mill, and William Cobbett. In his letters to his brother Alexander, it is clear that he was particularly impressed by the critique and suggestions offered by Cobbett in his pamphlets and speeches.[37] Throughout this period, Turgenev recorded in his letters the upheaval that England was undergoing; he detailed protests by rural farmers as well as by urban workers and intellectuals against the opponents of full democratic representation. For him, the two issues of industrial and political reform were inseparable; any compromise on permitting popular rule in Parliament was directly related to resistance to improving the economic condition of the poor.

Turgenev was also keenly interested in the Irish Question and the Chartist movement; his letters are filled with firsthand observations and analyses of these protest movements. Despite his acknowledgment of the benefits of the realization of full parliamentary democracy in England, the dominant mood in his thinking at this time was one of criticism of the existing situation. Turgenev, the exile from autocratic Russia, was not unaware of the obvious superiority of this system over the Russian and French monarchical forms of government, but he preferred to ally himself with the people, the oppressed, the "internal exiles" of his host society, rather than with the privileged interests of his own social class.

If the influences in England were significant, the revolution in France in 1830 and Turgenev's experiences in Paris once he relocated there were to affect him even more powerfully. Indeed, the impact of the 1830 revolution on Turgenev can properly be compared to the more well known effects of the 1848 revolution in France on his émigré successor, Alexander Herzen. Interestingly, the uprising of 1830 was not unexpected by Turgenev. He had been following French events from newspaper reports since his arrival in England. Beginning in 1828, his comments on France in his diary and letters increased as his attention turned more and more toward the Continent. In December 1829 he wrote to his brother, in a remarkably accurate prediction, that in France "they expect the start of the struggle between the court and the people."[38] On 20 July 1830, a week before the outbreak, he went further: "The menace of a *coup d'état* fills the newspapers from Paris. This will turn into a revolution. And the Russian government may interfere in this revolution and forbid Russians to be in France."[39]

Once the revolution was a reality, Turgenev began to clarify his overall interpretation of the events in Paris as he became increasingly absorbed by them. He was convinced that conditions in France would substantially improve, and indicated that he was seriously considering moving there. By August, the news from Paris had "captured [his] complete attention." He considered the July upheaval "a merchants' revolution" (*revoliutsiia v pol'zu kupechestva*). The popular forces opposing the Restoration convinced him that neither a Bourbon ruler nor a Bourbon administration would be acceptable to the French population. He called the July Revolution "an unparalleled achievement of the people of Paris. . . . The world must see the foundation of the people's salvation and prosperity that has emerged in France as a result of the July

[Revolution]."[40] He also speculated on the international significance of these events, considering separately the possibilities for Belgium, Holland, Germany, England, and Russia. His view of Europe was of an interconnecting web of centralized nation-states subjected to similar opposition forces from within. The results of the explosion in Paris, therefore, not only would decide the fate of France but would stir parallel outbreaks elsewhere, which was the case in Poland even as he wrote.

Turgenev hoped that the change of regimes in France would result in the new government's granting him permission to enter the country. Upon receiving a positive response to his request to visit Paris in the fall of 1831, he went there immediately. He was welcomed in Paris as warmly as he himself had welcomed the July Revolution. Unlike his more isolated relationship to English society, which he had not really managed to overcome, in France he had access to several key figures in power. He quickly made the acquaintance of Lafayette and Guizot in spite of his awareness of "the greater likelihood that the Russian government will be more concerned about me. . . . That is obvious."[41]

Turgenev's initial enthusiasm for the July Revolution was soon tempered, however. Gradually, he began criticizing the new regime of Louis Philippe. In November 1830 he wrote his brother that Guizot and his party wanted "to stop the [revolutionary] movement, but that is not in their power. The movement from the start was strong only in Paris; but with Paris, almost always, moves the fate of France." By 1832, Turgenev noted that as the government continued to suppress opposition journals, popular anger, "especially against the king, continues to strengthen. . . . The position of the government is becoming more and more difficult."[42]

As was the case in his critique of the English situation, his attack on the July Monarchy in France was a blend of political and economic objections. On the one hand, he found the new regime moving further from, not closer to, a commitment to widening the electoral representation of the country; on the other hand, he criticized the government's economic policies of protectionism in international trade while ignoring the growing plight of the factory work force. The popular uprisings in Lyon in 1831 and 1834 further convinced him of the dangers to the regime from below if it continued on its present course. Throughout the 1840s, Turgenev explored alternatives that might help resolve this conflict. He read the utopian socialists more seriously, but found the disciples of Saint-

Simon to be too removed from everyday problems; he was equally critical of the followers of both Lamartine and Lamennais. He met frequently with Louis Blanc in the early 1840s and was more positive in his opinion of Blanc's book, *L'Organisation du travail*, than he was about any other socialist work. However, the revolutionary events of 1848 shattered Turgenev's hopes for a peaceful evolutionary path from economic crisis to social improvement and from monarchy to a republican government.[43]

Turgenev's interest in European affairs remained connected to, but never replaced, his involvement with Russia. This concern for Russia, which increased markedly in the 1840s, was consistently expressed in his writings throughout his long career abroad. All of his published works on Russia revolve around two central themes: the realization of a constitutional government and the abolition of serfdom. Although these themes can be found in his first book, *Opyt teorii nalogov*, they were discussed in greatest depth in the third volume of his most substantial work, *La Russie et les Russes* (1847). This book, clearly Turgenev's magnum opus, was completely neglected by both Western and Soviet historians until quite recently; one scholar who has studied it has called it "the first monograph devoted to the history of the Russian liberation movement, its roots and prospects."[44]

In *La Russie*, Turgenev divided his suggestions into two periods of reform. The first period would bring the enactment of those reforms judged to be "compatible with the autocracy." These included, above all else, peasant emancipation, with land arrangements for former serfs and provisions for indemnity to former landlords. In addition, he included a number of associated reforms, such as the reorganization of the judiciary and of local administration. A new administrative order, based on an elected local self-government, was to be established at this time. This period would then be followed by a second stage, "the creation of a representative constitutional regime," with guarantees of equality before the law, freedom of the word (private conscience, the published press, and public meetings), ministerial responsibility, and an independent judiciary with judgment by peers. Turgenev also proposed national elections to establish a parliament with full legislative authority. He envisioned a group of 200 persons, elected on the basis of education and property qualifications out of a population of 50 million, sufficient to work out the initial problems of making the transition to a constitutional government. Ultimately, there were to be two houses in the parliamentary body, modeled on the English system of an aristocratic upper house and a popular lower house, which would represent the needs and aspirations of the entire nation. Turgenev's explicit constitutional model, to which he refers repeatedly in this discussion, is *Russkaia pravda* (Russian Justice), written by his former Decembrist comrade Pavel Pestel. Pestel himself had been strongly influenced by French revolutionary and British political institutions, and Turgenev is clearly endorsing this earlier document as a framework for the development of a constitutional structure in Russia.[45]

Turgenev was aware that there would be resistance to his plan, but he firmly believed that only those who profit individually from employment in an absolutist government would be irreconcilable opponents to such a political order.[46] As for revolutionary opposition to the proposed regime, Turgenev assumed that this would be an unnecessary phenomenon so long as the institutions of the constitutional government remained truly representative and continued to perform their fundamental tasks—ensuring "the material well-being of the people and the moral perfection of the individual."[47] He also took note of the danger that existed in Russia with regard to the peaceful realization of a constituional government in a country where the population had known only absolutism. Russia may not proceed, as Turgenev put it, at a pace and with the regularity "that one admires among the peoples most advanced in civilization."[48] Nevertheless, he concluded, all these difficulties can be overcome if the Russian people sufficiently desire this new political system and if they are willing to act on their desire in good faith to achieve it.

This, then, would assure Russia's participation in the progress of European civilization, which Turgenev believed was a necessary condition for advancement beyond forms of political and cultural barbarism. Europe, for Turgenev, was the apogee of modern civilization, and the future liberty of the Russian people depended on their ability to end their isolation from Europe. The very concept "civilization" was at the heart of Turgenev's world view. Other nations had to decide whether to embrace advanced forms of European civilization, to imitate them, to select discriminatingly among various influences, or to resist all such forms. Those who chose the latter course of action—and here he indicted the rulers of Russia for centuries—were what he called the *"anticivilisateurs,"* whose efforts led to decadence and backwardness.[49]

Why did Turgenev not only abandon but reverse his critical

attitudes toward Europe in his major published work? While there is no conclusive explanation in his writings, it seems reasonable to assume several possibilities. First, the sheer passage of time was quite significant between the period 1826–34, when he was most critical of Europe, and the middle 1840s, when he wrote his praise of European civilization in *La Russie*. During the first period, Turgenev was in an insecure psychological state as a recent émigré trying to cope with the personal problems of life in exile. At this point, he was still planning to return to Russia and did not imagine that he would spend the rest of his life in Europe. In his criticism of England and France, he may have been projecting some of the inner hostility he felt at his inability to return to his homeland, his resentment of his enforced (albeit initially voluntary) confinement in Europe. By the time he was writing *La Russie*, his personal circumstances had altered considerably. He had adjusted to his émigré existence in Europe and had come to depend on Europe for his own future; without a free, advanced "civilization" in Europe, Turgenev would have had to face the prospect of surrender to the tsarist *"anticivilisateurs."*

Second, Turgenev had different notions of Europe in mind in each of these periods of his career. In the earlier period, particularly during his residence in England, he wrote primarily about the English economy and government; he did not at that time examine the foundations of his criticism to the point of trying to understand the relationship between economic and political forms on the one hand and levels of civilization on the other. In the 1840s, when he did do this, he saw that industrial capitalism and parliamentary representative government were aspects of a historically evolving civilization which determined the distinctive kind of politics and economics (as well as cultural forms such as levels of education, science, the arts, etc.) a free society desired and its government guaranteed.

Third, Turgenev sensed he was a front-line witness to a struggle of extraordinary proportions. As a Russian, he stood on the battleground of the future in London and Paris, where societies of the most advanced civilization were fighting to determine the destiny of nations. The rest of the world, Russia included, waited in the wings, where policy decisions on democracy and capitalism had not yet been made. Thus, the aspects of European states and societies which he criticized in the late 1820s and early 1830s were individual components of a large-scale process that was to involve Russia as well. By the 1840s, when he was writing *La Russie*, his purpose was to address himself exclusively to Russia in this context. He conceived of his task here as not to compare Russian and European forms of government but to place Russia's more primitive political structure in the framework of Europe's higher civilization.

After trying to come to terms with the tumultuous international situation in 1848, Turgenev began turning his attention to the peasant problem in Russia. He published a political brochure during that revolutionary year, *La Russie en présence de la crise européene,* in which he expressed his fears of a world divided between the two extremes of destructive socialism from below and repressive monarchism from above. He was disappointed by the weakness of the liberals in the Frankfurt Parliament, whom he believed to be the main constitutional current in Europe. Turgenev was also deeply concerned about the rising influence of the "socialist and communist doctrines that would return the people to barbarism."[50] A few years before, he had written to his brother somewhat more favorably about socialist ideas, admitting that they represented the "first bursts of the human conscience toward the farthest completion of the condition of man and of human society."[51] Now, however, confronted with the reality of socialism in a revolutionary situation, he foresaw great dangers as governments, threatened and provoked by socialism, would respond with more repressive measures against the citizenry as a whole. Nowhere was this danger greater than in Russia. The practical lesson of 1848 for Turgenev was that Russia was falling further behind Europe in the development of constitutionalism. While Europe managed to incorporate aspects of the new popular demands into the existing framework, Russia reacted by strengthening the institutions of autocracy. Russia seemed to be moving away from the possibilities of constitutional politics while Europe increasingly moved away from the politics of monarchical authority. Turgenev concluded that he must devote himself to the transitional phase he had outlined in *La Russie*—peasant emancipation—without which constitutionalism could never be realized.

Turgenev's concerns for the abolition of serfdom were articulated in a series of brochures and articles. In an 1859 brochure, he wrote that the abolition of serfdom was for Russia "the most major problem, more important than all others, and without the resolution of which it is impossible to proceed toward further improvements. . . . Prosperity, honor, let us say directly—the salvation of government—depend upon the destruction of serfdom!" The liberation, he continued, must be completed at one time, it must be total, and it must be done without further delay.[52] He also emphasized the importance of emancipating the peasantry with land, and advised against a process of gradual transfer of land from lord to peasant; the latter, he believed, would produce only discontent and the continuation of the landlords' exploitation over their former serfs for decades to come.[53]

Once the Emancipation Decree was announced in 1861, Turgenev focused his criticism on the inadequacies of the government's plan. He objected to the financial arrangements, which favored the landlords and led to enormous peasant indebtedness. He was also unhappy with the allotments of land made available for peasant purchase since they were usually too small to support the families working them, and were often in comparatively unproductive areas. In addition, he was critical of the authority given to the peasant communes. Having been freed from servitude to private landlords, Turgenev predicted, the peasantry would now face a similar servility under the rural communes. As a result, a class of individual peasant landowners, bound neither to the aristocracy, the state, nor the commune, would be prevented from coming into existence in the foreseeable future.[54]

In the late 1850s and early 1860s, during Turgenev's most prolific period of publishing articles criticizing the terms of the emancipation in Russia, he also published a number of smaller essays on this subject in Herzen's *Kolokol*.[55] Despite Herzen's ambivalent attitudes toward Turgenev, which we have already noted, he did respect Turgenev as a figure who had knowledge of the peasant situation in Russia. Herzen (with Ogarev) wrote Turgenev a congratulatory letter on the occasion of the announcement of the Emancipation Proclamation in 1861. It was a tribute to Turgenev's entire career:

You were one of the first to begin to speak about the emancipation of the Russian people; recently, deeply moved, with tears in your eyes, you celebrated the first day of that emancipation. Permit us, disciples of your union [i.e., the Decembrist Union of Salvation, to which Turgenev belonged], brotherly, or better filial love, to clasp your hand and to embrace you warmly, in the fullness of [our] heart[s]. . . . With vibrant, tender emotion, we have written these lines and have signed our names with that profound religious devotion which we have retained throughout our lives for the veteran activists of Russian freedom.[56]

Turgenev responded with praise of his own for the editors of *Kolokol* in his return letter to them. "The Russian people," he wrote, "will recognize someday your feats, and your passionate zeal for their well-being."[57] In this same letter, he also discussed some further aspects of the problems facing landlords and peasants which certainly were concerns of Herzen's as well. Beyond all the financial and institutional arrangements lay the personal and psychological difficulties that had to be overcome if individual peasants were to gain respect from their former masters. He noted how hard it would be for landlords to learn to address peasants in the more formal language used for peers. He believed it was necessary to abandon familiar forms of address when speaking with peasants (to shift from *ty* to *vy* in Russian) if the existing class barriers were to be transcended in the reality of everyday life. Perhaps it was the experience of emigration itself which lay behind this comment by Turgenev—a rather personal perspective, incidentally, which one does not find very frequently in the literature on the emancipation of the Russian peasantry.[58]

There are two other aspects of Turgenev's career which should be mentioned. Both also happen to be characteristic of a number of émigrés of his generation. The first is his persistent effort to persuade the tsarist government of his innocence of the original charges made against him in 1825, and to return to Russia as a citizen of his homeland. The series of letters which Turgenev wrote to Alexander II poignantly reflects his unsettled conscience and his refusal to accept the identity of a political criminal confined to exile for crimes committed against the state. He repeatedly attempted to argue his case in his desperate search for imperial forgiveness. He denied that he had ever been a member of a secret society dedicated to provoking an uprising for the purpose of replacing the autocracy with a republican form of government, as the commission of inquiry had stated in 1825. The group he did belong to was concerned instead with a problem that, Turgenev wrote, he had "dedicated his entire life" to solving—"the emancipation of enserfed people."[59] He also emphasized his support of the preservation of the autocracy because of his belief that it was necessary for the tsar to initiate and carry out the emancipation of the peasantry.

At this same time, he also spoke to Prince A. F. Orlov, the Russian ambassador, who was leaving Paris, about the circumstances of his case. Orlov, upon his return to St. Petersburg, repeated the substance of his discussion with Turgenev to Alexander II.

This personal influence, together with Turgenev's letters, helped convince the tsar to permit Turgenev to return to Russia under limited conditions.[60]

After his three visits (in 1857, 1859, and 1864), Turgenev wrote another letter to Alexander II. This time, he attempted to persuade the tsar that he should move forward with a more ambitious reform plan. Now that the serfs were liberated, Turgenev argued, it was possible and desirable to begin plans for a national assembly.[61] This proposal, needless to say, was not received favorably by the tsar.

Nevertheless, the letters to Alexander II indicate Turgenev's need to be redeemed by the autocracy as well as his continued faith in its legitimacy and in the necessity for the tsarist government to play an active role in reform. Although he conceived of the politics of imperial rule as a transitional stage prior to the introduction of representative government in the future, Turgenev remained bound to the tsarist regime to justify much of his own political identity and to carry out the responsibilities of guiding the country toward "higher levels of civilization." He was not ready, as later generations would be, to renounce the autocracy completely and devote himself to a new political alternative.

The second aspect concerns Turgenev's familiarity with members of his social class in Russia despite his legal status as a pariah. Although he had relations with Herzen, Bakunin, and other radical émigrés who passed through Paris,[62] he also maintained contacts with aristocratic Russians and government officials whom he met either through family or through friends from the pre-Decembrist period of his life. During his visits to Russia in 1857, 1859, and 1864, he renewed and expanded many of these associations, and left very positive impressions on various members of upper-class society in Russia. F. N. Glinka, speaking on behalf of a number of people, was ecstatic in a letter to Turgenev at this time: "Your authority, your name, have remained in your fatherland . . . and have not been blotted out from the depths of the hearts of your friends.[63] Turgenev also corresponded with representatives of official circles such as A. F. Orlov, chairman of the state Committee on Peasant Affairs; A. V. Golovin, Minister of Education; N. A. Miliutin, Minister of Interior; and many others.[64] This activity is another indication of Turgenev's recognition of the legitimacy of the existing regime, regardless of his criticism of its methods of handling certain problems. Moreover, he believed that he could influence prominent men in positions of power in directions he desired. He chose to maintain these contacts in the hope of bringing about change in Russia in a peaceful, orderly manner rather than through more drastic measures. He did not want to see 1848 erupt in Russia.

Turgenev never joined an opposition organization during his four and a half decades abroad. The last political society he belonged to was the first he ever joined—the Union of Salvation, during the 1820s in St. Petersburg, before he emigrated. He remained, to the end, an independent reformist critic, at once suspicious of applying socialist theories and opposed to the eternality of autocratic authority. He often wrote that there was something of greater significance for him, beyond governments and theories of change. He called it "the desire for the good of mankind."[65] Yet despite this humanistic hope, Turgenev's letters reveal the hopelessness he felt in his life-long attempt to play a role in ending serfdom and bringing Russia into the higher world of European civilization. In one such letter, written in 1859 to the Russian Minister of Interior, A. M. Gorchakov, Turgenev reviewed his work on peasant emancipation and openly expressed the twin malaises of pessimism concerning his reform proposals and despair over his émigré existence. He had not found a way to connect his life in exile with a means to affect social change in Russia:

Russia is distinct from other countries by its continuance of the redemption system (le système de rechat). . . . God knows where Europe would still be at this hour if redemption had been the sine qua non of the emancipation of the agricultural class in different countries. . . .

I still desire that my writings and my emancipation plan would be better known in Russia, that they would be examined, discussed. But that is precisely the difficulty. This publicity is not permitted among us. I have written well, published, but no one reads me, no one knows what I have written. . . .

In touching on the delicate question of publicity, which is at the foundation of my thought, I feel that I will never finish if I enumerate all the advantages. It hardly bears repeating my passionate regret that the efforts and works of my whole life, which have been summarized recently in numerous publications . . . remain sterile and without access to my country. And that is why, my Prince, I am a discouraged man.[66]

I. G. Golovin: Emigré Individualism

The characteristics of the first generation of the Russian political emigration were still in the process of formation during Nikolai Turgenev's most productive years abroad. Another important member of this generation, who made a different kind of contribution to this emerging phenomenon, was Ivan Gavrilovich Golovin. He was, as we have seen, subjected to severe criticism by both Annenkov and Herzen, who portrayed him as a petty, wasteful, indulgent, and opportunistic mediocrity. Their judgment has been carried forth into scholarship by Lemke, whose two articles on Golovin represent the only serious study of his career by a Russian historian in this century.[1] Lemke concentrated on the unpublished correspondence between Golovin and various Russian officials (including Alexander II) regarding their desire for Golovin to return to Russia from his residence and his intention to do so; Lemke described little of Golovin's writings, and his demeaning tone makes it difficult for any reader to take his subject seriously. None of the editions of the *Bol'shaia* encyclopedia has a single entry for Golovin, and thus he has been buried in historical oblivion in his own country. Outside Russia, he has fared better, there having been some recent interest in his life by scholars in France and Poland.[2]

Ivan Golovin was born on his family's estate in Tver gubernia on 9 September 1816 (O.S.), twenty-seven years after Turgenev and four years after Herzen. His father died when he was only two months old. He was the youngest of seven sons, his only sister having died in infancy. In his memoirs, he recalled the military ethos of Alexandrian Russia following Napoleon's defeat by the tsar's army. Golovin looked admiringly to his two eldest brothers, who were army officers; with seventeen years separating him from them, however, they took little notice of him as a child.[3] He was sent to several boarding schools for his early education, and at the age of sixteen enrolled in the diplomatic department of the University of Dorpat. Confused and aimless by his own admission, he led a typically privileged student's life dominated more by duels and drinking than by serious study. In 1835 he went abroad for further study and heard lectures in Berlin by Ranke, Ritter, and other prominent German professors of history and philosophy. He then returned to St. Petersburg after receiving his degree at Dorpat, the first Russian ever to be awarded a degree there.[4]

In the summer of 1835, he traveled to Sweden, collecting material for his first book, *A Journey to Sweden in 1839,* which was published in 1840. This travelogue was to be the only book he ever published in his own country. He returned to Dorpat for a Master's degree and wrote a dissertation on political economy. He then went back to St. Petersburg to take up a state service post in the Ministry of Foreign Affairs under Count Nesselrode; this was to be his last stay in Russia. Clearly dissatisfied with his position, Golovin applied for a promotion to another section in the Ministry. Nesselrode's response was the following: "I agree to find Golovin a better position, but on the condition that he take lessons in calligraphy for six weeks." Golovin took this as a personal insult and as an obstruction in the path of his advancement in state service. More important, he had by this time begun to formulate his future in terms of writing. "But I was born to be a writer, not a scribe, and thus could not regret abandoning a career which demanded such servility, conceit, and, above all, deceit."[5] He expressed the motive behind his decision to leave service in another passage: "I thought I might be more useful to my country as an author than as a copyist, and accordingly withdrew from service."[6]

Thus, after serving eleven months at the rank of collegiate secretary, Golovin resigned. With no other position available, he decided to go to Europe in the fall of 1842 for reasons of improving his health. There is no indication of any serious medical problems and we know that Golovin was to live a very long time. However, the two most frequently stated reasons for seeking passports to travel abroad during the early 1840s were to improve one's health and to conduct international commercial transactions. Passports were issued for these reasons usually without any investigations, and Golovin was certainly aware of this when he put poor health on his passport application.[7]

Settling in Paris, Golovin quickly turned to his new career as a political critic of the tsarist regime; his initial conflict with Nesselrode over the service post which he took so personally was transformed into a critique of the entire regime. He first published two transitional works that did not deal with Russia at all. One was an expanded version of his Dorpat thesis on political economy[8] and the other was a brochure analyzing contemporary economic conceptions and theories, including those of the utopian socialists.[9] These were then followed by two large books critical of Russia[10] and by a pamphlet that has been considered "the first revolutionary brochure" in the history of the Russian emigration.[11]

These works established Golovin as the leading critic of tsarist Russia, a reputation which won him support abroad but also brought him under surveillance by Russian agents. Even before his first émigré book on political economy was published, reports were being filed on Golovin from Paris by Iakov Tolstoi, who headed the Paris branch of the Russian political police abroad. In January 1843 Tolstoi wrote to Count Benckendorff, chief of the Third Section in St. Petersburg, that Ivan Golovin was preparing to publish a book on political economy which was full of "doctrines detrimental to our governing order." He even quoted several passages to prove that Golovin's intentions were "of an inappropriate spirit."[12]

Action followed immediately. In March 1843 the Russian chargé d'affaires in Paris informed Golovin that he was ordered to return to St. Petersburg by imperial decree. Golovin tried to stall, to appeal, and finally realized that he was faced with a most difficult choice: he would either have to return, or renounce his country. Another émigré, P. V. Dolgorukov, had been summoned from Paris at the same time. (Indeed, Tolstoi discusses both of them in his letters from Paris.) Dolgorukov decided to obey the order and was rewarded with a term of exile to Siberia. Golovin, when he learned of this, resolved not to subject himself to a similar fate. He not only refused to return but went ahead with the publication of his book in spite of efforts by the Russian government to prevent it. "I loved, and still love, my country as much as any man," he wrote of this turning point three years later. "And because I loved it, I was desirous to contribute to the utmost of my power to efface the epithet of *barbarism* by which we [Russians] are stigmatized all over Europe."[13]

The stalemate ended in July 1844 when the Russian Senate confirmed Nicholas I's order to sentence Golovin *in absentia* to "banishment to Siberia, privation of all my civil rights, and the confiscation of my property."[14] At the same time, Nicholas also issued a decree prohibiting Russians from going abroad before the age of twenty-five and imposed a heavy tax on foreign passports in order to discourage further emigration.[15] Golovin was in this way declared *persona non grata* in his own country for planning to publish abroad thoughts considered by the Russian government to be dangerous and antithetical to the regime. He thus followed Nikolai Turgenev in becoming the second Russian émigré of the century, though they were shortly to be joined by Alexander Herzen, Michael Bakunin, and Nikolai Sazonov as the nascent Russian radical community abroad gradually expanded.

Golovin then joined a circle of émigrés from other countries who also had come to Paris to work for political causes prohibited by their governments. He collaborated with the German poet Georg Herwegh and James Fazy, who was soon to become president of the Swiss Confederation during the 1848 upheaval. Their intention was to establish an international journal of critical opinion, but the effort was unsuccessful.[16] Golovin also met many French journalists and socialists, who helped him publish articles in the democratic French press. His most well known piece at this time was a memoir devoted to the poet Evgeny Abramovich Baratynskii, which appeared in the *Journal des Debats* on 16 September 1844.

In May 1845 Golovin's major book was published in French and English. With the appearance of his *Russia under the Autocrat,* Russian opposition opinion took a large leap forward. Golovin's *Russia* was the first study by a Russian to condemn the tyranny of Nicholas I and his entire regime, antedating the work of his more prominent compatriots Herzen and Bakunin. As a result of this book, Golovin occupied a unique position as the spokesman for an alternative Russia which the emerging émigré community was later to represent collectively. Nikolai Turgenev's *La Russie* (which had been completed earlier than Golovin's book but was not published until 1847) is perhaps the only work to which it might be compared, but Golovin's critique of Russia went far beyond Turgenev's.

In his preface to the book, Golovin placed himself in an unusual historical tradition. He identified his own situation with that of one of his ancestors, who had refused to return to Russia when summoned by Tsar Boris Godunov at the end of the sixteenth century. Choosing to remain in Lithuania, the earlier Golovin is quoted as having said he "would return to Russia when three proverbs have ceased to be current in Russia: 'Everything that is mine belongs to the tsar'; 'near the tsar, near death'; 'do not fear the judgment, fear the judge.'"[17] Ivan Golovin then continues: "I am not the first, nor shall I be the last to deplore the servitude of Russia and to protest against its oppressors."[18]

In addition to his emphasis on the notion of tsarist opposition in a historical context, Golovin also introduced another concept that was to become part of the ethos of the Russian emigration: "My happiness could not be complete without that of my fellow citizens. And as I could not expect to see this wish speedily recognized, and was unable efficiently to contribute towards it in my own country, I renounced it with the less regret, because I trusted that I might render it greater service in a foreign land."[19] In short, he essentially redefined the notion of state service. Having been raised in an age when state service was the primary career for men of his social class, he was excluded from that career in part because of his critical attitude toward the values and practices of the Russian bureaucratic officialdom. He therefore combined the old notion of service with his critical views to fashion this new perspective of serving Russia abroad by dedicating himself to opposing the existing regime.

Russia under the Autocrat is a two-volume, 645-page comprehensive criticism of the impact of autocratic rule upon the Russian Empire. Golovin also included material on resistance to despotism within Russia which had never before been discussed in a published work by a Russian. Perhaps the best example of this point can be seen in the chapter on Nicholas I's accession to the throne, which contains a history of the Decembrist societies and their aborted rebellion on 14 December 1825. Golovin is strongly and unequivocally on the side of the conspirators. He ridicules the efforts of the Commission of Inquiry, which was appointed by Nicholas to investigate the affair, as a travesty to any sense of justice. For the "crime" of desiring to introduce a constitutional regime in Russia, the Decembrist leaders were executed by imperial order. "But who at that time had not drawn up some sketch according to his own notions [of a constitution]? There was not a man capable of thinking who had not the draft of a constitution in his pocket, in his desk, or in his head."[20]

The other historical event of significance in Nicholas's early years on the throne, according to Golovin, was the unsuccessful Polish uprising of 1830–31. Here also Golovin stands squarely on the side of rebellion, defending the Poles who risked their lives to obtain freedom from Russian domination. Golovin writes that Nicholas's vengeance was severe in the aftermath: "Every species of punishment was inflicted [upon the Poles] and neither property nor the ties of family were respected."[21]

Surveying the government and the social class structure in Russia, Golovin writes that "barbarism, tyranny and immorality are born and thrive in unworthy promiscuousness. . . . To study the melancholy effects of this combination of these three elements, we must go to Russia."[22] The basic problem, in Golovin's view, lies in the exclusivity of the autocracy. Without any political alternatives, without any access to independent appeals on the judgment of the sovereign, Russia cannot escape from the shackles of Nicholas's despotism. Russia is a land of serfs and functionaries where "the virtues which accompany or flow from liberty are unknown."[23] Nevertheless, Golovin believed that radical change was not imminent: "No revolution is possible in Russia, except in the palace, and only with the consent or by the command of the heirs to the crown themselves. . . . To judge by all appearances, one generation, if not two, must pass before there can be a revolution in Russia."[24]

Yet, he believed that the situation in Russia was potentially volatile: "Revolutions have always taken kings by surprise. The great mass of the people is excessively inflammable; a spark coming perhaps even from the government itself will speedily kindle a conflagration."[25] By this, Golovin had in mind the ever-expanding role of the police in Russia's internal affairs. "The distinctive characteristics of the Russian government," he wrote, "are despotism and rapacity. . . . The Emperor Nicholas is the declared enemy of liberty, and his entire policy is concentrated to persecute it to the utmost. He believes that liberty is equivalent to disorder."[26] In proving his case, Golovin ranges over the gamut of Russian institutional life. In addition to his lengthy treatment of Nicholas, his court and government, Golovin devoted many chapters of his book to social class structure, industry and agriculture, the legal system, provincial administration, and aspects of Russian culture. He even discussed the conflicts in the Caucasus between Russian military imperialists and the Circassian tribes, who "defend most obstinately every foot of ground, and they are still far from acknowledging the superiority of Russian arms and civilization."[27]

Although Golovin does not propose a concrete political alternative to the despotic authority exercised by the tsars, he indicates a strong faith in the liberating potentialities of public exposure and denunciation. Autocracy's power is preserved by its ability to keep its citizens isolated and the outside world uninformed. In this way, Russia need not adhere to the civilized standards of Western Europe so long as secrecy continues to surround its practices of abuse and injustice. Golovin recommends subjecting Russia to the glare of international opinion as a means to begin to counteract the present situation. He is convinced that important influences emerge when representatives of separated societies become familiar with one another. Referring to the Marquis de Custine's descriptions of cruelty that he witnessed in Russia, Golovin writes: "Europeans have become cannibals by living among savages; let the Russians be allowed to become free with free men." Thus, he continues, "publicity is the salvation of the world, and would be that of Russia if it were allowed to penetrate there. Open the doors of the tribunals, and justice will take her seat there. Publish the acts of the government, and it will become better. . . . There is a tribunal at the bar of which we must appear, even during our life—it is the tribunal of public opinion; let the wicked tremble, and let the good rejoice!"[28]

Golovin defined his own role in this context. By being abroad, "living with free men," as he had put it himself, "I perceive that I grow better." By writing critically of Russia, he hoped to expose the tyranny of the government to the world and thus to weaken its power. He knew he was taking risks by choosing this path, but believed he was serving a higher cause: "I love my country as much as any man, but I love mankind more; and should I even make enemies of my dearest friends, I shall not cease to oppose everything which is a violation of the universal and imperishable laws of social order."[29]

Russia under the Autocrat catapulted Golovin into public prominence in Europe as the book received widespread reviews in the press.[30] At the same time, pressure mounted against him. The French government was disturbed not only by the Russian government's persistent efforts to have Golovin extradited, but also by Golovin's controversial reputation. On the one hand, he seemed to be attracting excessive attention from the democratic and socialist left, which alarmed some members of Louis Philippe's administration. On the other hand, he also acquired an unsavory reputation as a *debauché* and philanderer who wasted the bulk of an inherited fortune on gambling and stock speculations. Ultimately, he was banished from France. He then went to England, where, in six weeks and with the help of the Tory leader Duddley C. Stuart, Golovin obtained a certificate of naturalized citizenship in 1846. This was a step which few Russian émigrés took.[31]

In 1847 Golovin published his next work, *Types et caractères russes,* or, as it appeared in English, *A Russian Sketch-Book.* Here he moved into another genre of writing, a combination of the techniques of the short story and journalistic reportage. The book is divided into a number of sketches of Russian life which are fictionalized representations of problems faced by ordinary Russians. While the stories deal with a variety of fascinating situations and individuals, one tale concerning the experiences of a group of rebellious peasants is of particular interest. The story, called "A Revolt of the Peasants," leaps beyond the depiction of Russian peasants as found in Radishchev and Ivan Turgenev in the same way that Golovin's criticism of Nicholas I in *Russia* transcends all previous political criticism of the autocracy published by Russians. Indeed, the subject matter and the attitudes of its author in this story foreshadow the political radicalism and social realism that we find much later in the work of the populist Stepniak-Kravchinskii. The story concerns a landowner who rapes one of his peasant women and suffers a terrible retribution. Already near the breaking point as a result of terrible burdens performed for the master, the peasants are stirred to overt rebellion by the humiliating seduction. After setting the estate on fire, several of the peasants heave their hated master into the flames to his death. Golovin writes that the master's merciless cruelty and contempt for his peasants "made them look upon his murder as an act of justice." They then "took possession of his chateau without opposition on the part of the servants." Finally, the revolutionary seige was brought to an end, and the three peasant leaders were condemned to death by firing squad. All other participants were flogged and "many banished to Siberia." Still, the story closes with a sense of symbolic victory for the peasants. We are told that the surviving widow of the murdered landowner cannot return to her estate because fears from the revolt haunt her. The local priest is transferred to another locality (he too is identified with the established order), and the estate is left abandoned. Although the new order was defeated, restoration of the *status quo ante* also was blocked. This was clearly a new interpretive twist to the traditional tale of lord and peasant in Russia.[32]

Golovin's involvement in the 1848 revolution is not entirely clear. We have only his account, with no objective corroboration. Nevertheless, we do know that he returned to France and participated in the upheaval that year, if not always in the somewhat heroic pose he presents in his memoirs.[33] He believed he was the representative of revolutionary Russia in Europe as the *ancien régime* was being extinguished. While such a reality is obviously questionable, what is significant is that Golovin certainly was one of the first Russians to conceive of such a role abroad. He did take part in a number of democratic clubs that sprang into existence after the February Revolution in Paris, published articles and open letters in the French press, and spoke publicly at political meetings, often for the cause of free Poland. Golovin belonged to a group called the Brotherhood of Peoples, and at its rally in November 1848 he spoke on behalf of Poland and against the tsar.[34] He dreamed of a new political career in France as a result of the revolution, and intended to seek election to the National Assembly. How a Russian-born, English-naturalized citizen would have managed to sit in a French parliamentary body will never be known, for Golovin was eventually expelled once again from France following the consolidation of authority by Louis Napoleon. Golovin's identification with the democratic left was too threatening for the new regime. Also, his support for the Polish cause was viewed as contributing to a disruptive international situation.[35]

In the summer of 1849, before leaving Paris, Golovin published a brochure entitled "The Catechism of the Russian People." Once again he broke new ground as he switched to yet another genre of writing—the revolutionary manifesto. For the first time, an émigré Russian openly preached "subversion of tsarist power by force."[36] Obviously influenced by the events in Paris, Golovin advocated the tactics of the barricade struggle and direct confrontation with the forces of autocracy. In the preface to his brochure, he sets forth the role of the revolutionary émigré in unmistakably clear terms. In Russia, he writes, those who sought change found only persecution. Because of the "fanatical animosity of the tsarist regime, we have gone abroad to carry on our work, to countries which recognize the sufferings in Russia and where support can be obtained." We shall bring Russia's cause "before the court of enlightened Europe." Even though official Russia "regards us as dead," he implores his readers "to listen to us so that the dead may reveal the truth."[37]

Set in the form of a Socratic dialogue of questions and answers, the brochure is divided into four topics: the tsar, the gentry, the soldiers, and the government. The orientation is clearly antitsarist as Golovin proposes a republican form of government for Russia. The initiative for this movement for change must come from the intelligent and the well-born people," who understand that "the first enemy of Russia is the tsar." Golovin continues: "Revolutions are not so difficult as you presume. One person muses about it, a second acts, and the people will gradually come to join the initiator." The weapons for the coming struggle can be found "among the soldiers, in the arsenals, in the shops, in the homes of private citizens." The revolt will begin in the cities, but "the countryside will be with us."[38] The last line of the brochure is a response to the question of whether some compromise with the tsar is not possible. The answer is unequivocal: "He is unredeemable, stained by the blood of sacrifices." Finally, Golovin warns that "a bad peace," by which he meant accepting servitude under autocracy, "is worse than a good war"—i.e., a struggle for liberation.[39]

The Russian government's response to this inflammatory brochure was swift and predictable. The Russian chargé d'affaires, Kiselev, went to the French police to determine who the anonymous author was and to have further printing and distribution cut off immediately. The French police were very cooperative as they helped the Russians establish the identity of the brochure's author, prevented publication of further editions, and ordered all unsold copies confiscated.[40] Golovin's brochure was thus fully recognized by the Russian authorities for its revolutionary language. As one scholar has stated, "[The] Catechism [is] the first work of this kind later destined to be propagated among the Russian people, opening their eyes to the true nature of tsarism and inciting them to overthrow the reigning dynasty in the name of a republican order."[41] The Russian authorities began to take reprisals as well against anyone suspected of affiliation with Golovin or his writings. Some copies of Golovin's books were smuggled into Russia,[42] but most were confiscated from travelers returning to the country from Europe. Vasilii Vysotskii, a captain in the General Staff, was arrested at the border because of police reports that he had been in touch with Golovin while abroad; the officer received a sentence of six years in prison and was forbidden to leave Russia ever again.[43] Also, among the evidence submitted to prove cause for the sentencing of Herzen to exile *in absentia* was his contact with Golovin.[44]

This was the zenith of Golovin's career as the pioneer of the Russian émigré opposition movement. After his expulsion from France in 1849, his life took on a confused, disoriented pattern. He wandered from country to country, an exile without moorings. First he went to Geneva, where Fazy, now head of the Swiss confederation, invited him to accept a university teaching position. The job carried the condition that Golovin could not engage in political activity; he refused.[45] Then, in 1851, he traveled to Nice, where he briefly collaborated on a journal, *Carillon,* designed for tourists interested in scandals of high society. Golovin's contribution was a feuilleton entitled "Les Prussiens, les Russiens, et les autres chiens à Nice." It was during this period that he was on cordial terms with Herzen, having met with him first in Paris during the 1848 revolution and again in Geneva and Nice.[46] From Nice he journeyed to Belgium, from which he was expelled, and then he went on to Turin. There, in 1852, he published a series called "Portraits et equisses russes" in Cavour's *Le Journal de Turin,* and also a brochure, *La France et L'Angleterre comparées.* The latter, dedicated to Richard Cobden, contained a strong denunciation of the police regime of Napoleonic France.[47]

Forced to leave Turin as a result of diplomatic pressure (this time from the Austrian ambassador, who may have been acting with the Russian government), Golovin returned to London, where he attempted once more to launch a new journal. He wrote to Victor Hugo about his project; the journal would be called *La Revue internationale* and it would serve as "an intellectual center for representatives of various nations."[48] When this did not materialize, Golovin began work on a book which he called *L'Oncle Tom blanc, ou l'esclavage en Russie;* this too was never realized. He did finish a book on Russia in 1854 in which he criticized Nicholas I's foreign policy regarding Turkey. Here he argued for the right of each nation to an independent existence, and warned against Russia's imperialistic designs on the provinces of the decaying Ottoman Empire.[49]

In 1855, Golovin crossed the Atlantic for a tour of America. He spent nine months traveling from region to region, and reported his impressions first in a series of articles in the *New York Tribune* and then in a book, *Stars and Stripes.* In his preface to this book, Golovin made his mood quite clear when he wrote, "The exile is nowhere at home and his stay is bitter everywhere."[50] His account of life in the United States is a critical one, and there is indeed a bitter edge to the tone of his writing. He finds little of redeeming virtue in the New World. Compared to de Tocqueville's far more illuminating perceptions, one is tempted to say that Golovin did not—or perhaps could not—see American society with real objectivity. The exile had wandered too far.

Back in London, his sense of homelessness reemerged and dominated his writings in sometimes contradictory ways. At this time, he married Alexandra Hesse, the daughter of a lieutenant general in the Russian army, who soon bore him a child. She was concerned about her husband's unwelcome status in Russia, and the marriage was clearly strained from the start over this problem. His financial situation continued to be unstable. In addition to an earlier inheritance of 70,000 francs, he received another 9,000 rubles in 1855. Seven years later, despite his sporadic but continuing income from his writings, his wife wrote in a letter that his finances had disappeared "in various speculations. At the present moment, my child and I are deprived of all means." Fearing for the future, she applied for a passport to return to Russia on her own because "I have absolutely nothing on which to live abroad."[51] She was granted her request; Golovin agreed to a separation and she left him for her homeland.

During these years, Golovin began to correspond with Emperor Alexander II about the possibility and conditions of his own return to Russia. These letters to Alexander II and other Russian officials, which he began to write soon after the tsar's coronation, gravitate between uncompromising assertions of independence and subservient dependence regarding his relationship to the crown. Just as Alexander II's accession had produced a wave of optimism in Russian society about the prospects for peasant emancipation and other reforms, it also awakened longings for roots among émigrés like Nikolai Turgenev and particularly Golovin. These feelings were expressed in Golovin's earliest letter to the tsar, written on 18 March 1855. Here he virtually begged for permission to return to his homeland, although he was careful to mention that he expected the permission to include amnesty and the restoration of his civil rights. He closed this letter by saying, "The hopes of my whole life have been placed upon you."[52]

This was followed by a letter to Gorchakov, the new Russian chargé d'affaires in Paris, in which Golovin noted that he had "never raised a weapon against Russia" and pointed out that "love for the fatherland cannot be extinguished even in the heart of the most caustic and bitter exile and writer."[53] Still fearing that he might be arrested if he set foot on Russian soil, he wrote in another letter that "16 years of exile life abroad [have] made me unfit for such a life of exile in Russia."[54] The letters continued, and at times expressed greater desperation. In April 1857 he stated he was renouncing his English citizenship and pleaded for, at the very least, "the hope that I will no longer be counted among the exiles."[55] Curiously, Golovin was granted an amnesty with permission to return to Russia, but it was made conditional upon his returning to state service. This he could not accept, and he refused the entire offer.[56] As late as 1877, Golovin telegraphed the tsar as follows: "Sire, permit me to spend my last days in Russia."[57] None of these communications apparently were ever answered.

At the other end of the spectrum, Golovin frequently informed Alexander II of the conditions *he* would accept if he returned, and on occasion advised the tsar on various reform proposals which the Russian administration was studying. He made it quite clear, for example, that he wanted permission to publish his writings in Russia without censorship. He also indicated that this should not be a privilege for him, but ought to be a condition for all citizens of the country. The abolition of censorship, together with the other reforms planned by Alexander II, would make Russia a land with "space for free people, who do not have to submit to surveillance and who are not locked up in exile."[58] He also wrote a letter to P. A. Valuev, Minister of Interior, in which he suggested, in bold style, a wide-ranging series of reforms concerning the reorganization of the legal system and the role of the police and the army in Russia. "I have recently assumed for myself the role of peace mediator between the government and the people, and I must state that dissatisfaction grows according to the lack of fulfillment of expectations. Without radical changes, you will not prevent the emerging crisis. The longer [you ward off] bankruptcy by stitching things together, the more terrible will the bankruptcy be. The tsar did not listen to the gentry, and now the peasants do not hear him. Beyond the edge of the abyss lies the plunge."[59] In 1866, he wrote a sharp letter to the tsar complaining that the Russian government and the Russian embassies abroad were dominated by Germans to such an extent that one could reasonably assume that "your Majesty is really not a Romanov but a Holstein-Gottorp. . . . The true Russian is to be found in exile."[60]

Golovin's last effort to stabilize his career and regain prominence as a radical publicist and writer was centered on a journal he established in 1859 after many previous unsuccessful attempts. The historical moment he chose to found his journal, *Blagoname-rennyi,* was an important one. Herzen's *Poliarnaia zvezda* had already been in existence for three years, and a new polarization of radical opinion was beginning to emerge. A more militant social movement was forming, with goals and conceptions far beyond those which Golovin was prepared to accept. He was, in short, about to be surpassed by political reality at the very time he decided to make a sustained venture into émigré opposition journalism. As one historian has put it, "If, in the preceding period it sufficed simply to declare one's opposition to the despotism of Nicholas I in order to be considered a progressive, henceforth it became necessary to pay a much higher—often an excessive—price for that [opposition]."[61]

The journal was indeed moderate. In a rare explicit reference to political categories, Golovin admitted in one of his editorial essays that he was not among the advocates of a republic for Russia, though he did not make his reasons clear. Revolution, which he had once defended so passionately in his 1849 "Catechism," had disappeared from his political vocabulary, with the exception of a brief reference in which he indicated his discomfort with the concept. In this particular instance, he defined revolution awkwardly as the consequence of discontent with "rapid changes in laws" and indicated that he considered "tolerance a superior form of politics."[62] Golovin appeared to be directing himself in a confused manner to issues that were of secondary importance to the new generation in Russia. Without the insight, commitment and coherence of Herzen's *Kolokol* abroad and Chernyshevskii's *Sovremmenik* at home, his readership declined sharply.

After the collapse of his journal, Golovin continued to publish articles, brochures, and letters to newspapers denouncing autocracy in Russia, but he was engaged more and more in a monologue.[63] The Russian government faced far greater dangers during Golovin's last years, dangers from which he, incidentally, seemed quite removed. There is little in his last works about the major opposition currents of the 1870s, like the Paris Commune in Europe or the populist movement in Russia. Instead, in his final book, *Russische Nihilismus*—a kind of memoir supplement to his earlier *Zapiski*—he returned to a past period of his life in an effort to salvage the remnants of his reputation, which Herzen had so viciously attacked in *My Past and Thoughts*. Yet even this effort to reconstruct and reinterpret his former relationship with Herzen and Bakunin fell largely on deaf ears. It is important to note in this regard that the book was published in German, and was never translated into Russian or any other language. Unlike his previous books, there is no evidence that this one was widely read.

Golovin tried to remind his readers in *Russische Nihilismus* that there had been a time when he, Herzen, Bakunin, and other leading émigrés worked together on behalf of Russian and Polish freedom. Speaking of their involvement on a political committee in 1848, Golovin referred to the bilingual pun on his and Herzen's names when he stated that they were "the head (*golova*) and heart (*herz*), if not of all Russians, then at least of the Russian emigres."[64] Nevertheless, however much he tried to point out the justness of his own efforts, no one in 1880 was prepared to believe his criticism of Herzen; his taking to task the man who epitomized the Russian revolutionary emigration sounded like the wounded and embittered voice of the vanquished. Golovin admitted that Herzen was "a great propagandist," but that his influence paled before Pushkin's "Ode to Freedom." He also said he disagreed with Herzen's joining "*dvorianstvo* and communism," that Herzen too squandered money (a charge Herzen had leveled against Golovin), that Herzen had been personally cruel to Golovin in rejecting the latter's attempts to help Herzen and contribute to his Russian Free Press, and that Herzen "frequently parted from the truth."[65]

Golovin died on 4 June 1890 in complete obscurity and isolation. According to one scholar, his chief contribution lies merely in the fact that "he familiarized, as much as was possible within his power, Russia and the tsarist government with Western Europe."[66] Another historian has written what is in fact a far more fitting evaluation of Golovin's career: "He was one of the first Russians who had the courage to rebel against the regime of Nicholas I and to expose him to those, especially, who maintained illusions about him, or who, quite simply, did not know everything that was happening in Russia. This is why, in spite of his personal faults, Golovin deserves to be rescued from oblivion."[67]

4

N. I. Sazonov: Marx's First Russian Follower

While Turgenev and Golovin were struggling to shape their roles as émigré opponents of the Russian autocracy, a new figure appeared in Western Europe who would soon develop a political critique of the tsarist system which substantially differed from that of his predecessors. The originality of Nikolai Sazonov's critique has not been appreciated in the historical literature; neither Soviet nor Western historians have succeeded in moving beyond Annenkov's and Herzen's unflattering portraits of Sazonov, which we have examined. E. H. Carr, however, is by far the most elegant of Sazonov's detractors. "Sazonov," he writes, "was one of those gifted young men whose brilliant future recedes imperceptibly into the past without ever having been realized in the present." Admitting that Sazonov was "one of the most brilliant and daring members of Herzen's group in Moscow," Carr sees the rest of his career as a "record of continuous decline." Sazonov's intelligence was subdued by his more powerful obsession with political illusions, and his financial inheritance as a member of the landowning gentry was squandered by "his disreputable manner of life," according to Carr.[1]

The noted Soviet historian B. P. Koz'min has indicated in an article on Sazonov that "it is time to recall such half-forgotten people," but he nevertheless repeats Herzen's original negative evaluation of Sazonov. Talented and intelligent, Sazonov wasted his gifts because, Koz'min writes, he lacked the discipline of work; this deficiency is traceable to his social class background and indulgent upbringing amid the landed aristocracy. Koz'min places him among "the ranks of the numerous Russian talented failures, one of the most colorful figures in the gallery of the Russian 'superfluous men.'"[2] Another Soviet historian concludes, after agreeing with Koz'min, that Sazonov represents the ideology of "gentry-landlord liberalism."[3] It is interesting to note that neither of these Soviet scholars makes any reference to the pioneering study of Sazonov by D. Riazanov, which was published shortly after the 1917 revolution. This neglect is all the more significant since Riazanov portrayed Sazonov not only as an authentic émigré revolutionary but also—and more importantly—as the first Russian Marxist.[4]

Contemporary opinion of Sazonov, apart from Herzen's, is of a different tone and view. Even Bakunin in his confession to the tsar, written while in prison, was more balanced than Herzen in discussing Sazonov.[5] Peter Chaadaev wrote to a friend in 1841 that "there is in Paris a Russian of unusual intelligence by the name of Sazonov."[6] Konstantin Aksakov, who knew Sazonov during their student years in Moscow, noted that Sazonov, despite his egotism, was an exceptionally bright man who finished first in his class. Aksakov also mentioned that Sazonov was very well read, particularly in French literature, which was later to become one of his most absorbing concerns.[7]

Nikolai Ivanovich Sazonov was born in Riazan on 17 (29) June 1815, three years after Herzen's birth. Beyond the fact that his father was a comparatively wealthy landowner, little is known about his earliest years. In 1830 he entered Moscow University, and a year later joined an intellectual circle that included Herzen, Ogarev, N. M. Satin, N. Kh. Ketcher, V. P. Botkin, and K. Aksakov. The members of this group dedicated themselves to the writings of Saint-Simon, Jacob Böhme, and the Russian Decembrists.[8] At the beginning of 1834, Sazonov formulated a project for "a new encyclopedic journal" together with Herzen and Satin. Their intent was to use the journal to chart "the main phases of the development of humanity. . . . and to focus attention on its aspirations." Their tasks were to be divided as follows: philosophy of history was to be handled by Ogarev, Herzen, and Sazonov; the theory of literature was to be guided by Ogarev; and the statistical section—to which the group attached great significance—was to be the responsibility of Herzen and Sazonov.[9] Although police arrests prevented the project from being realized, this serious planning for an activist journal devoted to social and intellectual change reflects the commitment of the circle's members to radical endeavors. More specifically, the project foreshadows Sazonov's involvement with progressive journalism during his émigré years.

In the summer of 1834, Sazonov graduated with a degree from the physical-mathematical faculty of Moscow University. He knew four languages and had already published a scholarly article on historiography.[10] This academic distinction, together with the intervention of his mother in influencing officials, helped Sazonov avoid the fate of his comrades during the arrests of July 1834. Whereas Herzen, Ogarev, and Satin were condemned to administrative exile in Siberia, Sazonov was granted permission to travel abroad. He spent the winter of 1835–36 in Germany, Italy, and Switzerland. He was enthusiastically impressed with Western culture, particularly in Germany, as is evident in a letter to his friend Konstantin Aksakov.[11] Yet, at the same time, his excitement about experiencing Europe should be set against his special appreciation of having avoided arrest and a period of Siberian exile. The sense of exultant liberation he expresses in the letter to Aksakov is in marked contrast to a guilt-laden letter he wrote to Herzen at the same time, where he expressed concern over the fact that he had managed to avoid arrest while Herzen had not.[12] Returning to Moscow, he renewed his friendship with Ketcher, the only other active member of their university circle who had escaped arrest and exile. A surviving letter to Ketcher from this period reflects Sazonov's continuing involvement with Europe. As a result of his trip abroad, he now sharply dichotomized the cultural ethos of St. Petersburg and Moscow, and in his argument with Ketcher, stood firmly on the side of the capital city as the embodiment of the civilization of the future. He saw St. Petersburg as Russia's progressive European center, while Moscow clung stubbornly to the traditions of the archaic past. As new trends from abroad were absorbed in St. Petersburg, the dichotomy would become more severe and irreversible. "Whoever wants to know Russia must live here [in St. Petersburg]," he wrote.[13] The debate between Sazonov and Ketcher over this issue is a good example of the division between Slavophiles and Westernizers that was dominating intellectual circles in Russia. More personally, however, the argument signified that Sazonov had come into conflict with his two remaining friends in Russia, Ketcher and Aksakov, both of whom had gravitated toward the Slavophile position. In 1840 Sazonov learned that Ogarev and Satin had been released from Siberian exile and had gone to Europe. He suddenly left for Paris at this time, perhaps encouraged by the example of his former comrades, never to return to Russia again.

Sazonov's life as an émigré differed substantially from the patterns established by Golovin and Turgenev. Instead of the more isolated, individualistic, and settled existence preferred by his émigré compatriots, Sazonov "threw himself into Parisian revelries."[14] Although he did have money from his family estate in Russia, he carelessly spent what he had in excess—at one point, according to a contemporary, he was "spending around 100 francs a day."[15] He was a frequent figure at various restaurants, cafés, and bars. One of the more vivid reminiscences of him at this time recalls him in an inexpensive restaurant habituated by Russians, in the midst of a heated argument with Bakunin over French politics.[16] At one point, in 1846, his financial problems got so out of hand that he was forced to serve a sentence in the Clichy prison in Paris because of his inability to pay his creditors. He was also prevented from returning to Russia with Ogarev and Satin at the end of 1845 because of his debts.

Sazonov was also far more influenced by the advanced political and intellectual currents in Paris during the 1840s than were Turgenev and Golovin. Although his career as a journalist did not coalesce until after the 1848 revolution, there are indications from his correspondence in these years of his involvement with Left Hegelianism, utopian socialism, and Marx's emerging communist theory. One of his closest friends in the mid-forties was the German poet Georg Herwegh, who later introduced him to Marx. Herwegh, for whom Sazonov had enormous respect and admiration at this time, played an important role in bringing into focus for him many of these new social theories. With the possible exception of Bakunin, Sazonov was the first Russian to become seriously absorbed in these ideas. Paris was, in the 1840s, the only place on the Continent where it was possible for individuals and groups freely to explore what were then called "questions of practical action," that is, problems directly concerned with the nature and transformation of society. Paris provided the best milieu for the formulation of these problems. The most discussed intellectual issues among the various exiled nationalities in Paris concerned the critique of modern religion along the lines being worked out by David Strauss and Ludwig Feuerbach (Strauss's *Leben Jesu* was published in 1836 and Feuerbach's *Das Wesen des Christentums* appeared in 1840), and the critique of modern society as theorized by the French utopian socialists and the Left Hegelians. The more radical members of the latter group argued that Hegel's philosophy should be reoriented to try to resolve concrete problems facing the lower classes of Western society; Herwegh was an integral part of this intellectual movement, and through him Sazonov became familiar with the issues.

There was, as a result, a curious blend of interest among intellectuals in questions of spiritual faith on the one hand and social transformation on the other. Sazonov's interest in these matters from his perspective as an émigré can be seen most clearly in a letter he wrote to Herwegh in 1844. In this letter, he compared Herwegh's position as a poet and philosopher to the "glorious role of the holy Justinian, the first apologist of Christianity; I, having been born in a barbaric land, have the modest mission of St. Dionysius, the first bishop and first martyr of France."[17] France was then barbaric in the sense that Russia is today, Sazonov explained. He pointed out that Justinian brought a new faith to Rome which challenged all established beliefs and that he was martyred there publicly for his commitment, while Dionysius died in obscurity, having wandered far from his native city with his new faith. Thus, Sazonov strongly identifies himself and Herwegh with the early Christian martyrs; he sees his own and Herwegh's critical theories as occupying a similar relationship to the values and authority of the existing order as did those of the early Christians under Roman rule. He goes beyond this, however, in drawing a link between the Christian martyrs as radical individuals in their time and those groups who fought for the revolution in France in 1789. He describes himself, Herwegh, and all other progressive people as the martyrs of their era in carrying on this revolutionary challenge to existing authority to the point of death.[18]

Sazonov was also close to Ogarev at this time. In a very revealing letter to Ogarev, written around the same time as the letter to Herwegh, Sazonov continued to examine some of these ideas. The letter is essentially an argument by Sazonov against the socialist views advanced at the time by Ogarev. In stating his own position, Sazonov not only discusses most of the leading French socialist thinkers of the 1840s but also makes what in all likelihood is the earliest reference to Marx's ideas in the correspondence of any Russian intellectual. Although it is difficult to reconstruct the background of the letter, Sazonov is obviously conversant with the split between Marx and Ruge over their interpretations of the significance of French utopian socialism. In addition, Sazonov is very familiar with Ogarev's socialist ideas as well as his practical plans to form a communist agricultural colony and factory in the Russian countryside with 2,000 freed serfs from an ancestral family estate.

Herwegh also is mentioned in Sazonov's critique of Ogarev, but this time more negatively than positively. Indeed, the letter is in some ways evidence of a rebellion against Herwegh's enormous influence on Sazonov.

Sazonov tried to address himself to what he saw as the absurdity of Ogarev's emerging populism. He claimed it would be unrealistic and unproductive for Ogarev to "devote himself to the people and live together with them as one of them." The gap between Ogarev and the Russian people in education and styles of life could not be bridged so easily.[19] Sazonov made it clear that he was not opposing the concept of improving the material condition of humanity in general or the Russian people in particular, but rather was criticizing the means by which Ogarev planned to obtain this desired end. He used a familiar religious analogy to make his point here: "I passionately hope that they [i.e., the peasants] will be extricated from this situation, but I see no need to throw myself at the mercy of natural necessity and chance. Christ, in order to expiate mankind, took upon himself the sins of the world, but he did not consider it necessary to sin himself."[20]

In discussing the theories of "socialism and communism" which had influenced Ogarev, Sazonov stated unambiguously, "I do not recognize communism, nor an equality of compensation either in the moral or the industrial world."[21] He then indicated aspects of the theories of Proudhon, Louis Blanc, and Cabet that he found objectionable. Cabet's book *Voyage en Icarie* he considered "a crazy confusing of Christian morality with the dreams of utopians of all centuries and all peoples."[22] He also pointed out the authoritarian potentialities inherent in forming "various communist sects." Socialists often propound aspirations of harmony and brotherhood that they believe will exist under the new system. "This is the kind of communism my friend Herwegh dreams about," Sazonov writes.[23] Blinded by ideals, they fail to realize the possibilities of despotism when their theories are put into practice. He calls this enforced leveling process "the communism of tailors and shoemakers"; to illustrate his point, he quotes the doomed rebel Jack Cade of Shakespeare's *Henry VI* on egalitarianism: "And when I am king . . . there shall be no money, all shall drink and eat on my score, and I will apparel them in one livery, that they may agree like brothers."[24]

This led Sazonov to return to the experience of emigration itself, which he had also mentioned in his letter to Herwegh in identifying with the exilic wanderings of St. Dionysius. He tried to explain to Ogarev the destructive aspects of emigration upon the thinking of men like Marx, Ruge, and Herwegh. As they moved from Germany to Switzerland, their previous notions touched on socialism and communism, but they still had not abandoned themselves to these theories. "Here [in Paris], on soil which was for them new and foreign, deprived of the structure of daily activity to which they had been accustomed, isolated and exasperated, they completely surrendered themselves to these extreme theories. . . . The first result of their enthusiasm was disagreement among them; from then on, they were unable to cooperate on tasks in common—nothing was accomplished; they lost time, opportunities, sympathy, and confidence which, perhaps, they never will retrieve."[25]

That is why, Sazonov concluded, he was begging Ogarev not to commit himself to these theories, but instead to stand on firm ground and find the appropriate and realistic means to make a contribution to the problems of oppressed people in Russia and Europe. He was advising his friend that caution and patience were necessary in this search, and that the certainty gained from an impetuous commitment could be far more disastrous than the insecurity of a search without end.

Within the next few years, Sazonov began to reevaluate some of the notions he expressed in his 1844 letter to Ogarev. The revolution of 1848 certainly played an important role in the reshaping of his political ideas, but Sazonov could not possibly have responded as he did to the events of that year unless he had already undergone a prior challenge to his beliefs. Unfortunately, there is no direct primary evidence for the years leading up to 1848. What we do know is that Sazonov actively participated in the 1848 revolution, that his career as a radical journalist took shape in the years immediately following the revolution, and that he developed a relationship with Marx at this time which reflects an acceptance of the very kind of socialist commitment that he had earlier warned Ogarev against.

In the years just preceding 1848, Sazonov had cultivated a wide network of associations with French democrats as well as with foreign exile groups. Together with Bakunin and Golovin, he was an active supporter of the Polish emigration. Through his friendship with Herwegh, he also worked with a number of German exiles in Paris (including Carl Vogt). He was a member of the democratic society, Fraternité des peuples, as was Golovin; Herzen also joined this society after his arrival in Paris in May 1848, probably through his contact with Sazonov. In addition, Sazonov was on the editorial board of Mickiewicz's *Tribune des peuples* during 1848–49 and wrote several articles for the paper, which was the chief organ of the Polish emigration in Paris during the revolution. Sazonov was also on the editorial boards of Proudhon's *Voix du Peuple* and Lamennais' *Réforme* in 1849, in addition to participating in various demonstrations, banquets, and public meetings on behalf of the revolutionary movement.[26]

It was against this background of revolutionary involvement and prominence that Sazonov began his correspondence with Marx in 1849. The two men knew of each other as a result of their common friendship with Herwegh, and it is possible that they met as early as 1844.[27] Sazonov's first letter to Marx, written on stationery from *Réforme,* is dated 6 December 1849, just prior to Sazonov's expulsion from France. Sazonov said he was writing to Marx at the request of Ferdinand Wolff, one of the editors of the *Neue Rheinische Zeitung,* to help organize a "democratic correspondence for German newspapers." Such a venture is needed at this important moment in history when "citizens propose and the police dispose." In his capacity as foreign editor of *Réforme,* Sazonov was soliciting contributions from knowledgeable democrats. From his vantage point in London, Marx could write about German problems as well as on "the situation of the working class in England. I know how deeply you have studied these questions and I would be happy to familiarize readers of *Réforme* with English social life with the aid of your pen," Sazonov wrote. He made it clear to Marx, however, that should he agree to write for *Réforme,* his articles must be free of both ideology and slander—"doctrine and personalities," in Sazonov's words.[28]

We do not know Marx's response to this proposal, but the plan was never realized, for Sazonov was expelled from France by order of Louis Napoleon's government. He resettled in Geneva, with the aid of James Fazy, who as head of the Swiss confederation was also responsible for helping Golovin and Herzen after their forced departures from France. Sazonov resumed his correspondence with Marx on 2 May 1850 when he wrote a long and highly revealing letter in which he openly declared himself Marx's disciple. Sazonov explains in the letter that "an attentive study of the latest works of Proudhon and reading his compromising articles in *Voix du Peuple* compelled me to take the final step in your direction." Sazonov continues: "I subscribe to all essential points which you have expressed in the [Communist] *Manifesto.* . . . I have come to the conviction that a serious revolutionary can only be a communist, and I now am a communist."[29] This decision, he continued, is the result of a process of "natural development" emerging from his ongoing involvement with contemporary social change. Having analyzed and rejected other theorists of society such as Saint-Simon and Proudhon, Sazonov now agrees with Marx that European civilization is progressing primarily in the area of industry. While other economic and social forms are disintegrating, industry increasingly dominates modern society. Yet, he adds, European civilization cannot, as it presently functions, resolve all the complex problems that contemporary industrial development places before it. The chief characteristic of modern society is its individualism; in the economic sector, it is individual labor, which is the most salient form of development. The tendency of the current economic system is to "exchange one individual's labor for another's, with the result being injustice and exploitation."[30]

Sazonov wants to take action and suggests reviving the idea of "a democratic journal" to propagate these views as widely as possible. He suggests several people who might collaborate with them, including Mazzini, Ledru-Rollin, and Considerant. The failure of the revolutionary situation in Europe must be reversed, he writes. New conditions must be created, not only for leaders but also, and especially, for the masses if future upheavals are to be successful. For this "a central organ must be established" and located in Paris if at all possible.[31] For this new task, new people are needed. It is necessary that they be young, strong, knowledgeable about, and deeply committed to, working for "a united Europe in the name of the great idea of communism." Further clarifying the role of these "new people," Sazonov writes that they must be "the bearers of conscious ideas," people who are not afraid to act on their own in defined groups and who, above all, are "capable of scientifically establishing the means to realize these ideas." The task of the proposed journal, with the support of these "new people," consists in "creating a European force for the achievement of communism and pointing out the practical means for this."[32] Sazonov envisioned here a grand scheme for the transformation of the European state system into a close federation of peoples striving in unison toward progress, a federation led by France, Germany, and Italy against all existing regimes. This he called "the collosal, centralized force for the realization of our ideas in the future."[33] The new journal was to play a vital part in this process of change, according to Sazonov. He outlined the contents of the first issue, which was to include contributions on specific countries not only from convinced communists like Marx but also from sympathetic Proudhonists and nonaffiliated progressives like Herzen. The second issue was to be more theoretically oriented, based on the data supplied in the first issue on individual European nations. It is here that Sazonov believed Marx could make his most significant contribution.[34]

Once more, however, there was only silence from Marx, as far as the available evidence shows. A year later, Sazonov again wrote to Marx, this time from Paris, where he traveled illegally for a firsthand look at the impact of Louis Napoleon's consolidation of power. He recorded his observations for Marx, who was then at work on his *Class Struggles in France*. Paris, Sazonov writes, "has never represented such interest as at the present moment. The Old World finds itself on the eve of its own complete disintegration." Sazonov perceives Paris to be a storm center radiating from all sides "a multitude of various projects, hopes, intrigues, and conspiracies that change and disappear just as suddenly as they arise." The savage struggle for power among legitimists, Orleanists, Bonapartists, and democrats resembles what Sazonov calls "this most confused and amusing comedy."[35] All factions are relying on the support of the army, and Sazonov points out the very real danger of a Bonapartist conspiracy to seize power. At the same time, however, he relates to Marx the more hopeful stirrings, from their standpoint, of the masses, who "more and more are liberating themselves from the prejudices of the moribund world." Militant workers' associations continue to attract recruits; indeed, he finds that their activities "are far more progressive than could be presumed on the basis of their statutes." He mentions the work of Cabet, Lerroux, and Louis Blanc in this regard, and indicates that he is translating Marx's *Manifesto of the Communist Party* into French for distribution to these workers' groups. He applauds Marx for using the international exhibition in London, the showpiece of bourgeois achievements, as evidence to point out that middle-class progress leads inevitably to its own decline and to the coming of communism. This theme, he concludes, is an example "of your genius." He asks Marx, to whom he refers as his "dear Teacher," to keep in touch with him about these matters.[36]

Sazonov sent one more letter to Marx some years later, despite the fact that he had assumed a more moderate political orientation. In May 1860 Sazonov wrote to Marx: "You have given to the scientific world the first part of an excellent work, which will recognizably transform economic science and establish it on new, more solid, principles." He tells Marx not to pay attention to the "fruitless polemics" directed against him and his work; "all serious, all honest people are on your side." Instead of becoming involved with these petty intrigues, he urges Marx to continue his work on the *Critique of Political Economy.* "You have achieved enormous success among thinking people," Sazonov writes, including the people of Russia. Sazonov informs Marx that this success in Russia has been aided by the lectures in Moscow by Professor I. K. Babst, who regularly teaches a course on political economy. Sazonov promises to send Marx a newspaper article describing "the respect surrounding your name in our country."[37]

Was Sazonov "the first Russian Marxist" as Riazanov claims he was? Soviet commentators unhesitatingly conclude he was not. Sazonov's admission that he was a communist in his 1850 letter to Marx is seen as a passing intellectual fancy, an effort by an unsuccessful opportunist to become associated with a prominent socialist. Koz'min points out that Sazonov was still too closely tied to a variety of moderate socialists and their positions for him to have made a serious commitment to Marx. More significant for Koz'min is his charge that Sazonov never truly understood Marx's ideas. Sazonov speaks of "civilization" instead of "society," "people" instead of "class," "evolution" instead of "conflict"; this was clearly not the vocabulary of a Marxist thinker. Koz'min also believes that there is little in Sazonov's letters to indicate that he truly comprehended the notions of Marx which he claimed to have accepted. Furthermore, "Sazonov arrived at his 'communism' not by the path of the study of the economic development of contemporary society but rather as a result of his disillusionment with the principle of individual freedom. . . . Sazonov searched for the path to the 'realization of communism' not in the development of the workers' movement but in the literary activity of groups of intelligentsia-revolutionaries." Koz'min concludes that Marx himself would be the most astonished of all if he knew "that there were historians who, on the basis of Sazonov's letters, were persuaded that Sazonov had taken a step in the direction of proletarian communism and had transformed himself into a 'real Marxist.' "[38]

There is a certain degree of overstatement in both Riazanov's assertion that Sazonov was the first Russian Marxist and Koz'min's argument that he was not. It would be difficult to define very clearly what a "Marxist" would have been around 1850 since Marx himself had not yet fully developed his ideas in any comprehensive manner, nor did he head a political party with an ideology and a widespread recruiting process. Thus, it is unreasonable to demand of Sazonov that he comprehend Marx in the manner of Marxists or Leninists a half-century later in order for the label "Marxist" to be applied legitimately to him. What can be safely stated is that Sazonov was genuinely attracted to Marx's critique of society at a time when Marx was formulating and refining many of his fundamental conceptions, and that Sazonov certainly understood Marx better than—and well before—any other Russian intellectual of his time. The motives behind his temporary commitment to Marx's theory are therefore perhaps less important than the more concrete fact that he respected Marx intellectually as a serious thinker and critic of society for the rest of his life, as the final letter to Marx so forcefully indicates.

Sazonov had a far more problematic relationship at this time with his former student comrade, Alexander Herzen, who arrived in Paris in May 1848 amid the revolution to find his old friend deeply immersed in revolutionary activities there. Although there was some mistrust between them from the start,[39] their relations were quite cordial for several years after their remeeting in Paris. They were in contact with each other over a variety of concerns, ranging from cooperating to support Proudhon's paper, La Voix du Peuple, to arranging for passports to Switzerland through their common friend James Fazy.[40] Concerning their plans for "democratic" journals, they also worked together with Herwegh, to whom they were both close at this point, and Golovin, with whom they were less enamored. Although Herzen made some of his own contacts in Europe, Sazonov had built up a fairly wide network of socialist antimonarchical comrades as a result of his participation on various newspapers and journals prior to Herzen's arrival in Paris.

In 1852 Herzen's reaction to the discovery of the affair between his wife and his friend Herwegh spilled over into many of his relationships. Sazonov's exact connection to the affair is not known, but Herzen turned against him venomously. He wrote to another friend, "My friendship, my familiarity with [Sazonov] has ended forever."[41] Sazonov was deeply disturbed by Herzen's severing of their relations. He wrote to Herzen to try to calm his passionate outbursts and to urge him not to discontinue their political projects. Sazonov also admitted that he had a heart condition which was worsening, and that he "might not have long to live."[42] Because of this, he felt it was imperative that they put aside personal suspicions and devote them-selves to their political work. He reassured Herzen that "from my side, I know that nothing in our friendship has changed" and he expressed the hope that "from your side, nothing [be allowed to] destroy our long-standing friendship."[43]

Indeed, relations between them did improve for a time as Sazonov contributed to Herzen's newly established Russian Free Press in London. Some of these writings reveal aspects of Sazonov's thinking in the mid-1850s. Sazonov wrote a proclamation for Herzen in October 1854 concerning the outbreak of the Crimean War.[44] He drew a contrast in the proclamation between Russia and France, explaining how the French "liberated the peasantry" during the 1789 revolution and why there was so much sympathy toward the Polish cause in France. The proclamation urges Russians "to overthrow the yoke of the 'German' government" in St. Petersburg and calls for the emancipation of all peasants in Russia, with land. This, together with the realization of Polish independence from the Russian Empire, is listed as the main task confronting the Russian people.[45]

Sazonov wrote a more substantial piece which appeared in the second issue of Herzen's *Poliarnaia zvezda* in 1856, a wide-ranging article called "O meste Rossii na vsemirnoi vystavke." Here he tried to clarify his views on the relationship between Russia and Europe, a problem which had concerned him for some time. Sazonov charac-terized Western European "civilization" as having despotic govern-ments coexisting with comparatively independent public opinion. This interplay between government and society is largely the cre-ation of the bourgeois class, which has achieved preeminence in the economic—but not the political—sector of European life. Bour-geois Europe's distinctive trait is reflected in its established forums for discussions of views and trends that are often in conflict with the government. The best examples of these forums, according to Sazonov, can be found in the press and in public meetings. By contrast, Russia differs from Europe in a number of important ways, including the lack of industrial development. The main reason for this, Sazonov argues in very Marxist overtones, is that "industry in Europe is now emerging in the bourgeois epoch, and in Russia there is no bourgeoisie."[46] Probing behind this, Sazonov finds the cause in the system of jurisprudence which has been established over the course of centuries in Russia and the West. In the West, there has always been a different structure of property and different conceptions of justice from those which developed in Russia. Whereas common (*obshchinnoe*) property has largely been overcome by individual property in the West, in Russia it remains a central feature of ownership patterns. Without a legal system which responds to, reflects, and consolidates these new developments in social class mobility and economic change, Russia remains mired in the past.

Russian civilization, Sazonov continues, is primarily defined by its own history—by the facts of the Tartar occupation, the power of the Orthodox Church, and the separation from many of the transforming forces of the West. His point, however, is that neither Russia nor Europe is superior—they are different cultures and societies, and as such have to be understood on their own terms. Similarly, he states that his argument does not predispose him to either the "despisers" or the devotees of the West. He admits, on the one hand, that having lived for years in Europe, he has become accustomed to a European way of life—especially in France, "which I consider my second homeland."[47] On the other hand, he wants to indicate his deep attachment to Russia in spite of his disagreement with messianic notions of Slavic dominion over the West: "A renewed Russia will take its place in a transformed Europe; then the reconciled popular masses will no longer reproach one another as the privileged classes of various nations now do. Western Europeans have ceased to regard liberated Russians as barbarians, and we must cease to dream about the approaching collapse of a decadent West and about the global reign of the Slavic tribes."[48] He closes his essay with a call for a unified opposition movement for change in Russia: "There is room on this earth for each generation, for all ideas and for all labor. Let us unite our forces so that nowhere will there be dens sheltering slavery, ignorance, and lies."[49]

Aside from attempting to transcend the categories of the Westernizer versus Slavophile debate within the Russian intelligentsia, Sazonov was also engaging in a lightly veiled polemic with Herzen over the notion of disillusionment with post-1848 Europe. Sazonov did not share Herzen's loss of faith in the future of European civilization. They also disagreed on the role of communal Russia. Herzen was moving closer to embracing the *obshchina* as a revolutionary conception, while Sazonov looked in a semi-Marxist manner at the evolution of property and industrialization in the West as keys to radical change. They continued to cooperate and correspond for a time, but soon drifted irreparably apart.[50]

In 1854 Sazonov published a small book, *La Vérité sur l'empereur Nicholas*. The book, which was issued anonymously "par une Russe," has been considered "the most brilliant and successful," in literary terms, of Sazonov's works.[51] Although it contains a number of factual inaccuracies and some questionable interpretive statements, the book was favorably received in France. During the Crimean War, it was widely used by the French press to portray the tsarist regime in an unfavorable light. The book is primarily a broad-scaled attack on the government of Nicholas I, and reveals the author's deep hostility toward the emperor who was responsible for revoking Sazonov's Russian citizenship. Its popularity for the contemporary French-reading public in Europe lay not so much in its factual particulars as in the general characteristics of Nicholas's personality and the policies of his government as presented by a Russian revolutionary with apparent access to firsthand sources on the emperor and his personal milieu. As the book's subtitle stated, its purpose was to reveal the "intimate history of [Nicholas's] life and reign."

Sazonov's book must inevitably be compared to Golovin's *Russia under the Autocrat*, which appeared about the same time. If Sazonov's book seems to have been more popular, this may be due to its brevity and readability; Golovin's study of Nicholas and his regime was written in a more demanding manner and filled two large volumes. Sazonov, incidentally, was quite aware of Golovin's book and made reference to it in his discussion of Golovin's conflict with Nicholas. In a chapter comparing the politics of Nicholas with those of Ivan the Terrible, Sazonov drew a parallel between Prince Kurbskii's flight abroad to escape from Ivan's tyranny and Golovin's refusal to return from Paris at Nicholas's command. Both Kurbskii and Golovin brought to the attention of Europe the nature of Russia's autocracy in a manner that would have been impossible within the country, Sazonov observes.[52]

One of the more interesting sections of Sazonov's book concerns the area of Russian literature which was of special significance to him. He indicated to his readers how Nicholas had not only systematically destroyed an authentic literary culture but had also replaced it with his own artificial, official literature. He listed Ryleev, Bestuzhev, Kükhelbecker, Pushkin, Lermontov, and Dostoevsky, among others, as writers who had been executed, exiled, or imprisoned by the emperor. In place of the literary journals to which many of these individuals (and other writers) had contributed their poetry and prose, Nicholas "created an unbelievable mass of government journals" under various state ministers designed to influence the content and style of Russian culture. One of these new journals was a journal of "public enlightenment," another was a journal devoted to the nation's "internal affairs," another to finance, and still others to technical subjects; the range of coverage and distribution was vast and nationwide, extending from the capital cities to the remote provinces. At the same time, periodicals from abroad were placed under strict controls, Sazonov explains, and Russians were discouraged from subscribing to them in general.[53] Sazonov was in effect portraying a kind of culture of official propaganda, *avant le mot;* for Sazonov's European readers, this was the first time such a charge against the tsar had been published by a Russian émigré.

In his conclusion, after an analysis of diplomacy, finance, serfdom, and other aspects of Nicholas's regime, Sazonov turned again to a work of literature to make his final interpretive statement on the Russian emperor. On the one hand, Nicholas aspired to a grandeur which involved comparisons with historical figures no less than Louis XIV, Frederick the Great, and Napoleon Bonaparte; on the other hand, there was a pathos visible in Nicholas's pedestrian character, hopelessly in search of that grandeur. This situation of unattainably lofty goals being pursued by a man incapable of achieving them was best epitomized for Sazonov in Gogol's play, *Inspector General.* Indeed, Sazonov strongly believed that Gogol intended the caricatured hero of the play to be "Nicholas himself, transformed into a petty official." As Khlestakov assumed a role beyond the ability of his character in the play, so did Nicholas in reality; as Khlestakov convinced himself that lies were truths, so too did Nicholas.[54]

In 1855 Sazonov became an editor for *L'Athenaeum français,* one of the superior literary periodicals of the age. He wrote a number of review essays for the journal on a variety of topics from the origins of Muhammed to Western philosophy, but his main field of specialization (and his best articles) concerned Russian and European literature.[55] He also published articles in Russia on literary and political themes in the *St. Peterburgskie vedomosti, Nashe vremia,* and *Otechestvennye zapiski;* these articles appear under the *noms de plume* of Karl Stachel and Feopatel'.[56]

In 1859 Sazonov became one of the main editors of the weekly Parisian paper *La Gazette du Nord,* whose stated goal was to familiarize Europeans with the life of Russia and Scandinavia. He published an extraordinary number of articles in this journal during 1859–60—twenty-eight by the count of one historian.[57] His articles concern many subjects, including the emancipation of the Russian peasantry, the condition of Jews in Russia, and recent developments in Russian literature. Soviet historians interpret these articles as evidence of Sazonov's gravitation in his last years away from radicalism and toward a more moderate political position.[58] It is true that he argued in his *Gazette* articles that the Russian peasantry was no longer subject to mass rebellions with leaders like Razin and Pugachev,[59] that Russian society should "preserve national traditions,"[60] that he defended constitutionalism,[61] and that he wanted Russia to avoid "the proletariat, that gaping ulcer of contemporary societies" as he now saw it.[62] This, to be sure, is a clear indication of a changed position and, in some instances, a renunciation of his earlier statements to Marx. Nevertheless, a sense of searching for new categories and new interpretations also emerges from Sazonov's *Gazette* articles. His discussion of gentry interests with respect to the peasant emancipation may be less a defense of traditional aristocratic rights and privileges than a recognition of the realities of class relationships in Russia. Thus, when he argued that peasant liberation would not be possible without adequate compensation to the landlord class, he was pointing out a path between the two camps of gentry conservatives and "revolutionary democrats."[63] Similarly, Sazonov changed his views about the rural commune in Russia. Now he defended the notion of collective ownership of agricultural land, but not only because of his fears of an emerging landless proletariat; an appreciation of the importance of communal land among the peasants also led him to argue for a network of independent communes and other producing associations in the Russian countryside.[64]

Sazonov's ideas, then, certainly were veering away from some of the more radical aspects of his earlier critique of contemporary society, although his general position around 1860 cannot easily be identified with any of the prevailing viewpoints in Russia any more than it can be considered typical of the Russian emigration as a whole. His conceptions were changing according to his own eclectic reasoning, subject of course to the impact of existing European and Russian trends. A good illustration of his independent thought at this time was an evaluation of his own revolutionary commitment which he made in the context of a comparison of tsars: "Yes, I love freedom more than slavery, law more than arbitrariness, a legislative order more than personal caprice, progress more than stagnation, science more than superstition—in a word, I prefer Alexander II to Ivan the Terrible. It is in this sense that I am a revolutionary."[65]

Although Sazonov expressed many of his ideas in his articles on political affairs, his most perceptive work was done in his essays on literature—especially those on Russian literature. In an age when literary criticism in Russia was developing into a sophisticated art form as well as a weapon against the autocracy, Sazonov's articles on Russian writers represent the analogue of this trend abroad. He was fully conscious of the important work done in the field of literary criticism by Belinskii. Like the essays of Belinskii and his successors in Russia—particularly Chernyshevskii and Dobroliubov—Sazonov's reviews of specific books or authors were occasions for a wide-ranging analysis of the evolution of Russian literature, Russian society, and Russia's relationship with the West.

Two of his most representative essays on Russian fiction concern the writings of Herzen and Ivan Turgenev. It was not accidental, of course, that he chose two Russian exiles to portray the most creative developments in Russian national literature. He interprets Turgenev's career as a writer in the context of a "crisis in the international development of Russia," which began after the defeat of the Napoleonic army in Russia and ended in 1856, when, in the midst of the Crimean defeat, Alexander II revealed his intention to liberate the peasantry. This period of crisis, Sazonov argues, was severe for the country, and Turgenev's fiction was a new means of expressing the efforts to resolve that national crisis. In *Notes of a Sportsman, Nest of the Gentry,* and *On the Eve,* Turgenev attempts to bring to life Russia's problems as a nation in the characters he creates. Sazonov also sees no contradiction between Turgenev's living abroad and his devotion to Russia. Perhaps identifying with the problem himself, Sazonov quotes a statement by Turgenev in which he explains why he believes he could best serve Russia by writing beyond its borders.[66]

Sazonov's essay on Herzen in the *Gazette du Nord* is actually a review of the French edition of part of the first volume of Herzen's memoir, *My Past and Thoughts.*[67] Instead of confining himself to the book, however, Sazonov discusses Herzen's upbringing and background as a way of understanding more fully the significance of the memoir. He presents Herzen as an advanced intellectual who led a small circle of university friends into an exploration of the leading European ideas of his time. This, then, is shown to be a process affecting Russia's national evolution.[68] In Sazonov's view, Russia required the stimulation of Hegelian philosophy and French socialism during the 1830s and 1840s in order to escape from the heavy weight of traditional culture and to achieve "originality of thought. To Herzen belongs the high honor of being one of the pioneers who opened up this path." Sazonov then shows how Herzen's memoir itself is the fulfillment of those earlier years of intellectual quest, and how it has become a source of new values. The book's greatest achievement lies in its ability to both affect and reflect the internal development of Russia; it is "an expression of the existing turning point" confronting the Russian nation and "a trailblazer of the new era."[69]

Sazonov's personal relations with the growing Russian colony abroad were not harmonious while he worked for the *Gazette*. In December 1859 a literary reading and musical concert benefit performance was arranged, with the proceeds to be donated to needy Russians in Paris. Sazonov was first invited and then, at the last minute, disinvited. The organizers of the benefit were the French journalist Ferri de Pigny and a priest from the Russian embassy in Paris named Vasiliev, who was also an agent of the Third Section. Both were worried about Sazonov's "revolutionary tendencies" and feared he might use the occasion to castigate the Russian government.[70]

At the same time, Sazonov was in verbal combat with Herzen over the latter's publication in *Kolokol* of part of a book by the moderate Russian émigré P. V. Dolgorukov. Sazonov wrote Herzen that he was shocked that the pages of *Kolokol* would be open to, and supportive of, Dolgorukov's political ideas: "Just take his book—it isn't a book, but a memoir-notebook about people who played up to him or who despise him. He extols the genius of the charlatan . . . and abuses many honorable people. Everything revolves around personalities. And his ravings about constitutions! God forbid. And this landlord writes the 'truth about Russia.' "[71]

To this private statement, Sazonov added a public one when he wrote a highly critical review of Dolgorukov's book in *Gazette du Nord*. The book, which admittedly was gaining popularity, was for Sazonov a superficial work utterly without serious content. At a time when Russia was experiencing "a profound revolution," it was disturbing to find a new book on Russia which was based merely on acecdotes and proposed utopian projects rather than on a genuine examination of the crucial issues of peasant emancipation. Sazonov charged Dolgorukov with being motivated primarily by "state interests," not by real concern for the improvement of the Russian people.[72]

Sazonov's last years are confusing, and in the absence of sufficient primary sources from this period of his life, the contradictions cannot be disentangled. One fact is indisputably clear, however, and it is true of all émigrés of this generation—despite all his involvements in European affairs, Sazonov remained deeply attached to Russia. The evidence for this conclusion is very convincing and ranges from family letters to police records. One important part of this evidence is the correspondence Sazonov maintained with his sister, Maria Ivanovna Poludemskaia, who had married into a family of high officials. Sazonov admitted the great intellectual influence his sister had on him in one of his letters to her: "It is to you that I send my first letter from Europe. It is to you that my first impressions belong . . . because you have had such an impact on the formation of my opinions and my beliefs."[73] The correspondence unfortunately does not elaborate on exactly what kind of influence she had, but it does reveal Sazonov's strong concern for family and for Russia. Most of the letters are about his wife, his children, and their domestic triumphs and travails. Since Sazonov suspected quite correctly that his letters were being read by the police, he could not discuss any ideas or events that were potentially controversial.[74]

Another problem that Sazonov discussed in this correspondence in passing references beginning around 1859 was his desire to return to Russia. This was also a matter that the Russian police were particularly interested in for obvious reasons. The police had been watching Sazonov closely since the 1840s. Their reports charge him with writing articles in "democratic journals" which are inimical to the Russian government, and with "participating in revolutionary plots." When the government demanded that he return to St. Petersburg in 1849, he was threatened with loss of estate, civic rights, and other "consequences of disobeying government orders."[75] He claimed he needed to remain abroad longer for reasons of health,[76] which was the excuse most émigrés used in responding to government ultimatums to leave Europe.

The police continued to report on his associations, meetings, and publications through the 1850s even after he was declared an émigré. So matters stood until 1857, when a report mentions that Sazonov submitted a petition to Grand Duke Konstantin during the latter's visit to Paris that year "in which [Sazonov] recognized his

faults and solicited authorization to return to his fatherland."
Sazonov admits himself to be, the report continues, "the author of
writing hostile to our government, but he professes patriotic sentiments."[77] To resolve the matter, the government turned to their
chief police agent in Paris, Iakov Tolstoi, whom they asked to write
an evaluative report on Sazonov in 1858. Tolstoi's opinion was both
highly respected and informed since he had been a close and loyal
observer of Russian opposition figures in Europe for decades.
Tolstoi appropriately reviewed Sazonov's career in comparison with
those of Golovin and Nikolai Turgenev. Sazonov's writings for
French liberal periodicals were at times critical of the Russian government, according to Tolstoi, but he concluded that there was
nothing in his writings expressing the "abhorrence of the Sovereign
that one finds on every page in the books of Golovin and Turgenev."
Tolstoi therefore recommended permission for Sazonov to return to
Russia.[78]

The government also took note of other reports of police agents,
which stressed Sazonov's commitment to his family and the fact that
much of his journalistic writing was done to earn money to support
his family. Finally, in the fall of 1858, Sazonov was pardoned and
granted permission to return to Russia by a decree of Alexander II.[79]
Officials in the government also reported that, to their knowledge,
Sazonov's intentions were to leave for St. Petersburg "within two or
three months" after closing out his affairs in Paris.[80] For reasons not
made clear from the evidence, however, Sazonov's passport was not
sent to him until the spring of 1861, two and a half years later.[81] The
file then reveals nothing for another year, but reports dated 1862
mention that Sazonov has left Paris and is residing in Geneva. The
government assumes that he is en route to Russia, and that he has
not gone further because he is "devoid of the [financial] means" to
continue his journey.[82]

The evidence does not permit a definitive resolution of
Sazonov's intentions at this point. While in Geneva, he renewed his
contacts with Fazy and with Johann-Phillip Becker, whom he knew
from his earlier visits to Geneva. Among Becker's papers an essay
written by Sazonov in April 1862 was found which may have been
composed for Becker and his German comrades. In this, his last
known work, Sazonov chose to explain the significance of the peasant reforms and the role of the intelligentsia in Russia in grandiose
terms. He defined the 1861 emancipation decree as "a complete
economic transformation of the very foundations of Russian soci-

ety. . . . World history knows of no other example of such a collosal economic revolution. Seventeen eighty-nine remains completely in the shadows [by comparison]." Sazonov foresaw vast changes inevitably taking place in Russia as more land gradually passed into the hands of free peasant proprietors. He suggested that these currents would reach beyond the realm of solely economic forces. In a passage that reflected his earlier concerns in his letters to Marx, Sazonov now wrote, "History teaches us that economic changes necessarily are accompanied by political and social changes." An important example of these intersecting areas of change could be seen, according to Sazonov, in the demands being expressed by gentry officials in the Tver, Moscow, and Petersburg gubernia meetings. Here one finds the shape of the future as these gentry meetings produce proposals seeking "the abolition of all class privileges and the convening of a national government elected by the entire nation." Another crucial development, Sazonov observed, was the formation of a new social group in Russian society as a further by-product of the emancipation of the serfs. This group, he wrote, was distinguished from all existing social classes in that it did not define itself "according to its own interests." Furthermore, this group did not belong to any single existing class. Instead, it consisted of people from various classes and was characterized by the tendency "to represent and defend with passion and enthusiasm the general currents of contemporary civilization." He found a comparison in the eighteenth-century "Englightenment party" in France, "but today it exists only in Russia."[83]

Sazonov was optimistic about the possibilities of progressive change in Russia in part, at least, because of the rise of this intelligentsia, which was committed to the success of these new forces unleashed by the emancipation. He nevertheless warned against the possibility that the future realization of freedom for the Russian people might "be compromised, on the one hand, by the ignorance of the popular masses and, on the other, by the irresponsible and utopian tendencies of the gentry."[84]

Regrettably, Sazonov did not have any further opportunities to expand on these ideas, nor did he develop any further his concept of the "revolutionary" changes affecting Russia as a result of the emancipation. With these unpublished notes—a kind of spiritual testament to his talented and creative mind—his career came to an end. He died on 5 (17) November 1862 in Geneva, probably from the heart condition that had worried him for years. He died in virtual obscurity, forgotten by most of his former comrades. "No one came to his grave," wrote Herzen, "no one mourned over his death."[85] By digging Sazonov's grave very deep in his memoirs, Herzen tried to ensure that no one would ever want to know who Sazonov was and what he had accomplished. Despite the fact that Sazonov never had the tenacity or the will to create a lasting monument of political or intellectual inspiration, Herzen clearly misjudged Sazonov's abilities and achievements.

5

P. V. Dolgorukov: The Republican Prince

The career of Petr Vladimirovich Dolgorukov is filled with so many exceptions to the established modalities of Russian émigré life in this period as to make efforts to set up such generalizations almost futile. He emigrated not once but twice; unlike all other first-generation émigrés, he actually returned from Europe when summoned by Nicholas I before leaving Russia forever. He was the most committed émigré journalist of his generation, with the pardonable exception of Herzen; while his émigré compatriots concentrated on publishing books, brochures, and articles, Dolgorukov established a periodical press that functioned alongside Herzen's more prominent Russian Free Press. Dolgorukov's ancestry was not only so princely that he stood above his aristocratic émigré comrades, but so ancient that his family lineage far antedated that of the ruling Romanovs. As he wrote on one occasion to Alexander II, "You know, sovereign, that my ancestors were Grand Princes and rulers of Russia at a time when the ancestors of your Majesty were not yet Counts of Oldenburg."[1]

Unlike Turgenev, Golovin, or Sazonov, Dolgorukov had a consistent political program, which he reiterated in his numerous writings. Other aspects of his life are quite unique among the émigrés. Dolgorukov may have been responsible for the death of Pushkin, albeit indirectly and doubtlessly unintentionally; nevertheless, no other émigré had to defend himself against allegations of involvement in a dual that was fatal to Russia's greatest poet. In terms of careers prior to emigration, no other émigré had achieved so prominent a reputation as a scholar as Dolgorukov did with his distinguished publications in the field of genealogy. Once abroad, he achieved a more unsavory notoriety in several scandals, one of which was actually brought before a Paris courtroom, causing embarrassment for many Russians abroad. Despite this, he was, ironically, the only Russian political critic abroad whom Herzen publicly defended and celebrated.

Nevertheless, Dolgorukov is not mentioned in Herzen's memoir, primarily because he came to Herzen's attention after the book was completed. As a result, Dolgorukov has suffered the identical fate of the other Russian émigrés of his generation who have been ignored by historians; his contributions to the antitsarist opposition abroad and his place in the Russian emigration have gone largely unrecorded and unevaluated.[2]

Petr Dolgorukov was born on 27 December 1816 (8 January 1817) to an illustrious family whose origins stretched continuously back to Mikhail Chernigovskii, one of Russia's ancient rulers in the thirteenth century.[3] He was orphaned very young as his mother died giving birth to him, and his father, a major general in the army, died before he was a year old. He was raised by his grandmother until he was ten. When she died in 1827, young Dolgorukov was sent to the elite Imperial Corps of Pages school. He performed brilliantly at the school, achieving the title of *page d'chambre*, an honor given to the top student in the junior year class. Dolgorukov was soon stripped of this title for some offense he committed, the nature of which has never been made clear. Although he might still have recovered his loss and gone on to a career in the top ranks of the government had he so desired later on, there is no doubt that this dark event severely limited his chances for such a post.[4]

Dolgorukov then accepted a minor job in the Ministry of Education, but he was clearly dissatisfied with his situation. Moreover, he was mocked not only for his dishonorable loss of title at the Corps of Pages, but also for his limping, bowlegged gait. He soon dropped out of service entirely and began associating with a group notorious at the time for "insolent debauchery."[5] The patron of the group was the Dutch diplomat Baron Heeckeren, who devised pranks and schemes for his aimless disciples. One of these mischievous intrigues for which Dolgorukov was personally responsible was the composition of an insulting lampoon in 1836 at the expense of Alexander Pushkin. The lampoon, anonymously written, identified an alleged lover of Pushkin's wife. As a result of the lampoon, the outraged poet challenged the man he suspected, Georges Dantes, to a duel and lost his life in February 1837. Although Dolgorukov argued for the rest of his life that he was not the author of the insulting and provocative Pushkin lampoon, he was hounded periodically by charges that he was in fact responsible for the death of the renowned poet.[6]

Apparently unable to overcome the depression of his shattered hopes by continuing this dissolute life-style, Dolgorukov shifted his attention in the late 1830s to serious scholarly research in the field of Russian genealogy. He completed a four-volume study of Russian aristocratic genealogy at the end of the decade which was very favorably received when it was published.[7] At this critical moment, when he was on the edge of recovering his reputation and respect, he went abroad and published a book which decisively altered the future course of his life. There is no concrete evidence to indicate why the sharp change occurred, but clearly Dolgorukov was at a crossroads. He certainly enjoyed the easy acceptance into intellectual circles in Paris which his aristocratic background and his newly acquired reputation as a genealogist won for him. This access to French intellectual life and rapid recognition of his work with respect there contrasted sharply with his failures in Russia, where he found ridicule far more often than admiration. Whether out of revenge against his real and imagined enemies from the aristocracy, or for other, unknown reasons, Dolgorukov published the provocative *Notice sur les principales familles de la Russie* under the pseudonym "Count d'Amagro" early in 1843.[8]

The critical nature of the book and the real identity of its author were the subjects of a long letter by Iakov Tolstoi, the tsarist police agent in Paris, to the head of the Third Section in St. Petersburg. Although the book had produced, according to Tolstoi, a "disagreeable impression on the small number of people who might be interested in such a subject," he felt it his duty to bring this work to the government's attention. The book is dominated by "irreverent descriptions of people in high positions." Dolgorukov, Tolstoi went on, was attacking men of long and eminent service, whose loyalty to Russia "has been recognized by their sovereign and their fatherland." The aristocracy is presented "in the most odious of colors, like a band of traitors and assassins." The book is "completely inimical to the interests of my government," and will provide ammunition to Russia's enemies against which it will be difficult to defend if Dolgorukov continues to publish such writings. Thus, Tolstoi concludes, Dolgorukov is a man with "an impetuous and confused character" who is dangerous to Russia so long as he is free to attack his country from abroad.[9]

The Russian government, on orders from Nicholas I, took immediate action. Dolgorukov was ordered home without delay and the Russian ambassador in Paris, Count Kiselev, was instructed to speak to the French administration about helping them extradite

Dolgorukov in the event that he refused to comply. To the surprise of the Russian authorities, Dolgorukov left Paris on 21 March 1843 to return home as requested. Kiselev nevertheless did speak to Guizot, the French prime minister, who was reportedly relieved that Dolgorukov had gone voluntarily and that further moves against him were thus unnecessary.[10]

On his way to Russia, Dolgorukov wrote personally to the tsar in an effort to explain his actions and intentions. He said that he had written the truth about Russia in his book, however unpleasant it was to admit. There was a time in the grim past "when tsaricide was [ingrained] in the mores and habits of Russians," and when succession to the throne was determined by "night rebellions and bloodshed." But the horrors of the past, the oligarchic excesses and aristocratic intrigues, were eradicable. Dolgorukov ended his letter with a plea to Nicholas I to learn from the past for the benefit of the country's future. Exposure of the truth leads to a hastening of the success of Russia's "intellectual and moral development," he concluded.[11]

If Dolgorukov was hoping to have some influence on Nicholas and the running of the Russian government by leaving the safety of France, he miscalculated completely. Neither his family connections in government nor his reputation as a respected genealogist could save him from Nicholas's wrath. On 2 May 1843 he was arrested upon his arrival at Kronstadt and all of his possessions were confiscated. After a hearing in St. Petersburg, he was sentenced to administrative exile in Viatka, where Herzen earlier had been exiled. The Third Section archives contain a number of reports on the books, letters, papers, and visiting cards taken from Dolgorukov at the time of his arrest. The books included such unsubversive items as works by Thierry and Chateaubriand, histories of Europe, royal almanacs, travel guides, and a book on the English peerage.[12] Dolgorukov was processed like a common criminal. Not since the arrest of the Decembrists had a member of one of Russia's most distinguished families been imprisoned and exiled in such a manner.

Dolgorukov's exile, however, was commuted a year later when he was permitted to live anywhere in the empire with the exception of St. Petersburg. Upon his release, he composed an obsequious letter to Benckendorff, asking that he "carry to the foot of the throne the expression of my profound gratitude" for the clemency granted by Nicholas. It was Dolgorukov's most ardent wish to "consecrate my entire life in service to the Emperor," he wrote.[13] Exactly how he was to do this was not clear to him though. He had no desire to enter the ranks of the civil service at the ninth level, which was where he was entitled to begin. The only other possibility was to be selected for some advisory position close to the seat of power, which was doubtful.

In any event, Dolgorukov spent the next fifteen years relatively quietly, marrying, becoming a father, and living mainly at his Tula estate with frequent trips to Moscow. During this period he again turned to genealogical research. In 1853 he published the first part of his *Rossisskaia rodoslovnaia kniga,* which the government censor found entirely acceptable and commendable.[14] As a result, the ban against his residing in the capital was lifted. In 1857 a second edition of his *Notice* was issued in Berlin, but Dolgorukov wrote to a relative who now headed the Third Section that this publication occurred "without my consent and against my wishes. The brochure of Count Amagro was a sin of [my] youth. Who has not been young?"[15] He also managed to gain both government cooperation for information and a personal endorsement from the new tsar, Alexander II, to produce a biographical dictionary of the Russian aristocracy. The commissioned project was completed on schedule and the book was published in 1858.[16] It is likely that Alexander II approved of this book, which was published only in French, in the hope that it would counteract the negative impressions left by Dolgorukov's *Notice.*

Through family contacts and his own experience, Dolgorukov was on personal terms with a number of influential Russian statesmen during the 1850s. Those he knew included his cousin, V. A. Dolgorukov (head of the Third Section), A. M. Gorchakov (foreign minister), A. V. Golovnin (minister of education), and D. N. Bludov (president of the State Council). Dolgorukov was later to utilize his association with these individuals in positions of authority by writing highly critical essays about them. At this time, however, he was more interested in them as a means of having some input into policy decisions regarding the reforms announced by Alexander II after his coronation.

In November 1857 Dolgorukov composed a long memorandum, "On the Internal Condition of Russia," which he presented to Grand Duke Konstantin on 2 December for consideration by the government. The memorandum's stated purpose was to alert the government to what Dolgorukov considered an alarming situation developing in the country which could be reversed only by enacting bold reforms. Dolgorukov warned the government that without a rapid and appropriate resolution of the peasant question, Russia would face popular discontent that could result in a massive peasant *bunt*, an upheaval directed against the state and the nobility of the proportions of the late-eighteenth-century "Pugachevshchina." Most fundamental and critical of all reforms, therefore, was the abolition of serfdom. Dolgorukov favored peasant emancipation with land, and with provisions for compensating the gentry land-owners.[17] In addition to making specific proposals on emancipation, he also outlined a number of political reforms that went well beyond what the government was prepared to permit. In the words of a historian who has recently examined Dolgorukov's memorandum,

He proposed reform of the courts, the table of ranks, budgetary procedures and the granting of titles; he recommended that the corporate institutions of the nobility, renamed *zemskiye*, be thrown open to all landowners and given a vastly enhanced role in provincial administration. He also recommended the formation of a committee of ministers to coordinate the government's activities. In regard to the censorship, Dolgorukov argued for *glasnost'*, or latitude for the press; he argued that the existing censorship system was harmful, since it depended on information provided by self-seeking police spies, and also pointless, since the government was powerless to stop the influx of Russian publications from England and Germany.[18]

During the next year and a half, Dolgorukov continued to involve himself in the reform process, but began to exhibit signs of discontent with the existing legal channels. In 1858 he refused an appointment as one of the government representatives on the Tula provincial committee because he feared these committees would not be free enough of bureaucratic restraint to be effective. His letter of rejection to the Tula governor, with its criticism of the government's procedures, was passed around and read "in large quantities" according to Third Section officials, who were cautiously keeping Dolgorukov's activities under surveillance.[19] Dolgorukov also criticized the government commissions as absurd because "the majority of the members do not live in the countryside and are utterly unfamiliar with the conditions, desires, and necessities of rural life."[20] At the same time, he published a statement with his redemption plans for the emancipation of the peasantry in the December issue of *Sovremennik* and circulated a more detailed version of his plan; the latter was blocked by the government before Dolgorukov could have it published. The problem of censorship was the most unsettling aspect of the government's policies for Dolgorukov personally. He wrote in 1859 that "literature had passed into the jurisdiction of the Third Section," and was convinced that the government had "a deep, inveterate hatred . . . for anyone who writes and thinks. Now doubt is as impossible as hope; the present situation is at an impasse and the future is ominous."[21]

No clearer statement could possibly reflect Dolgorukov's own situation. With little hope that his reform plans would be accepted by the government, and confronted with the specter of life-long censorship of his future writings on politics and reform, Dolgorukov decided to go abroad for a second time—this time permanently, as an émigré. In May 1859 he left Russia clandestinely, abandoning his wife and young son. Some scholars believe that Dolgorukov's main reason for leaving Russia was his realization that he would not be offered a high post in government, which he had coveted for years.[22] A more convincing case has demonstrated that Dolgorukov's motives for emigrating had far more to do with his desire to escape from the constraints of censorship and that both his writings and his activities in the period 1857–59 indicate he "had no basis for expecting an important government post."[23]

After his flight from Russia, Dolgorukov traveled through Italy, where he had discussions with Count Camille Cavour and other Italian political figures before settling in Paris. He immediately plunged into the writing of a new book on Russia, *La Vérité sur la Russie,* which was published in April 1860. Dolgorukov's purpose in publishing this book, as one historian has put it, was "to open Europe's eyes to the horrible situation in his country and, in this way, to induce the Russian government to embark decisively on a path of fundamental reforms."[24] This had also been the motivation for Nikolai Turgenev and Ivan Golovin in publishing their books on Russia abroad, but Dolgorukov's critique of the Russian state was at once different in content from theirs and a more devastating attack. The book was, in addition, an extension and elaboration of the ideas Dolgorukov first developed in his 1857 memorandum, now free of restrictive censorship.

La Vérité sur la Russie won considerable popularity for Dolgorukov in Western Europe. Not only was it acclaimed by Herzen in the pages of *Kolokol,*[25] but it was widely and favorably reviewed in European newspapers and journals.[26] The official Russian response was quite the reverse, however, and Dolgorukov's portraits of corruption and venality in administrative and aristocratic circles were strongly condemned.[27] P. D. Kiselev, the Russian ambassador in Paris, wrote an alarmed letter to the Third Section in St. Petersburg about Dolgorukov's book, which he called "a scandalous work." He also noted the potential impact of the book, given Dolgorukov's background. "Under the pretext of healing by means of publicity, the book exposes all the weak sides of our position. While these have been discussed by foreign writers, their lack of sound knowledge fundamentally undermined the authority of their judgments in the eyes of foreign governments and of society. But from the pen of a Russian author, and one, moreover, with a high social position, these disclosures of weakness acquire a serious importance and give the entire work a significance it undoubtedly does not possess, but which is imparted to it by these exceptional circumstances."[28]

Under orders from the Russian government, Kiselev requested Dolgorukov to withdraw the book from circulation and demanded his return to St. Petersburg under penalty of losing his civil rights and facing a sentence of exile to Siberia. Faced with almost the identical situation he had confronted in 1843 when he published his *Notice*, Dolgorukov this time responded quite differently. He rejected the ultimatum in defiant and mocking terms. "My emigration," he wrote to Kiselev, "is not the result of momentary passion. . . . It is the outcome of a plan, of deep conviction, worked out over many years with the greatest caution . . . so that I might speak the truth about my fatherland." Since this cannot be done inside Russia, it must be accomplished abroad. He says his intention is not to criticize individuals but to attack an entire system built on "personal caprice and the abuse of legality." He is writing critically "as a free man, a true patriot"; this is his duty and that is why he continues to regard himself while living abroad "as a Russian citizen."[29] Concerning the Russian government's demands that he return to defend himself, he said he could not because he had no respect for the legal system in Russia, where courts are "a caricature of justice." Sentencing him to Siberian exile was useless, he continued, as useless as sentencing him "to exile on the moon." He offered to send, in place of himself, his photograph, which the Third Section could send "to Viatka or Nerchinsk or any place [of exile] of your choice; I myself, forgive me, will not be caught in the clutches of your police force."[30]

After receiving Dolgorukov's sardonic reply, the Russian authorities promptly sequestered his estates in Russia, and on 5 June 1861 the tsar confirmed the government's decision to deprive Dolgorukov of his title and rights and sentenced him to "eternal exile." Dolgorukov thus legally became an émigré on this date.

At the same time that he was combatting the tsarist government, Dolgorukov was brought to trial in Paris by Prince Semyon Vorontsov, who sued him for defamation of Vorontsov's father's character. The evidence brought against Dolgorukov to support the charge included private letters as well as his books. Vorontsov won his court case in January 1861, but Dolgorukov managed to emerge from the scandal with the continued support of Herzen when he claimed that the entire trial was a conspiracy of the Russian and French governments to silence his critical voice.[31] The writer Ivan Turgenev, however, came away from the trial with a different view. He wrote to Herzen that Dolgorukov was "a morally dead man" and advised Herzen to stay away from Dolgorukov's "damaging tendencies."[32]

With the trial behind him, Dolgorukov plunged into a series of journalistic enterprises designed to spread more widely his criticism of Russia and also his reform proposals. *Budushchnost'* (The future), the first journal he wrote and edited, began to appear in September 1860. The journal was dedicated to "the denunciation of administrative procedures in Russia and to the propaganda of moderate constitutionalism."[33] A change at the head of the Leipzig press that published his journal forced him to close down *Budushchnost'* at the end of 1861; the new publisher was opposed to printing material critical of Russia.[34] Dolgorukov then created another journal, *Pravdivyi* (The truthful, or The just) which was published in Brussels; a companion version in French, *Le Véridique,* was printed simultaneously with the Russian edition.[35] This journal was superseded in November 1862 by *Listok* (The sheet), which was printed at first in Brussels (the first five numbers) and then in London, where Dolgorukov moved in the spring of 1863 to continue his campaign against Russia; *Listok* survived until July 1865.[36]

Dolgorukov also published several books during this period which expanded his criticism of Russia. In 1862 his *Des reformes en Russie* appeared, which was an elaboration of the attack on the Russian political system which he had presented in *La Vérité sur la Russie.* He also published a collection of political essays in 1862, *O peremene obraza pravleniia v Rossii* (On change in the form of government in Russia), a two-volume study of France under Napoleon III in 1864,[37] and a volume of sketches of Russian historical personalities in 1867.[38] In addition he published many smaller essays and brochures, and contributed occasionally to *Kolokol.*

Although Dolgorukov did not experience any difficulties in finding publishers abroad willing to print his books, he did encounter serious problems in trying to publish his journals. As obstacles to these ventures mounted, Dolgorukov began to assume the role of a militant combatant in what he saw as a war for freedom of expression. He also developed the sense of political paranoia that was characteristic of the émigré mentality of his time. He was outraged when the French authorities announced that they were prohibiting publication of any further editions of his two critical books on Russia in France—*La Vérité* and *Des reformes*. Convinced that the Russian government was behind this move, Dolgorukov wrote a letter of protest to an official in the French administration. He warned the French government that if his Brussels-based journal *Le Véridique* was prohibited in France, he would place on the masthead of each issue the following line: "This review has the honor of being banned in France."[39] Both France and Dolgorukov held firm to their announced intentions and carried out their threats: *Le Véridique* was prohibited in France, and Dolgorukov did put the promised phrase on the masthead of the journal.

Dolgorukov also wrote directly to some of the highest officials in the Russian government about these matters. He accused the Russians of having primary responsibility for the change of editors at the Leipzig firm which led to the closing of his earlier journal *Budushchnost'*. At the same time, he boldly proclaimed to the Russian vice-chancellor that he would never be "reduced to silence" by censorship or coercion. If he was halted from publishing in Brussels by Russian pressure, he would move to London and continue his struggle there against the autocracy and its dominating "Petersburg camarilla." Indeed, he threatened the Russian administration with a form of blackmail in reverse: "Moreover, if I am compelled to relocate in London, I will publish in French the biographies of the members of the imperial family and their entourage."[40] By announcing his intention to publish in French, he was saying, of course, that his attacks would reach a far wider European audience than if he were to write in Russian. This was no idle threat, for Dolgorukov had a good deal of privileged information on the royal family and its court appointees. Again, both sides carried out their threats: Dolgorukov was forced to leave Brussels for London because of publishing problems, and he did publish a series of damaging biographical portraits in his journal as promised.[41]

In a revealing correspondence with Iurii Gagarin, who had emigrated from Russia for religious reasons,[42] Dolgorukov discussed in some detail his plans to fight Russia from afar. He spoke at one point of forming an émigré committee "composed of trusted people like you, Nikolai Turgenev, A. Golitsyn, myself, and others," specifically to expose Russian attempts at censoring émigré publications in Europe. It was absolutely vital, he believed, to have free access to published organs abroad.[43] "My banner still remains," he continued, "a constitutional monarchy on republican foundations." He also proclaimed to Gagarin that his journals and his entire career as an émigré were principally devoted to the establishment of this form of government in Russia.[44]

Dolgorukov's letters to Gagarin are also full of disturbing information received from Russia—the increase in the number of arrests and exiles to Siberia, the closing of Chernyshevskii's *Sovremennik,* and rumors of threats to the university faculties in the wake of an outbreak of fires in St. Petersburg in the summer of 1862. He wrote, in addition, about his contacts with recent, younger émigrés such as Leonid Bliummer, who was publishing a new journal in Berlin called *Svobodnoe slovo* (The Free Word), as well as about his meetings with more prominent émigrés like Herzen, Kel'siev ("horrible fanatic"), and Bakunin ("hero of the barricades").[45] Dolgorukov was also informed about the Russian student colony in Heidelberg, with which Herzen was in contact to raise support for Bakunin and for his own London press.[46] Surveying the overall situation in another and particularly perceptive letter to Gagarin, Dolgorukov wrote that "Russia is now in the mire, and in several years will surely be in blood." He feared this bloodshed would erupt because of the widening gulf between the Russian government and the increasingly radicalized youth. Russian students in Heidelberg and in St. Petersburg were an indication of frightening new currents of revolt at home and abroad, reflections of the substitution of radical politics for the more traditional values of church and state that were being eroded by the government's persistent refusal to embrace necessary reforms. He saw a process of evolution from the Decembrist uprising of 1825, from which there emerged "the youth of our pathetic generation, cowed, trembling, and groveling, for whom the Anichkov palace balls formed the purpose of life." The frivolity and idleness of his own generation, now in positions of power, had finally reached its zenith; Dolgorukov predicted the rise of a new generation that was already beginning to oppose the previous generation's "horrible nonsense" and irresponsibility, and that would continue to do so with increasing violence.[47]

In 1863, shortly before preparing to leave London for Switzerland, Dolgorukov was accused in a book of having been the author of the anonymous lampoon that led to Pushkin's death, an accusation that involved him in yet another public scandal.[48] Once again he escaped with only minimal damage to his reputation. In 1865, when Herzen left London for Geneva, Dolgorukov followed him and lived out his last years there in luxurious splendor. He turned away from his journalistic enterprises and gradually began to fall into episodes of bizarre behavior. He published a brochure gratuitously attacking Bakunin, argued frequently with Herzen while claiming he could trust no one else, and even made several conciliatory gestures toward the Russian government he had condemned so furiously in the past.[49] He also refused a request for financial support from a recent émigré, Mikhail Elpidin, who wanted to establish an émigré journal in Switzerland. Dolgorukov saw this as an effort "to preach assassination."[50] One of his strangest outbreaks occurred when he was visited in Bern by his son, Vladimir, whom he had abandoned in Russia a decade before. In a state of heightened anxiety and already gravely ill with dropsy, he denounced his son as a Russian police agent who had been sent to seize his papers. This fear was especially irrational in view of the fact that Dolgorukov had just written to his cousin in the Third Section to assure the Russian government that his son had no political intentions and gave his word that his son would not emigrate during his stay abroad.[51] Dolgorukov sent for Herzen to rescue him once his son arrived, and appointed Herzen as his executor for the safekeeping of his papers. In his letters to Ogarev, Herzen poignantly described Dolgorukov's terrible condition and his agony as he awaited death in alternating moments of clarity and hysteria.[52] Death finally came on 6 (18) August 1868.

Dolgorukov's political orientation, as presented with great consistency in his books on Russia and in his journals, was centered on the demand for a constitutional government to succeed the autocratic tsarist administration. His critique was rooted in a historical context in which he argued that Russian rulers had permitted centuries of abuse and privilege exercised originally by Russia's leading aristocratic families and, more recently, by the court bureaucracy that had been built up since the time of Peter the Great. Government had been corrupted because of the tyranny of these ruling elites.[53] In the course of his critique, Dolgorukov tried to demythologize the nature of autocratic authority and aristocratic power in Russia. It is a serious error, he wrote, to believe that the Russian emperor is an omnipotent autocrat, since in reality "the emperor reigns, the bureaucracy governs."[54] The emperor has been unable to exercise the authority that is vested in him because of the encroachment into the political process by members of the high-ranking officialdom, who are often ill-trained and are motivated more by self-interest than by national concerns. Similarly, the Russian aristocracy long ago ceased to be a ruling class in any legal sense of the term. Instead of evolving into a class with rights and duties defined and protected by law, Russia's aristocracy became "serfs of the tsars." Russia has no real aristocracy; "we are only slaves who may, by whim of a master, be deprived of our fortune, our liberty, our life."[55] The void left by the demoralization of the aristocracy has been filled by the "court camarilla" and the despised bureaucracy of self-serving officials. Without a press independent of the government, the information on which the tsar bases his decisions on national problems comes almost exclusively from these functionaries. Without an independent judiciary, justice itself is defined solely in terms of the ideas and values of whatever individuals are in power at a given time period.

What choices did Russia have to alter this despotic state of affairs? Dolgorukov foresaw the possibility of a revolutionary situation similar to 1789 in France if the gap continued to widen between the frustrated hopes of the population and the abuses of the privileged elite. The only realistic solution was the establishment of a constitutional government. As he indicated in a long, open letter to Alexander II in the initial issue of *Pravdivyi,* without a constitutional structure of rule, the Romanov dynasty was doomed "to destruction and exile." He called on Alexander II to enact the bold legislation required to save the country from revolutionary upheaval. The emancipation of the peasantry with land was the *sine qua non* of Dolgorukov's reform proposals. Together with this, he also demanded an end to corporal punishment, recognition of the equality of all citizens before the law, freedom of religious belief, freedom of the press, and the creation of an elected legislature to govern the country by law.[56] Dolgorukov was as strongly opposed to socialist solutions as he was to oligarchy and autocracy. He also was not interested in a rapid transition to a republican government. Thus, he favored a gradual evolution from autocracy to republicanism via a constitutional monarchy.[57]

Dolgorukov's sense of urgency about this situation was repeated many times. To Alexander II, he pleaded, as Russia stumbled closer to its 1789, "In God's name, save us from a 1793."[58] In his journal, he wrote that "without state freedom, without a constitution, there is no possibility of a peaceful way out of the confusion, out of the chaos into which Russia is now plunged."[59]

Dolgorukov was particularly concerned about the terms of the emancipation because he was convinced that the way in which serfdom was abolished would directly affect future constitutional reforms. In his discussion of the process of peasant emancipation, he reemphasized the two factors he had argued for in his 1857 memorandum: the peasants should be freed with land, and the landowners should be adequately compensated. Without land, the peasantry threatened to develop into a rootless proletariat capable of bringing to Russia the problems of mass unrest and social dislocation already experienced in Western Europe. Without appropriate compensation, the former rural landowning class would lose its economic power base and thus be unable to play a responsible role in the transition to constitutional government; this would in turn create a lacuna of authority which could endanger the entire structure of local administration that Dolgorukov believed was so crucial to the success of any constitutional regime.[60]

Although his ideas of emancipation linked him to leading advocates of peasant liberation in Russia such as B. N. Chicherin, N. A. Mel'gunov, and D. K. Kavelin, Dolgorukov's stress on political decentralization and constitutional guarantees separated him entirely from these contemporaries. Dolgorukov saw Russia as an empire in the throes of rapid "administrative disorganization": the political, economic, and social conditions of the country were in disarray—"in a word, anarchy was gaining ground."[61] To reverse this trend, Russia must promulgate a constitutional charter, convoke a "chamber of deputies" and create a "chamber of boyars"—in short, it must form a government that will legislate for the nation with the concurrence of the sovereign. In order to prevent a revival of despotic central authority in any form, Dolgorukov argued strongly for a comprehensive program of provincial autonomy and decentralization.[62] The Chamber of Deputies, or *Zemskaia Duma*, would be composed of representatives of the nation, its members freely elected by the entire population on a regional basis. Dolgorukov envisioned this legislative body as being directly linked to numerous elected provincial assemblies, which were to be responsible for running the affairs of the countryside. The Chamber of Boyars, or *Boiarskaia Duma*, was conceived of as a kind of Russian House of Lords, which

would be composed of members of the country's hereditary aristocracy and representatives of all religions in Russia.[63]

To ensure that regional self-government would not be overwhelmed by the two-house legislature in the central administration,
Dolgorukov proposed that Russia be divided into twenty-five
provinces, with districts to be established within each province,
cantons within each district, and communes within each canton. A
complex and elaborate system of self-governing institutions would
be set up from the communal level up through the provincial level.
The entire network of local institutions would also have a parallel
court system for both civil and criminal cases and would cooperate
with the legislature in the capital. Dolgorukov devised a complicated voting system for each of the two chambers, and there was to
be a restricted franchise based on age and property, although provisions were to be made for the participation of professionals with
higher education who did not possess property.[64]

Dolgorukov's proposals have been criticized by Soviet scholars
for being largely in the interests of the gentry landowners,[65] and also
for the maintenance of aristocratic authority through the power of
the Chamber of Boyars.[66] An American historian has charged that
Dolgorukov's plan for regional self-government is "greedy borrow-
ing" from two French theorists of provincial automony.[67] While it
may be difficult for us to see how Dolgorukov could have been
influenced so completely by both Russian and European currents in
his formulations, he himself had no such problem. Just as Russia was
for him "an immense edifice with a European façade, but with
Asiatic furniture and administration inside,"[68] he saw no difficulty
resolving specifically Russian problems with proposals informed by
both European and Russian historical experiences. His proposal for
a national legislature was an example of this fusion: he traced the
existence of a duma back to the seventeenth century, before Peter
the Great abolished the traditional Boyar Duma, while at the same
time he redefined the institution in light of modern parliamentary
structures in Europe. His ideas on self-government were indeed
affected by the notions of contemporary European theorists, but
they were also rooted in the pre-Romanov structure of the Russian
state, according to which separate states governed their own citizens
prior to the consolidation of the empire under Muscovy. Here Dolgorukov disagreed openly with Nikolai Turgenev over the issue of
self-government as well as on the interconnection between emancipation and constitutionalism.[69]

Dolgorukov's political program, which he considered to be a plan for the introduction of "a monarchical-constitutional regime" in Russia,[70] was accompanied in his writings by a series of critical sketches of many leading Russian statesmen. In this realm of criticism, Dolgorukov had unique talents among the Russian émigrés of his time. In addition to a sharp and witty tone set in an ornate vocabulary, these biographical portraits possess a convincing power born of Dolgorukov's familiarity with the ruling elite of his country. Because he personally knew (or knew of, through family connections) so many influential families, no one in government was safe or immune from being attacked—from within, so to speak—by Dolgorukov's pen. Ministers, senators, and even the emperor himself and his immediate relatives were all subjected to Dolgorukov's at times savage, but usually knowing, assault.[71]

Dolgorukov's political writings have been placed in the shadows of his more visible and dramatic public scandals. His career as an émigré journalist has been overlooked in favor of Herzen's more influential opposition organs abroad. In reality, however, Dolgorukov represents far more than another "romantic exile" who "flits" momentarily "across the pages of Herzen's life."[72] This man, for whom Ivan Turgenev aptly coined the term "republican prince,"[73] carved out a distinct constitutionalist ideology in the specific context of his position as an anti-autocratic force in exile. He firmly believed he was contributing to a growing "literature of émigrés" which "proclaims the truth" and "is in harmony with the aspirations and desires of the Russian people."[74]

In one of his last letters before his death, where he reviewed his original reasons for emigrating, he found he had not changed his mind about the high value he placed on freedom. "I came abroad to seek free activities, ideas, and the possibility to write in a way which was forbidden to me in my native land."[75] This was the credo with which Dolgorukov wanted to have his name associated.

6

Perspectives on the First Generation

At about the time of the emancipation of the Russian peasantry in 1861, the activities of the first generation of émigrés from tsarist Russia had come to an end or, as in Herzen's case, had reached their peak. Although the émigrés themselves were not entirely aware of it, the world in which they had come to political consciousness was about to be transformed. The forces that had led to their decision to leave Russia and create new careers abroad were also in the process of change. A new generation of émigrés was being born, one that would be dominated by new tactics and strategies. The new generation, however, was made possible by the existence of the first generation, even though the "men of the sixties" were to challenge virtually every aspect of the world their predecessors inhabited, and even though they often acted as if they themselves had invented the emigration.

What had become utterly clear at this point was that a permanent part of Russian politics and society had been established outside the borders of the empire. The main force behind this development was the need to resolve the central contradiction of Nicholas I's reign, which few educated members of Russian society could avoid confronting. This contradiction was the conflict that resulted from the collision of an aroused expectation of change generated by the forces of social progress, and the continued effort by the regime to restrain, control, and censor the manner in which these forces influenced Russian society. Thus, while the number of university students and the number of journals and books published (especially about the West) were on the increase, the government constantly attempted to contain the parameters of thought that accompanied this increase. To be sure, the obvious power of the autocracy to wield supreme and exclusive political authority over Russian society remained unchallenged, and the similarly obvious loyalty felt by the vast majority of that society not to overstep the established bounds of legality also had not been shaken. Nevertheless, Russia had grown increasingly complex and more unmanageable within the existing political framework. The popularity of professors like Timofei Granovskii in Moscow, the rise in prestige and influence of journals like *Otechestvennye zapiski* and *Sovremennik,* the stimulating debate that went on in public and private between Westerners and Slavophiles during the 1840s, and the greater number of Russians traveling abroad all led to the situation in which currents with an underlying and implicit challenge to the Russian state functioned within approved limits while simultaneously giving rise to ideas and questions that were beyond those limits.[1]

Unable to resolve this contradiction at home, a small number of individuals sought to transcend or escape it by emigrating to Western Europe. By taking this decision, men like Turgenev, Golovin, Sazonov, and Dolgorukov were extending the split that was in the process of developing between the values of the state and those of the questioning and critical segment of society. Each of these first émigrés went abroad for his own conscious reason, and several of them were, as we have seen, embroiled in personal controversies that appear to have been petty and devoid of any larger significance at the time. However, by refusing simply to accept the authority of their immediate superiors, they were faced with the problem of confronting the authority of the state. In the tight, interlocking patterns of authority in tsarist Russia, a challenge to an official anywhere in the bureaucratic hierarchy was tantamount to a challenge to the government itself.

The decision to go abroad entailed great risk. Each of the émigrés knew that it would be difficult to return to the homeland once they were abroad, though none of them ever completely gave up the dream of that possibility. As the months turned into years, and as they became more deeply involved with creating new roles as émigrés, the chasm between them and their country deepened. The distinguishing feature for all of them, including Herzen, was that they remained in some fundamental way committed to Russia while condemned to exile from it. For each of them, the moment of truth came when they were requested to return to Russia to face an inquiry into their activities. When they refused, they received a notice from the Senate in St. Petersburg that they were forever to be classified as "émigrés," deprived of all rights and properties.

None of the original émigrés had a clear idea of what it was they wanted to do once they arrived in the West. All they knew was that they were stifled and confined in Russia, and that in Europe they would be able to develop, learn, and think in a way that had proven impossible in their homeland. Although Herzen and Carr have exaggerated the frivolousness of the first émigrés, there was a degree of bravado and performance about their descriptions of their departures from Russia, and a clearly manifested degree of confusion about their decision to leave. Nevertheless, once abroad and faced with the realities of surviving there amid an entirely new set of problems for which they were ill-prepared, they became quite serious in their efforts to create a new career that would have significance for themselves as well as for their abandoned country.

They settled in Paris and London mainly because that is where the forces of progress that would aid them in their quest for an émigré role seemed to be at work. Although the Italian, Polish, and German émigré communities had preceded them, Turgenev, Golovin, Sazonov, and Dolgorukov established few enduring contacts with them. They also tried with varying degrees of success to find permanent positions with the progressive journals and newspapers in London and Paris, though only Sazonov seems to have managed to write for these organs on a regular basis. Mostly they found that they could express themselves best in books, and each of them did produce at least one book of importance which was critical of Russia in a style that was possible only in emigration. Even this, though, did not allow them to overcome the many barriers that existed among themselves. The most characteristic aspect of their existence is that they had so little contact with one another. There were Russian émigrés, but there was no Russian émigré community as yet. It is also true that Bakunin had been abroad since 1840, and that in December 1844, after refusing to obey a state summons to return home, he was stripped of rank and property and sentenced to Siberian exile *in absentia*. However, his circles consisted largely of émigrés from other countries, and his concern for Russia was secondary to his interests in Left Hegelianism and Pan-Slavism.[2] Golovin was expelled from Nice together with Herzen in 1851, but Herzen, as we have noted, did everything possible to dissociate himself from his émigré compatriot. These émigrés remained, to the end, supremely individualistic, uninterested in unanimity, and perhaps incapable of any sustained collective effort on behalf of the Russian cause, which itself was still largely undefined.

The individualism of this generation was undeniable. These first émigrés were as individualistic in life-style as in their politics. Turgenev remained a moderate, a reformer, throughout his career abroad. The revolutions he witnessed in the West only convinced him that Russia had to find a peaceful path "to a better civic existence," one "devoid of particular tranformations and upheavals."[3] Golovin, after several years of flirting with notions of radical upheavals inspired by the 1848 revolutions in Europe, turned to a more unfocused general critique of the autocratic regime in Russia. Sazonov also underwent changes, shifting ground from an involvement with Marx during the 1840s to a less radical stance later. Dolgorukov, living grandly and defiantly in exile, proposed variations on the theme of constitutionalism for postautocratic Russia. Only Herzen continued to conceptualize in a radical direction during the 1850s with Russia firmly in the forefront of his political plans. Unity among such diversity was truly impossible. Each of these émigrés had his own distinct personality and his own political perspective, which was primarily a politics of criticism. This was what they shared in common, but they were not ready to act as a group within an organizational framework, to develop their critique into a program of action with defined goals.

As to their influence in Russia, we do have some evidence that they were beginning to be heard, however faintly. Turgenev was read and known among members of the politically concerned aristocracy, as we have seen in our discussion of his ideas. He was also read with great interest by the leading literary critic, Vissarion Belinskii.[4] We know that Peter Kropotkin found Golovin's book on Nicholas in his uncle's library, and that Golovin's critique made a significant impression on him.[5] Dolgorukov's revelations of scandal at the Romanov court led readers to sort through his political program in the issues of his journals that reached Russia. Sazonov was undoubtedly read by Russians who were fluent in French, but since so much of his journalism was published pseudonymously, it was uncertain that they knew who he was. With the emergence of Herzen's periodical press, and its great success in the late 1850s, the names of the émigrés and the importance of the emigration as a political force became much more pronounced and much more of a phenomenon in the consciousness of both the established educated and the emerging critical sectors of Russian society.

The methods of bringing the illicit books and journals of the émigrés back to Russia clandestinely became more sophisticated and more successful during this period. A network of smugglers at the borders of the empire was established, which in turn was linked up with a growing number of booksellers in various cities in Europe (Berlin, Brussels, Hamburg, Leipzig, Naples, Nice, Paris, Vienna, and others) where émigré publications were stocked and sold. With the increasing number of Russians traveling abroad each year, it became easier to persuade some of them to return with the latest copies of Herzen's journals along with the work of other émigrés. In some cases, émigrés sent their publications directly through the open mail, in clear defiance of the official ban on these writings.[6] In this way, the process of direct interaction between the emigration and the empire began to intensify and to forge indelible links.

II

THE SECOND GENERATION

*Herzen was the last Russian
to act in isolation.
The time has come now for
clear thinking and collective action.*

BAKUNIN

The Origins of Collective Action Abroad

The first Russian émigrés were so individualistic that collective action was impossible. Turgenev, Golovin, Sazonov, and Dolgorukov were uninterested in and psychologically incapable of creating organizations dedicated to social and political change in Russia. They saw such behavior as a renunciation of the very liberty for which they had abandoned their homeland and come to Europe. They fought their battles alone, each according to his own idiosyncratic predilections. The same, of course, can be said for Herzen too, although he frequently substituted his collaboration with Ogarev for group activity.

A dramatic shift toward collective endeavors occurred in the 1860s. One of the important reasons for this change was that the "new emigration" of the 1860s came abroad with a background of radical activity in Russia. Many of the individuals who came to Europe at this time had already been involved in revolutionary events in Russia in some capacity, which had not been the case with the first generation of émigrés. The most significant of these events were the student disorders (1861), the activities of the first Zemlia i Volia group (1861–62), and the Kazan conspiracy (1863).[1] In some instances, Russian émigrés of the 1860s had been arrested and had experienced the political trials of this period as well prior to their arrival in Europe. Thus, for this generation—men like N. I. Utin, N. I. Zhukovskii, M. K. Elpidin, and Alexander Serno-Solov'evich—collective radical action and revolutionary commitment had become an accepted part of their careers before they became émigrés. They were not always successful in re-creating this collective experience abroad, but they were prepared to act within an organizational framework in a way the earlier émigrés were not.

Another distinctive characteristic of the new generation of émigrés concerns their social origins. Whereas the first generation was largely from an aristocratic social milieu, the new émigrés came predominantly from the ranks of commoners, the *raznochintsy*. M. Elpidin was the son of a priest, V. Zaitsev's father was an official, N. Utin and M. Sazhin were the children of businessmen, and P. Mart'ianov was of peasant origins. These men came to Europe with an entirely different cast of mind from that of the earlier generation, and this was in part a function of their class background. Their conflicts were not concerned with the necessity of freeing themselves from the ethos of the ruling class, as had been true for the first generation. For them, the aristocracy and its values were inextricably associated with the entire tsarist system. Their commitment to the political opposition necessarily entailed a distanced critique of the aristocracy as well. This dimension of "class struggle" emerged in full force in an émigré variation on the theme of the "schism among the nihilists," the division from within the opposition movement itself during the 1860s, which in this case alienated the younger émigrés from Herzen and the aristocratic first generation.[2]

Finally, the emigration of the 1860s was distinguished from the earlier generation by its size as well as its ideological scope. As protest against the autocracy on behalf of the *narod* gained momentum inside the empire, new recruits to the growing opposition came abroad to continue their struggle. The early 1860s, the time when upheaval in Russia over the emancipation was aroused so powerfully, were the years in which the most rapid expansion to date in the size of the Russian emigration took place.[3] These were also the years in which the range of émigré political strategies broadened in an unprecedented manner. Thus, not only was émigré individualism replaced by collective action in the 1860s but "émigré liberalism" was succeeded by a new radicalism abroad; both trends were, as we shall show, strongly informed by these factors of political experience and social background.

The Russian Colony in Heidelberg

The closest approximation to an opposition émigré organizational structure at this time was the colony of Russian students in Heidelberg during the early 1860s. The magnetic attraction of the university there for young Russians was first publicly expressed by the nihilist character Evdoksiia Kukshin in Ivan Turgenev's *Fathers and Sons*. When she told Bazarov she was planning to go to

Heidelberg to study, both Bazarov and Russian educated society suddenly were made aware of this advanced center of learning and its progressive atmosphere for Russian émigrés.[4] As more Russians learned about Heidelberg, the population of the colony grew. The largest stimulus behind the increase of Russian students there was the closing of the universities in St. Petersburg and Moscow after the student disorders in 1861. Many students went abroad in the winter of 1861–62, either to continue their studies or to escape arrest for involvement in the student uprisings. By 1863 the Third Section had sixty Russian students in Heidelberg under surveillance,[5] but the real number was significantly larger, for some Russian students enrolled there were not actively involved in the "cause of the emigration."[6]

The center of the colony's activities was the reading room (chital'nia), organized in the spring of 1862, which consisted of a large library of both legal and illegal works. The sixteen members who ran the reading room were not in complete agreement on political ideas. Some were sympathetic to Herzen and were in direct communication with him in London. A banquet was arranged to honor the visit of Herzen's son by this group that year, and occasionally, small articles by Heidelberg "Herzenists" appeared in Kolokol. Others in the colony, however, like A. I. Voikov, were critical of Herzen, especially regarding the Polish question, which flared up in 1863. Some of the Russians in Heidelberg affiliated themselves with new émigré journals that sought to counter Herzen's influential press. The most important of these émigré organs were Leonid Bliummer's Svobodnoe slovo and the colony's own publication, Letuchie listki, which reprinted the Velikoruss proclamation, N. A. Serno-Solov'evich's "Otvet Velikorussu," and N. V. Shelgunov's "K molodomu pokoleniiu." A. I. Linev and S. T. Konstantinov, two of the Russians in Heidelberg, were planning to establish a permanent émigré journal to be issued by the colony, but disagreements prevented this venture from succeeding.[7]

Among the active members of the Heidelberg colony, the names of two émigrés stand out above the others. The first is Nikolai Nozhin, a charismatic figure who exercised a tremendous influence over his contemporaries, playing a role not unlike that of Nikolai Stankevich during the 1830s in Moscow. Like Stankevich, Nozhin's own productive capacity was comparatively limited due to his premature death in 1866 at the age of twenty-three.[8] Nevertheless, Nozhin was involved in all the colony's activities in 1861 before he was expelled from Heidelberg for his radicalism. After leaving Heidelberg, he traveled to Italy, where he met Bakunin. In the context of the politics of the Heidelberg colony, Nozhin was on the extreme left. Meeting Bakunin in Florence, however, proved to Nozhin that he was a moderate when confronted with anarchist ideas.[9]

The other person, Vladimir Bakst, known as "the oracle of the Russian Heidelberg colony," was, with Nozhin, one of the leaders of the more radical faction within the colony. A participant in the 1861 student disorders in St. Petersburg, Bakst in Heidelberg was in direct contact with Herzen and Ogarev in discussing programs for social change in Russia.[10] Although Bakst gave credit to Nozhin for being the unifying force and moral inspiration behind the activities of the colony, Bakst himself clearly occupied a more active leadership role. In addition to creating "a perpetual center for debate" in the colony on the problems of the Emancipation Act of 1861, he also established an émigré printing press in Bern in 1862. Initially, Bakst felt that Herzen's press was not producing enough critical material for distribution in Russia. The new press in Bern was intended to supplement the output of Herzen's publications in London. Then, in the winter of 1862–63, an attempt was made to unite the London and Bern printing operations.[11] Negotiations were carried on with Herzen by Bakst and by Alexander Serno-Solov'evich, who later was to turn against Herzen publicly, sharply, and irreversibly. Herzen himself appears to have been most responsible for the failure of this publishing merger. He had neither faith nor trust in the abilities of these younger émigrés to carry out serious and enduring opposition ventures. Further, he had strong doubts about merging with a group so far from his direct personal control, and he was not anxious to sacrifice his own political independence. He also knew that there were financial problems associated with the Bern venture, and did not want to end up as the major, if not exclusive, underwriter of the Bern group. With the withdrawal of Herzen's backing, and in the absence of any other financial support, the Bern press ceased functioning by the summer of 1863.[12]

One other event of importance that occurred in the Heidelberg colony was the "trial of *Fathers and Sons*." When Ivan Turgenev's novel appeared in *Russkii vestnik* in 1862, members of the Heidelberg colony were critical of the portrayal of Bazarov and were shocked to read the following description of themselves:

"Kukshin too went abroad. She is in Heidelberg . . . fraternizing with students, especially with the young Russians studying physics and chemistry, with whom Heidelberg is crowded, and who astound the naive German professors at first by the soundness of their views of things [only to] later astound the same professors no less by their complete inactivity and absolute idleness."[13] The Heidelbergers' critique of the novel and the expression of their discontent with Turgenev's depiction of the colony were summarized in a letter sent by K. Sluchevskii to the author.[14] Turgenev decided to visit the colony to clarify his views in September 1862, but left feeling he had not succeeded. He spoke in later letters of the "wild Russian youths" he had met in Heidelberg and defended his characterizations in *Fathers and Sons* against the charges leveled at him by the Heidelberg émigrés. He felt as if he and his fictional characters had been put on trial by the colony. Indeed, this clash of views anticipated the storm of criticism over the novel that was soon to erupt in Russia, but it also symbolized the emerging conflict between a new generation of activist émigrés and the older generation of opposition critics which Turgenev and Herzen, in differing ways, represented. Heidelberg was, in the words of one historian of this period, "an independent laboratory of free Russian social thought" in which the growing contradictory currents within the opposition first came to the surface.[15]

The Russian colony disintegrated rapidly in 1863 under the impact of two external events—the Polish rebellion and the reopening of the university in St. Petersburg. The outbreak of the disorders in Poland split the members of the colony into two irreconcilable camps: the "Peterburgskie" or "Herzenists," who sympathized with the rebellious Poles, and the "Katkovists," who supported the Russian government's claim that it intervened to suppress a seditious rebellion in Poland. There was also a smaller group that was closer to the position of the "Herzenists" on the Polish problem, but that criticized them for not directly involving themselves; some of these Russians actually went to Warsaw to join the Polish rebels in their struggle.[16] Once the revolt in Poland was brought under control, the university in St. Petersburg was reopened. This led some members of the colony to return to Russia. Thus, by 1864, the combined forces of division and departure had destroyed the remaining effectiveness of the colony's activities and its center—the reading room in Heidelberg.

The Emigré Congress

During the winter of 1863–64, new recruits to the emigration arrived abroad, most of whom had been involved either in the student upheaval of 1861 or the first Zemlia i Volia organization in St. Petersburg. Nikolai Utin, a former student activist in the Russian capital and a member of Zemlia i Volia's central committee, escaped from arrest and came to London, where he was warmly welcomed by Herzen. Although Herzen invited Utin to join the staff of *Kolokol*, disagreements arose and Utin left for the Continent. Also at this time, I. I. Kel'siev and E. K. Gizhitskii escaped from prison and exile respectively and went to Switzerland; both had participated in the Moscow student movement. Historically, this was a moment of disorientation in the emigration given the failures of the Heidelberg colony, the Bern printing press, the Polish rebellion, and the demise of Zemlia i Volia. Herzen, to whom the émigrés looked for guidance and inspiration, ended up provoking further disillusionment.

The crisis between Herzen and the "young émigrés," which would soon approach a climax, was rooted in a polarization of attitudes that had been developing for several years. In 1859 Chernyshevskii and Dobroliubov had begun to challenge Herzen's politics in a way that had far-reaching implications. The debate on the nature of change and the shape of Russia's future which appeared in the pages of *Sovremennik* in St. Petersburg and *Kolokol* in London reached a wide audience of readers, many of whom were to join the growing opposition movement before emigrating to continue their work. The editors of *Sovremennik* expressed their discontent at what they saw as Herzen's moderate positions and pushed for more radical solutions to the pressing issues of how to oppose autocracy and serfdom in Russia. Less well known outside a smaller network of trusted intimates was the "reconciliation meeting" that took place between Herzen and Chernyshevskii in London in June 1859. Although there are no surviving documents from the meeting, it is clear that no rapprochement occurred. Each man came away more convinced of his own political position. In the next few years, Chernyshevskii turned more stridently toward relying on a peasant revolution as all legitimate alternatives appeared exhausted under the existing regime. Herzen responded with fears that such a popular uprising would only lead to reaction and a more powerfully entrenched autocracy. Herzen continued to believe in the possibilities of a peaceful transformation through legal reforms from above, and he also cautioned against a headlong leap toward accepting unrealistic comprehensive solutions that might themselves, however noble in inspiration and intent, lead to new forms of terror over the masses even if they were successful.[17]

The collision course between Herzen and the young émigrés was noted by perceptive visitors from Russia at this time. Discussions with Herzen, for those willing to listen, were dominated by his dazzling displays of erudition about the human condition and the situation in Russia, insights he had gleaned from literature, history, and politics. One of his most characteristic strengths was his ability to examine any question from all its sides. In addition, he "demanded the possibility not only to think freely but to express his thoughts freely." By nature he was continually in search of special conditions to maintain the space for this vital process, and just as continually wary of accepting commitments that might deny him that space.[18] At the same time, another visitor to London felt that Herzen "was already losing the real ground beneath his feet" because his absence from Russia was making it impossible for him to absorb the tremendous intellectual and social transformation then under way in his homeland.[19]

The new generation arrived in Europe with firm ideas about change, deeply scarred by the expectations first aroused and then crushed by the 1861 Emancipation Decree, and committed to a wholesale rejection of the world as they knew it, all of which Herzen could not fully comprehend. For Herzen, there was still an abiding connection to that world. Europe in particular possessed an importance for him as a historical factor in the evolution of civilization and as the birthplace of modern protest and revolutions. The post-emancipation émigrés, however, did not come to Europe out of historical curiosity or to participate in its culture or even to learn from its politics. They came because Europe was the only place where they could continue to function as an opposition force.

Nevertheless, Herzen attempted to redefine the direction and tasks of the Russian opposition, both at home and abroad, in a programmatic article in *Kolokol* which was circulated among the émigrés even before it appeared in print. Herzen expressed his conclusion in this way: "It is time to concentrate thought and force, to clarify goals and to calculate means. Propaganda, quite obviously, falls into two categories. On the one hand, the word, advice, analysis, unmasking, theory; on the other hand, the cultivation of circles, the building of pathways of internal and external relations. Regarding the first, we will dedicate all our activity, all our commitment. As to the second, this cannot [now] be accomplished abroad. Such work can only be anticipated for the *very near* future."[20]

With these carefully chosen sentences, Herzen was denying the last remaining dreams of the young émigrés who still hoped for the possibility of a unified opposition movement. Unwilling to accept the moratorium or restriction on action which Herzen's article seemed to imply, they went forward with a plan for the emigration to establish a new center of revolutionary activity with Herzen's involvement.

In an effort to create "an internationalized publication" of the Russian revolutionary emigration which would transcend the particularities of isolated communities and strategies, Utin, together with Alexander Serno-Solov'evich, Nikolai Zhukovskii, Lev Mechnikov, and other émigrés in Switzerland, decided to hold a congress in Geneva in December 1864 to which Herzen and Ogarev would be invited.[21] On the eve of this congress, Utin wrote an impassioned letter to Herzen in which he tried to make the most convincing case possible for the proposed united émigré center and its journal, which he called "a stronghold of force and of faith in force." He explained how he and his generation had come of age inspired by Herzen's and Chernyshevskii's writings. One of the important aspects of the agenda to be negotiated at the forthcoming congress was the opportunity to apply some of the principles that Herzen had always emphasized: propaganda, or the developing of ideas for criticism and change; correspondence, or the organizing of systematic lines of communication for the dissemination of propaganda; ties to people, specifically providing the means for individuals sharing similar concerns for change to join in collective action; and funding these operations.[22] In this letter Utin also reiterated the advantages to the general cause if the united émigré center and journal could be agreed upon, with Herzen and *Kolokol* as the focal points around which the "solidarity of parties or, better still, groups of revolutionaries" could coalesce.[23] Utin's use of the term "party" here is one of the first instances of its appearance in the documents of this period and is an accurate reflection of his thinking. He closed his letter by raising the possibility of Herzen's refusing to agree to this strategy, thereby leaving "the tragic alternative" of separate, disunited, and weakened forces.[24]

Herzen responded in a brief note as he prepared for his trip to the Geneva congress. Although he agreed to come to Geneva to hear the émigrés' proposals, it was clear that he was quite unwilling to venture very far toward accepting Utin's program. "To work with people who share one's spiritual and emotional concerns, I truly desire," he wrote. "But what is this new political business of the Russian emigration? The activity of propaganda within the movement must take place at home, in Russia."[25]

During the spring of 1864 Herzen went to Geneva to meet the young émigrés and returned to London with essentially positive impressions. Doubts soon emerged, however; Herzen's letters from this time show that he mistrusted the intentions of the émigrés.[26] Nevertheless, Herzen decided to attend the émigré congress, and arrived in Geneva on 28 December 1864 with his son to meet with Utin, Serno-Solov'evich, Zhukovskii, Mechnikov, and others. This was the first time a congress of Russian émigrés had ever met in Europe. About fifteen people attended the meetings, including moderates like V. F. Luginin, who had been a member of the Heidelberg colony, and F. N. Usov; the latter regarded *Kolokol* as too socialist, and has been quoted as saying "I do not rejoice at revolution, but rather look upon it as a sad necessity."[27]

One issue at the congress which reflected the divided mood concerned the use of the Bakhmetev Fund, which had been given to Herzen earlier by a wealthy landowner with utopian interests. Herzen categorically rejected the proposals of the "young émigrés" that the Bakhmetev money be appropriated to found an alternative "general émigré" publication. Herzen's argument was that he had no right to spend this money in this manner, but Serno, Utin, and their Geneva comrades refused to accept this and accused Herzen of trying to hold on to archaic political views and to a controlling monopoly of the émigré press. Herzen wrote to Ogarev at the end of the conference of his fears that Serno and the young émigrés were seeking "to seize into their own hands *Kolokol* and the Bakhmetev money." Of the émigrés themselves, he told Ogarev, "They have no ties, no talent, no education." He concluded: "Geneva before the break with these gentlemen was an excellent spot; they have sickened it like bitter horseradish. I don't want to prejudice your personal tastes, but to work with them I feel is impossible."[28] Herzen also noted that Serno was now his "main opponent."[29] Along with Alexander Serno-Solov'evich, Utin was the chief spokesman for the proposal of a unified emigration at the congress. Herzen reacted to Utin with undisguised scorn. "Utin," Herzen wrote to Ogarev on 4 January 1865 during the meetings, "is worse than the others when it comes to limitless egoism." On another occasion Herzen wrote that Utin is "the most hypocritical of our mortal enemies."[30]

Herzen left Geneva on 6 January 1865 in a mood of despair. The disappointment felt by the émigrés in the aftermath of this congress turned, in some instances, to overt combat with elements of rage. Alexander Serno-Solov'evich expressed this feeling in stronger terms than did the other émigrés, but he spoke for many of them when he wrote of his reaction to Herzen:

And concerning the emigration, and your relationship to it? . . . When these youths with their wounds, over which you shed tears, merged together as émigrés and, saved in Switzerland from hard labor and the gallows, worn to the bone and hungry, when they turned to you, their leader, a millionaire and an incorrigible socialist, turned to you not with a request for money and bread, which they urgently needed, but with a proposal for working together jointly, you turned away with arrogant contempt and replied, "What emigration? I don't know of any emigration! There's no need for an emigration!"[31]

The émigrés were actually attempting to do two contradictory things simultaneously. On the one hand, Utin and his comrades were inviting Herzen to collaborate with them in a united opposition effort with the purpose of moving beyond the failures of the recent past. On the other hand, they were also seeking to oppose Herzen and transcend the parameters of his political universe. The congress, far from resolving difficulties, only widened and exacerbated them. For the émigrés, Herzen was an antiquated figure for whom reverence was no longer necessary; for Herzen, the émigrés were political Frankenstein monsters out of control. Beneath the verbiage at the congress lay the psychological warfare in which each side sought unrealizable and, to a large extent, fundamentally unwanted demands from the other. The result was the recognition on both sides that a permanent schism existed among the émigrés.

I. A. Khudiakov

The émigré community continued to grow during the middle 1860s as new arrivals from Russia turned up in Geneva, but the goal of establishing an organizational center or a common, unifying cause seemed as remote as ever. The antagonism against the autocracy and the opposition to Herzen were shared widely by these émigrés, but an authentic movement required a positive program. One of the most unusual men of this generation who attempted to cope with this problem was I. A. Khudiakov, the son of a Siberian official, who established a national reputation as a scholar of Russian folklore before becoming involved with the conspiracies of Ishutin and Karakozov.[32] Khudiakov came to Geneva in the summer of 1865, financed by Ishutin, with the intention of creating links with the émigrés. He met Bakunin, Utin, and Herzen and was singularly unimpressed. Herzen knew of Khudiakov's earlier writings, and was particularly well disposed toward one of his books, *Samouchitel'* (The Self-Teacher, 1865), but Khudiakov was in disagreement with Herzen politically and was appalled by his luxurious aristocratic life-style. He considered Herzen "a liberal of the forties" with archaic political views.[33] Khudiakov, who lived like a religious ascetic, denying himself all but the most basic necessities of life, saw Herzen as a hypocrite who spoke of devotion to uplifting the impoverished *narod* while dining over an elegant French meal prepared by his servants. Moreover, Khudiakov's program called for a political revolution organized conspiratorially to precede the more fundamental social revolution affecting the entire society, a program that Herzen found offensive, wrong-headed, and somewhat frightening.[34]

While in Geneva, Khudiakov encouraged M. K. Elpidin, another recent émigré with a history of student radicalism, to establish a new press and an émigré journal.[35] With Khudiakov's financial support (in part, money entrusted to him by Ishutin and, in part, money from his wife's dowry which she consented to use for social causes), Elpidin published two issues of *Podpol'noe slovo* in 1866. Although the journal did not succeed, Elpidin became one of the important émigré publishers who managed to remain outside the factional battles that were to divide the émigré community so frequently in the future. Khudiakov returned to St. Petersburg and Moscow, where he was arrested after the Karakozov *attentat*. He was banished to Siberia in 1864, where, after resuming his interest in Russian folklore through a research study of the traditions of the Yakuts, he went insane and died on 17 September 1876.

The Kel'siev Brothers

Another "man of the sixties" who played a visible role in the emigration was Vasilii Kel'siev. Like most of the émigrés of his generation, Kel'siev, together with his brother, Ivan, was actively involved in the 1861 student uprisings and had been arrested prior to his coming abroad. At the same time, Vasilii Kel'siev was somewhat unusual among the Russian émigrés for three reasons. First, he was one of the few younger émigrés to have actually collaborated with Herzen on apparently friendly terms (initially at least). Second, Kel'siev's intense religious interests were not generally shared by his comrades abroad.[36] Third, Kel'siev ultimately decided to return to Russia voluntarily and to submit himself to the autocracy as a penitent who had renounced completely his revolutionary ideals. After his return to Russia, Kel'siev composed a long "Confession" in which he attempted to reevaluate his life's activities and commitments. His "Confession" is superficially similar to Bakunin's more well known apologia, but in fact this comparison is not appropriate. Bakunin was in transit from one kind of ideological opposition to another when he wrote his *Confession* to Nicholas I in 1851.[37] Kel'siev, however, was in the process of turning away from his earlier radicalism. He was, in effect, denouncing his revolutionary past. In this he more closely resembled (and in fact anticipated) the later conversion to autocracy of the revolutionary émigré Lev Tikhomirov.[38] Thus, Kel'siev, not Tikhomirov, was the first "renegade" among the Russian revolutionary émigrés. As we have seen, the desire to return to Russia, to escape from the painful difficulties of émigré isolation and despair, was present among some members of the first generation, particularly in the case of Golovin, but none of them carried this out. No one in the emigration before Kel'siev was as willing, able, or desperate to make the necessary compromises not only of returning— which symbolically implied that the revolutionary struggle was over—but also of writing a confession to the emperor—which was an explicit admission of the need to embrace the object of that struggle.

Kel'siev may have fled the emigration, but he did not escape from Herzen's pen. Herzen tells us that his purpose in devoting a chapter of his memoirs to Kel'siev was not to condemn him. "To cast a stone at Kel'siev is superfluous; a whole roadway has been thrown at him already. I want to tell others and to remind him what he was like when he came to us [in 1859] in London," Herzen writes.[39] Nevertheless, he engages in yet another patronizing portrait of the émigré community in his treatment of Kel'siev. "At the first glance, one could discern in him much that was inharmonious and unstable. . . . [He] had studied everything in the world and learnt [*sic*] nothing thoroughly, read everything of every sort, and worried his brains over it all fruitlessly enough. Through continual criticism of every accepted idea, Kel'siev had shaken all his moral conceptions without acquiring any clue to conduct."[40]

Kel'siev was, according to Herzen, a religious nihilist—a man who questioned all values in the manner of a spiritual fanatic. Religious mannerisms informed his behavior just as a religious vocabulary informed his discourse. He was skeptical of both Russian and European "methods." His driving passion was "the recognition of the economic iniquity of the present political order, a hatred of it, and an obscure yearning for the social theories in which he saw a way out."[41] Kel'siev settled in one of the most depressed working-class sections of London (which Herzen describes in chilling realism) together with his emaciated wife ("thin, lymphatic, with tear-stained eyes") and infant child, who was dying when Herzen visited them. Herzen tried to dissuade Kel'siev from staying in London. "I told him that he ought first to learn what poverty in a strange land meant, poverty in England, particularly in London; I told him that in Russia now every vigorous man was precious."[42]

Kel'siev told Herzen he wanted to write about the "Woman Question" and the organization of the family, to which Herzen replied that Kel'siev should first devote himself to the need for a peasant emancipation with land. Instead, Kel'siev became interested in Russian religious schismatics. Like the subjects he studied, "Kel'siev was a vagrant at heart, a vagrant morally and in practice. He was tormented by unstable thoughts, by melancholy." He moved from task to task, job to job, unable to satisfy "his restless temperment."[43] Yet Kel'siev did manage to complete a book on the *raskolniki* (which Herzen published at his Free Press in London, 1860–63) before deciding to return to Russia to work directly with the schismatics. Kel'siev's decision shocked Herzen: "This journey . . . was incredible, impossible, but it actually took place. The audacity of this trip borders on insanity; its recklessness was almost criminal."[44] Kel'siev surprised Herzen again by returning to London in 1863 after his Russian journey. Kel'siev believed he had been in touch with the very pulsebeat of holy Russia during his experiences with the *raskolniki,* but in London he became "bored by work and sank into hypochondria and depression." He then decided to go to Turkey to preach on behalf of a Free Church and a new form of communal life, a decision Herzen considered to have been motivated by Kel'siev's grandiose illusions about the significance of his cause. Now Herzen urged Kel'siev to remain in Europe (after earlier advising him to return to Russia), but Kel'siev's "desire to do great deeds and to have a grand destiny, which haunted him, were too strong."[45] He went to Turkey to work with a Don Cassock schismatic community that had emigrated from Russia during the time of Peter the Great. However, a series of family tragedies ensued which ended Kel'siev's religious work. In June 1864 his brother, Ivan, who had joined him in Turkey, died of typhus. Cholera claimed his two daughters, and his wife died of consumption. On 11 June 1867 the *Moscow News* reported that Vasilii Kel'siev had presented himself to the Russian diplomatic authorities in Turkey with the request that he be arrested and sent back to St. Petersburg.

This, then, is the story of Kel'siev's émigré career as Herzen presented it. There is, however, a great deal more to add to this portrait. The materials on Kel'siev's early years reveal a pattern quite different from that of most of his émigré contemporaries. Kel'siev was born in St. Petersburg in 1835 into a gentry family that had lost all connection to its landowning past. For all intents and purposes, Kel'siev was a product of the new middle-class world that dominated his father's life. Kel'siev's father served in the Department of Trade in the imperial bureaucracy and retired with the modest rank of collegiate assessor. Kel'siev's education began at a private boarding school, but in 1845 his father sent him to a commercial school *(Kommercheskoe uchilishche)*. The death of his father in 1852 created a financial problem for Kel'siev's mother and interrupted Kel'siev's plans for his own future. According to his brother, Kel'siev started to learn Chinese so that he could apply for an Asian post with an American trading company. He also read a great deal of medieval literature at this time, filling himself with visions of heroic knights traveling to uncharted territories to combat lawless brigands.[46] These impressionable images would later re-emerge to influence Kel'siev's career.

In 1855 Kel'siev completed his secondary education and entered the philological faculty of St. Petersburg University as an auditor. To support himself, he obtained a service post with the Russian-American Trading Company. For 25 rubles a month, Kel'siev's duties were to translate commercial correspondence for the company in English and German, languages he learned at the university. Kelsiev considered entering the army amid the patriotic fervor of the Crimean campaign, but decided against this when he learned he would be placed in the reserve force. He had some romantic notions about being an officer at the front, but these were dashed by the reality of this mundane appointment in the reserves.

During the winter of 1856–57, Kel'siev befriended Nikolai Dobroliubov, who was a student of the Main Pedagogical Institute in the capital at his time. Kel'siev made an enduring impression on Dobroliubov, as evidenced by Dobroliubov's perceptive comment in his diary: "He is a man who thinks seriously. He has a powerful spirit, and a thirst for action; very developed through wide reading and deep thought. . . . What I don't like about him is his excessive touchiness in personal life. Of course this may be a result of inner impulses which in the process of seeking a proper channel, burst out on every side."[47]

Dobroliubov also recorded some of Kel'siev's plans, hopes, and dreams. Kel'siev was seriously interested in traveling to China—so serious that he mastered Chinese to the degree that he could both read and speak it with some fluency. However, he abruptly shifted his concern first to natural science and then to Slavic philology, which he hoped he might someday teach. Dobroliubov viewed these changes skeptically, doubting that Slavic philology would remain the goal of his restless friend.

Unfortunately, there is no evidence to explain why Kel'siev went abroad when he did. There was, unquestionably, confusion in his life. He had come to the realization that professionally his path toward becoming an Eastern specialist for a commercial company had reached a cul-de-sac. He was unable to create a viable alternative, and after considering a teaching career, he decided to abandon Russia. In this, his situation recalls the dilemma of Ivan Golovin two decades before.

Kel'siev arrived in London in 1859, already radicalized through reading, with the intention of pursuing a literary career on the staff of *Kolokol*. This dream, however, was soon crushed. Kel'siev submitted several pieces for publication in *Kolokol,* but Herzen refused to print them because he found the writing and the research unacceptable. For a time, Kel'siev handled editorial tasks correcting and editing correspondence from Russia, though he knew this was a secondary role that would never advance him to a writing position on the journal. At some point during the winter of 1860–61, Kel'siev began to become very involved with the Old Believer sects, which altered his life completely. Ironically, it was Herzen who first introduced him to the Old Believer literature, but Kel'siev himself saw the possibilities inherent in focusing on the religious sectarian community as an object of revolutionary strategy. Kel'siev described this moment of conversion in his "Confession" in a rather dramatic manner:

I didn't sleep all night and carried on reading. I almost went out of my mind. My life literally split in two, and I became a new man. If Herzen had not given me these documents, I would perhaps have remained a revolutionary and a nihilist. They saved me. Reading them, I felt that I was entering an unknown, unexplored world, the world of Hoffman, Edgar Allan Poe or the *Thousand and One Nights*. Suddenly, in one night, there were revealed to me the emasculates with their mystic rites, their choruses and their harvest songs, full of poetry; the flagellants with their strange beliefs; the dark figures of the "priestless" sects; the intrigues of the leaders of the Old Believers; the existence of Russian villages in Prussia, Austria, Moldavia and Turkey. One sect after another, one rite after another appeared before me, as in a magic lantern show, and I read on and on and on. My head whirled, I stopped breathing. . . . In a flash I saw in front of me the peasants and bearded merchants, so scornfully despised by Europe and our educated classes: ignorant barbarians, sunk in primitive materialism. They were not all that bad, these people who, beneath social oppression and the terrible yoke of the seventeenth and eighteenth centuries, were able to keep awake, unlike the Western *paysan* and *bauer* or the Polish *chlop*. On the contrary they thought, thought of the most important problems that can concern the human soul—truth and untruth, Christ and anti-Christ, eternity, man salvation. . . . The *Raskol* reflected honour on the Russian people, showing that it does not sleep, that every peasant wants to keep a lively independent eye on dogmas, wants to think for himself about truth, that the Russian people searches for truth, and then follows what it has found, and does not allow itself to be frightened by floggings or by caves with their entrances blocked up, or by emasculation, or by human sacrifice and cannibalism.[48]

It was at this point that Kel'siev began his research on the Old Believers in earnest, which resulted in the four small volumes entitled *Sbornik pravitel'stvennykh svedenii o Raskol'nikakh* (1860–63), published in London by Herzen's press. Also at this time, Kel'siev met two Russian visitors to London who strongly influenced his interest in radical activity among the religious dissenters in Russia. The first was Petr Alekseevich Mart'ianov, an Old Believer of peasant origins who had written a pamphlet in which he argued for the tsar to call a Zemskii Sobor to free the people from the aristocracy.[49] The other was Pafnutyi Kolomenskii, Bishop of Kolomna, who lived in Kel'siev's apartment during his stay in London and with whom Kel'siev had many impressionable discussions about the problems of the Old Believers.[50] As a result of his talks with Pafnutyi, Kel'siev decided to travel to Russia clandestinely to agitate among the Old Believers. Pafnutyi arranged contacts with Old Believers for him in Moscow, while Kel'siev made plans for a newspaper devoted to the cause of religious liberty for dissenters in Russia.

Kel'siev was operating entirely on his own during this trip. He told no one but Herzen in the émigré community about his journey to Russia, and Herzen, as we have already seen, strongly opposed the trip as dangerous and futile. Kel'siev, however, was not to be deterred from his overall purpose: "I want to bring the *raskolniki* over to our side, to arouse in them political opposition to the government, to make use of their religious doctrines [to show them] that the tsar is the anti-Christ, that the ministers and the [bureaucratic] hierarchy are the archangels of Satan, that the [church] officials and the priests are the servants of the devil. I would would like to establish for the *raskolniki* a practical way out of their belief system, and to suggest some ideas to them concerning their goals, aspirations, and needs."[51]

Arriving in Moscow with a contrived Turkish passport, Kel'siev was greeted by a group of Old Believer merchants, with whom he proceeded to have a number of intensive discussions. When Kel'siev attempted to talk about politics with them, however, he found the Old Believers utterly unresponsive. He does not say they were afraid, but describes them as either not able to comprehend or simply uninterested. "A lot was said, and nothing was done," was his own assessment of the encounters. He could neither find nor create "political activists from the Old Believers."[52] He thus failed to accomplish the basic purpose of his trip, a grand notion that he conceptualized in his "Confession" as "the unification of the religious sects with the *Kolokol* party."[53]

The other purpose of Kel'siev's journey to Russia was to arrange for the transporting and distribution of various publications issued by Herzen's Free Press in London. At the same time, Herzen and Ogarev had asked Kel'siev to gather information on the possibility of forming a revolutionary secret society in Russia. To this end he went to St. Petersburg and stayed at the apartment of the Serno-Solov'evich brothers for five days.[54]

Kel'siev and the Serno-Solov'eviches held extended and detailed discussions not only on the specific proposals Kel'siev brought with him but also on the general subjects of the future of a revolutionary movement in Russia and the potential for cooperation between radicals inside Russia and the émigrés. The discussions, as reported in Kel'siev's "Confession," resembled a meeting of diplomats, with Kel'siev acting as the emissary of Herzen and Ogarev and as the representative of the émigré revolutionary movement, and with the Serno-Solov'evich brothers assuming the role of spokesmen for the radical movement on Russian soil.

At one of their meetings, Nikolai Serno-Solov'evich asked Kel'siev what Herzen's true intentions were regarding the organization of antitsarist strategy in Russia. Kel'siev responded by saying that Herzen conceived of his role not in terms of "throwing himself into practical activity but rather in an organizing capacity as a propagandist and as a leader of social opinion." Nikolai Serno-Solov'evich was outraged at this notion and angrily lectured Kel'siev on the need for a much stronger strategy. Noting that segments of Russia's youth were willing to sacrifice themselves in Herzen's name, he called for the creation of a powerful centralized organization with affiliated circles in Moscow, Kiev, and in the provinces across Russia, with a common, unified platform to be established and reaffirmed at periodically convened congresses. "The leader and dictator of this organization must be Herzen," he said.[55]

It should be noted that Serno-Solov'evich was not speaking for all of his comrades. V. I. Kasatkin took an entirely different viewpoint on the question of Herzen's role as "dictator" of the Russian resistance movement. "It is impossible," he told Kel'siev, "to carry on Russian affairs from abroad." He added that "in Russia itself [there are] talented activists who can conduct these matters better than anyone else."[56] Nevertheless, Kel'siev was very interested in Serno-Solov'evich's ideas. Shortly after his return to London he wrote an excited letter to Serno-Solov'evich to report that Herzen and Ogarev were discussing his plan, and he predicted that "they will finally stand at the head of the movement in the fall."[57] Indeed, Kel'siev's role as a mediator between Herzen abroad and Serno-Solov'evich in Russia did ultimately contribute to their involvement in the development of Zemlia i Volia in the summer of 1862, though Herzen never could (and probably never wanted to) assume any dictatorial leadership role in an extensive, nationwide movement.

Kel'siev was also able to establish border points for the transporting of Kolokol and other materials from Herzen's press into Russia. In addition, he engaged a number of people in Russia to act as contributing correspondents for Kolokol. In fact, as he wrote to his brother, "my main job right now consists of correspondence; letters come in to me from all corners of the Russian borders."[58] However, amid the details of smuggling antitsarist literature into Russia and distributing it throughout the country, Kel'siev became increasingly involved with the religious sects. In letters to his brother and to Serno-Solov'evich, he spoke of the need to extend their opposition activities to the Old Believers and other schismatics and religious dissidents. In particular, he wanted to make *Obshchee veche* (rather than *Kolokol*) more oriented toward this population's needs, and spoke of the need for Zemlia i Volia to develop close contacts with the sects in their provincial centers.[59]

Kel'siev did not remain in London for very long. His concerns for the revolutionary potential of the religious sects grew into an obsession with grandiose fantasies. He grew impatient with his position as a correspondence agent for Herzen's press in London, and left for Constantinople, arriving there in early October 1862. Bakunin, who was aware of Kel'siev's intentions, wrote Herzen and Ogarev in November 1862 of Kel'siev's plans to distribute propaganda to the Cossack troops throughout the Caucasus and the Don region.[60] Kel'siev's dream was to begin preparations for a military-peasant revolution in southern Russia.[61] As he became more absorbed in this vision of insurrection, references to any organizations like Zemlia i Volia disappeared.

Kel'siev's activities in 1863 are not entirely clear. We do know that he wrote several proclamations to prepare the masses for an uprising, that Ogarev printed them in *Obshchee veche*, and that copies were found by the Third Section as far north as Arkhangelsk gubernia.[62] Yet Kel'siev seems to have been acting increasingly on his own at this time. As we have seen, he returned to Russia in 1867 and was granted a full pardon after completing his "Confession." Alexander II recognized his potential "usefulness to the government"—that is, his knowledge of and familiarity with the Old Believer sects and the South Slavs.[63]

Kel'siev's last years were bizarre and sad. He briefly entered the salon world of St. Petersburg, where no émigré revolutionary had ever tread before. There he met and married Z. A. Verderevskaia, a beautiful woman who was professionally involved in the literary world of the capital and was also an accomplished pianist.[64] He had fantastic plans, one of which was to act as a mediator between the Russian government and the revolutionary milieu. He also dreamed of founding and editing a journal "with a purely Russian, patriotic orientation." All these plans went unrealized. There are entries in Nikitenko's diary about this strange and transformed man who had returned from abroad and from revolution. According to Nikitenko, Kel'siev was upset over the refusal of *Otechestvennye zapiski* to publish his confession.[65] Nikitenko called Kel'siev "a living Don Quixote," as though a prehistoric dinosaur had somehow survived into the civilized era. He was seeking to save the world, but "no one listened to him except the secret police. . . . He has experienced so much, but for what?"[66] In May 1869, after an evening at Kel'siev's home in which his wife entertained the guests with a performance on the forte-piano, Nikitenko noted that Kel'siev now planned to visit America, where he hoped to earn money by lecturing on Russia. In spite of the comfort and conviviality of the salon setting, Nikitenko was perfectly aware of the desperation and the tragedy of Kel'siev's situation:

His position here, in any case, has become impossible. They permit him to live in Russia, but deprive him of any possibility of work to earn a living for himself. This is utterly absurd. Either it was unnecessary to admit him to Russia, or he ought to be allowed the legitimate means to a livelihood. He wanted to publish a newspaper— they refused to allow it. In this instance, there may have been a sound basis [for the refusal]. But vacancies in civil service exist which he could occupy usefully for himself and to which he could contribute something; yet they reject him for every post.[67]

Kel'siev did manage to publish some articles, but mostly in relatively obscure newspapers and journals. This was obviously difficult for him to bear—a man who had once valued his significance as an agitator on a level with Herzen's role as a publicist.[68] He gradually lost touch with friends and acquaintances and sank into oblivion. As a former revolutionary, he could not be truly trusted or accepted by established society, and the government, as Nikitenko observed, had effectively blocked his access to positions of influence. As a "renegade," he could not be trusted by opposition elements. After the publication of his memoirs in *Russkii vestnik* in 1868, he was severely attacked and mocked by the influential critic Nikolai Mikhailovskii. As doors continued to close around him, he turned increasingly to drink. His psychological difficulties worsened. In the last year of his life, he fell into complete apathy. He was estranged from everyone he had known, and separated from his wife. Finally and mercifully, according to one of his former friends, relief came in the form of death on 4 October 1872: "It was so difficult, especially in his last years, for him to bear this fruitless, completely unnecessary, shattered, and failed existence."[69]

The significance of Kel'siev's deterioration after his return to Russia cannot easily be extended beyond his own individual case. Although earlier émigrés had sought to return to Russia after years of frustration and disappointment abroad, none had been willing to come back to the homeland on the government's terms. As mentioned earlier, Bakunin had written an apologia before Kel'siev did, but under very different circumstances. Most important, Bakunin did not return voluntarily, and once the opportunity presented itself, he fled Russia to resume his revolutionary career. Kel'siev returned of his own volition, wrote his "Confession," and received his pardon. Yet he had stepped too far beyond the boundaries of the established value system in Russia while abroad. He could not stay abroad indefinitely and continue his revolutionary activities, and thus he returned to Russia after having failed as an émigré radical. Failure at home followed. The two worlds of order and rebellion could not be lived in simultaneously, and the world of order would never forgive the rebel, even after a confession.

In spite of his renunciation of radicalism and the personal tragedy of his last years, Vasilii Kel'siev and his brother, Ivan, with whom he worked during the early 1860s from their exile base in Constantinople, represent the coming of both a new kind of revolutionary activity and a new type of revolutionary activist. After decades of individual endeavors to reshape Russia from abroad, the focus now began to shift toward *collective* social action in emigration. Indeed, Ivan Kel'siev (1841–64), though he died prematurely, long before he realized his full political potentialities, symbolizes the emergence of this new social group far more accurately than does his brother, Vasilii.

Ivan Kel'siev's brief career presages the constituency of the Russian radical organizations of the 1870s. Within a very short span of time, Ivan Kel'siev made the transition from membership in the antitsarist opposition social movement in Russia, influenced by Herzen, to becoming a severe critic of Herzen and a formulator of an entirely new revolutionary praxis.

After completing a commercial curriculum in St. Petersburg in 1860, Ivan Kel'siev enrolled as an auditor at Moscow University. During his first year at the university, the student uprisings broke out. Kel'siev not only participated in the uprisings but was among the activist leaders. He was arrested in October 1861 while leading a student protest on the square in front of the Moscow military governor general's residence. In 1862 he was exiled to a town in

Perm gubernia, where he composed an article that he intended to send to *Kolokol* for publication. The police discovered the article before it was sent off, rearrested Kel'siev, and detained him in the Peter and Paul Fortress in St. Petersburg. In May 1863, while Kel'siev was being transferred to another detention center prior to what was to be a second sentence of internal exile, he escaped and made his way out of the country to Constantinople. The article he wrote for *Kolokol* is an analysis of the liberal and radical currents that surfaced in Moscow during the student uprisings, and testifies to Kel'siev's commitment to an uncompromising opposition to the tsarist autocracy. In the articles, Kel'siev admitted that before the uprising he was uninterested in politics. He was involved instead in the philosophy of Hegel and its "extreme indifference" to social and political questions.[70] He depicted two enemies of the radical opposition—the loyal institution of the autocratic system of government, and the new liberal element that was forming around an acceptance of serf emancipation as the endpoint of social demands. Kel'siev made it clear that he considered himself a socialist and a republican at this time.

Another reason for Kel'siev's second arrest was his involvement in the activities of Zemlia i Volia in 1862. In fact, his escape to Constantinople was arranged and supported by the Central Committee of Zemlia i Volia.[71] Once in Constantinople, Ivan Kel'siev quickly became what one Soviet historian has called "one of Russia's first professional revolutionaries."[72] From his base of operations in Constantinople and later in Tulcea (where a substantial colony of dissident Russian Old Believers had settled), Kel'siev sent a series of letters to Herzen and Ogarev in London in which he defined his emerging revolutionary worldview and strategy. At least as interesting as the content of this strategy is the fact that Kel'siev seems to have arrived at his formulations without the explicit influence of any theories. He was, of course, working with his brother, Vasilii, who was in Constantinople with him, but the political differences between them were the dominant theme in their relationship by this point. Vasilii was beginning to doubt the possibilities of radical activities among the Old Believers, and was starting his ideological reevaluation, which would soon lead him to return to Russia to cooperate with the authorities there.[73] Ivan, meanwhile, was taking off in the opposite direction.

Ivan Kel'siev wrote to Herzen in 1863 of the need to support a single "revolutionary party," a role he believed Zemlia i Volia should occupy. All other groups and parties in Russia were, he believed, aspects of Russian liberalism. It was crucial to distinguish between these two political tendencies and not to make the mistake of supporting liberals. "The whole of liberalism," he wrote Herzen, "consisted of various petty improvements in the administration, designed to augment the enrichment of the aristocracy and the bourgeoisie's comforts of life." It would be hopeless and self-defeating to expect "sacrifices from [liberals] in the service of the general cause." One must seek to transcend the intentions of these social classes in the interests of "a democratic, even more, a social [sotsial'-naia] revolution."[74]

Kel'siev called for a reorganization of the revolutionary activities of Zemlia i Volia and was, essentially, warning Herzen that this was the wave of the opposition future. There had to be widespread efforts at propaganda and agitation by militants who would not be tempted by the moderate reforms of liberals. He also had in mind a network for the dissemination of Kolokol and other émigré materials, but argued that a new Kolokol was required to reach the masses. The success of an opposition movement without the masses was unthinkable, Kel'siev wrote. Kolokol, in its existing format, was not suitable for this task. "The place of Kolokol," he argued, "was in the seminaries, military corps, institutes, and the university"; there, "in the gentry dining halls," it would have its audience. This, however, was not a revolutionary organ.[75] Kel'siev considered Ogarev's Obshchee veche more appropriate "to carry out the present war," and proposed that it be reoriented toward the schismatic sects. In addition, he suggested that a new journal be created for the masses which showed a profound understanding of the life of ordinary people and which, at the same time, must strive "to correct the existing disorder."[76]

Thus, in the few months before his untimely death, Ivan Kel'siev constructed an elaborate strategy linking the émigré press in London with a distribution center in Constantinople and a network of militant revolutionaries working inside Russia on a full-time basis to disseminate propaganda, enlighten the people, and prepare the soil for the coming revolution. Kel'siev was not entirely pleased with the Central Committee of Zemlia i Volia any more than he was entirely satisfied with Herzen, but he believed it crucial to utilize the existing organizational nexus and strengthen it rather than begin on a completely new foundation. "I am not satisfied with the [central] committee," he wrote Herzen, "but it must be supported to the end. Things are bad now, but would be even worse without the committee; its demise would only weaken us and give strength to our enemies."[77]

Kel'siev's last effort was to organize a Russian émigré commune in Tulcea. Although he did not have time to carry out his plan, his intention was to establish a strong revolutionary center in the south of Russia as an alternative to the existing centers in Western Europe. This commune would be able to coordinate the flow of propaganda northward into Russia along routes that Kel'siev believed would prove less vulnerable to police infiltration than those emanating from Europe. In this way, the revolutionary emigration would be more closely linked to the Russian population, the object of its revolutionary aspirations. Kel'siev's ideal, he wrote, was "an aristocratic republic in which everyone is an aristocrat and where no one is a slave."[78] However, Ivan Kel'siev contracted typhus and died on 21 (9) July 1864, long before he could create the revolutionary web of which he had dreamed, stretching from London to Constantinople to Tulcea, a web that he had hoped would ultimately envelop all of Russia in a fiery upheaval and bring down the autocracy.

8

A. A. Serno-Solov'evich: Beyond Herzen

At the end of the 1860s, a new voice emerged amid the expanding Russian émigré community in Western Europe. Alexander Serno-Solov'evich is an example of a Russian radical who experienced, in a few years, a lifetime of revolutionary endeavor. He is reminiscent of Belinskii, Dobroliubov, and Pisarev, all of whom made almost fanatical use of the short span of time they had to give themselves to the cause of the antitsarist opposition. He also went far beyond his contemporaries who did not emigrate in that he not only published a body of significant and influential radical journalism but also became an activist in the working-class movement abroad. In addition, Serno-Solov'evich epitomized the growing discontent felt by the "young emigration" toward Herzen's acknowledged position as leader of the Russian opposition. We have already mentioned Serno's attack on Herzen, which was the most severe and most uncompromising of any Russian's of his time. Through this critique of Herzen, Serno established a new theoretical terrain, which irreparably broke apart the reigning political paradigm of the time. Most important, perhaps, as a result of Serno's activities, collective action became a permanent and dominant feature in the life of the Russian radical émigré communities.

Serno was born into aristocracy in 1838. Of his father we know nothing, but his mother was the sister of Andrei Nikolaevich Kirilin, a high military official under Nicholas I. Kirilin frequently spoke to young Serno of Nicholas's court, and he may have been instrumental in helping arrange for the admission of Alexander and his older brother, Nikolai, into the prestigious Aleksandrovsk Lyceum. It is clear from Alexander's early letters that he had been in revolt against his family for as long as he could remember. He also established a link between his hostility to his family and his later rebellion against Russia. When he was twenty-one, he reflected on these formative years of his "unconscious childhood," which he saw as dominated by "empty phrases, bombastic words." From the battlefield of the family, he moved to the struggle against authority in the lyceum, a world of "moral death and apathy." At the time that he wrote these words in 1859, he was in despair. "I cannot believe in a future order," he wrote, "because activity here for me is a question of life and death."[1] Deeply wounded by the arrest of his closest friend several years before,[2] he seems to have retreated into episodes of morose introspection filled with feelings of alienation and mistrust.

He traveled abroad in 1856 and 1859, partly to relieve his anxiety and partly to study. He had become interested in European progressive thought as a result of a study circle to which he belonged in 1855. The circle, which included himself, his brother, Nikolai, and his lifelong friend A. A. Cherkesov, met at the home of M. V. Trubnikova (daughter of the Decembrist Uvashev), where they read Proudhon, Lassalle, Saint-Simon, and Louis Blanc.[3] During the second trip, he announced in a letter that he was committing himself "to work for the future, for Russia,"[4] though he was still uncertain exactly how he would do that. The letters he wrote during this period indicate that he immersed himself in reading on a wide scale, though he appears to have been particularly interested in the work of Robert Owen and "the development of communism" in England.[5]

Serno returned to St. Petersburg at a propitious moment. In 1861 a number of illegal opposition groups were formed which then fused with the student protests of that year. His tendency to brood and his confusion vanished as he threw himself into this ferment. Together with his brother, Nikolai, Alexander quickly became one of the leading activists in the capital. He helped distribute copies of Shelgunov's manifesto "To the Young Generation" and worked personally with Shelgunov. Shelgunov had the highest praise for his collaborator: "The energy of his temperament, the fierce passion of his character, the speed of his intuition, the subtlety and irony of his intelligence, and the dedicated spirit with which he devoted himself to the cause without ever thinking of himself—all these put him in a class of his own."[6] Serno also joined the student movement working to push the dis-

sidents into a more political orientation. In the spring of 1862 he
organized with V. I. Kel'siev a system of transporting illegal literature from abroad into Russia. He was, in addition, one of the organizers of Zemlia i Volia, for which he worked exhausting hours
around the clock for months.[7] Not surprisingly, he attracted the
attention of the police and would surely have been arrested had
he not decided to go abroad for reasons of health.

He was physically and emotionally exhausted when he arrived in Switzerland late in the spring of 1862. Soon after his arrival, he learned that his brother, Nikolai, had been seized by the
police. At the same time, the Russian government demanded Alexander's return, but he refused and thus officially became an émigré. On 10 December 1864 the Senate deprived Alexander of all
civil rights and condemned him to "eternal exile" from Russia.[8]
His life now assumed a new dimension. As a survivor of Zemlia i
Volia, he bore the burden of responsibility to carry on the radical
work of his brother and his former colleagues now jailed and silenced forever.[9]

Alexander Serno's letters from abroad reveal one of the problems that would plague him for the rest of his life—his desperate
financial situation. He lived with friends because it was cheaper
and he ate modestly, but his anxiety over the need to support
himself in a foreign environment remained. He tried through his
friend M. V. Trubnikova to have translations published pseudonymously in *Birzhevye vedomosti* and other journals in Russia.[10]
With the help of Ogarev and Vasilii Kasatkin, he also attempted
to put together a collection of readings on Russian literature for
use among the émigré communities as well as in Russia. He
hoped this might be lucrative for him if it were successful. Another proposal of Alexander's which, while not designed for self-
serving purposes, certainly would have helped him, was to establish a cooperative bank specifically to aid needy Russian émigrés
in Europe. None of these efforts seems to have been realized,
however, and Alexander continued to seek money from friends in
order to survive.[11]

His letters also document his many efforts to reestablish his
radicalism in the new émigré context in which he found himself.
In the winter of 1862–63 he joined with his friend Cherkesov and
other émigrés in an effort to set up a new Russian printing press
in Bern, where Bakst, Nozhin, and members of the Heidelberg
colony had attempted a similar venture earlier. He was also in

touch with V. I. Kasatkin and M. Elpidin in Geneva in arranging to publish Chernyshevskii's writings.

Serno's intentions are not entirely clear at this point. Although he wanted to establish an émigré press in Switzerland, there is evidence to suggest that he was genuinely interested in cooperating with Herzen and Ogarev. He may ultimately have envisioned merging *Kolokol* with the new press on the Continent to create a unified émigré press with two operational centers. With a growing and increasingly dispersed Russian emigration in Europe, a single, united press would serve as a focal point around which all revolutionary émigré forces could rally in the struggle against the tsarist autocracy. Yet, at the same time, Serno, together with another émigré, Nikolai Utin, was convinced that for this unity to be achieved, *Kolokol* had to be "reformed" to reflect the ideas of the young émigrés. The content of *Kolokol* would have to be altered to include the posing of new questions, the proposing of new revolutionary strategies; it was insufficient, Serno argued, to propagate only one side of purely Russian socialism. He wanted greater cooperation with West European socialists, including having their theoretical articles published in *Kolokol*.[12] Herzen, however, refused all suggestions to reorganize *Kolokol* and saw Serno's efforts as an attempt to undermine his independence. He rejected the plan to unite *Kolokol* with a new émigré press in Switzerland, thereby embittering Serno's attitudes toward him.[13] Serno was unable to understand Herzen's tenacious desire to remain independent politically just as Herzen could not comprehend the idea of a new generation's need to go beyond the political framework of *Kolokol*.

Serno was visibly involved at the December 1864–January 1865 meeting of the "young emigration" in Geneva, and there, as we have seen, his opposition to Herzen became more pronounced. Then, in 1867, Serno brought the conflict with Herzen from the obscurity and privacy of the small Geneva meeting out into public view, where it was noted with great interest not only by the Russian emigration in Western Europe but also by both the Third Section and the revolutionaries remaining at large in Russia.[14]

The first of Serno's three political brochures in which he openly attacked the editors of *Kolokol* was provoked by an article on Poland written by Ogarev and published in *Kolokol* late in 1866.[15] The main issue of this article was the recent tsarist decree that punished Polish landowners who had participated in the

1863 uprising by forcing them to sell their land. Instead of condemning this decree, Ogarev saw in it a retreat from the policy of what he called "the religion of property" and entertained the naive hope that if this process were extended to the gentry class as a whole, it could lead to the liquidation of both the landowning aristocracy and Poland's large private estates. Further, Ogarev advised the Russian government to arrange for the transfer of this alienated land to the local Russian and Polish peasantry.

Serno's attack began in the title of his article: "Question polonaise: Protestation d'un Russe contre Le Kolokol." His primary argument was that a systematic transfer of land along the lines suggested by Ogarev would inevitably lead to the "Russification of the entire area," and that such a policy was in direct contradiction to Kolokol's previous commitment to the right of every nationality to self-determination. "I was silent for so long," Serno writes, "because I passionately loved and deeply respected Messrs. Herzen and Ogarev." Alluding to the Geneva meeting and other efforts at rapprochement, Serno argues that the intransigence of the editors of Kolokol has led to a political schism in the émigré movement. He had tried to make his objection known to Herzen and Ogarev regarding this article when he first saw it prior to publication. Specifically, he had asked Ogarev to remove the term "our Polish brothers," which he considered hypocritical, and raised a number of theoretical objections. Mockingly and with obvious resentment and bitterness, Serno continues: "I sent this protest in Russian to the free Russian journal Kolokol; the free journal refused to publish it. . . . 'O liberté! Que peu d'hommes savant te comprendre et surtout t'aimer,' I say to the editors of Kolokol."[16]

On the surface, Serno's objections to Ogarev's article had to do with serious differences over the Polish Question. According to Serno, there were three tacit implications in Ogarev's position: (1) the Russian government would be dictating policy to Poland and thus determining its future; (2) the Russian opposition movement would be absorbing, co-opting, and perhaps stifling an autonomous Polish resistance movement. Here Serno believed strongly that only after the Polish movement had made significant advances toward the goal of national independence could relations with Russia be conducted on a level of genuine parity; (3) finally, there was the threat of "the Russian peasantry colonizing Poland" through the acquisition of land seized from dissident Polish landowners, land that ultimately belonged to the Polish people.

Beneath the surface, however, Serno was arguing for something larger than personal political differences between two émigrés. He claimed to be speaking not solely for himself; "I am convinced that the Russian young generation will stand with me on this question, and not with *Kolokol*. . . . *Kolokol* can no longer serve as the representative of the generation of Russian youth, since it is now only the expression of the personal views of Messrs. Herzen and Ogarev."[17] He closed his article by introducing the theme that was to dominate his next and more celebrated brochure—the irreconcilable opposition between "the mighty words of the genius Chernyshevskii" and the archaic politics of the editors of *Kolokol*.[18]

Serno's second essay in this series of attacks on Herzen, *Nashi domashnie dela*,[19] was a response to Herzen's article "Poriadok torzhestvuet."[20] In his article, Herzen had discussed his relationship to Chernyshevskii in terms of their political world views. He considered himself a representative of an authentic Russian socialism with direct roots "in the land and in the peasant milieu." Chernyshevskii, in Herzen's opinion, represented "a purely Western socialism" that was oriented more toward the urban, university sector of Russian society, which consisted "exclusively of workers of the intellectual movement, the proletariat of the intelligentsia." However, rather than seeing his own socialist ideas as competitive with or in opposition to Chernyshevskii's, Herzen preferred to see the two of them serving as "the mutual complement of one another."[21]

Herzen's portrait of Chernyshevskii as a bookish man, removed from the realities of Russian life and espousing an abstract, theoretical form of propaganda, was completely unacceptable to Serno. To alter this interpretation of Chernyshevskii, Serno had first to combat Herzen. He did this with a venom that no one within the Russian opposition movement had ever before dared put into print. "You are a poet, a painter, an artist, a raconteur, a novelist, you are everything that you wish to be, but you are not a political activist and still less a theoretician or the founder of a school of thought." He reminded Herzen of the time he had left Herzen's home after a meeting with a friend who had previously been an admirer of Herzen and a member of Zemlia i Volia. Speaking of the 1863 Polish uprising, the friend had told Serno: "Herzen's only use now would be to get himself killed on the barricades, but he'll never go near them anyway." Serno claimed that Herzen had himself brought about this disenchantment on the part of the younger generation. So many Russians had come to Herzen begging for help, for work, for

inspiration, "and you turned them away." Continuing, Serno casti-
gated Herzen for discussing socialism over champagne and caviar
while "all around you, Russian émigrés were not eating week after
week."[22]

Concerning Herzen's conceptualization of Chernyshevskii
and himself as "mutually complementing one another," Serno had
this to say: "Between you and Chernyshevskii there was not, nor
could there ever be, anything in common. You are two contradictory elements that cannot coexist, friend beside friend. You are
representatives of two conflicting natures, not complementing but
destroying one another." Whereas "you [Herzen] are a specialist
in enthusiasm, Chernyshevskii is a man of science." It is Chernyshevskii who has founded a school of thinking and won the admiration of the young generation. Herzen, Serno goes on, is only
"a poet of freedom," while his adversary Chernyshevskii is the
creator of freedom.[23] Herzen, Serno concluded, was "already a
dead man" [uzhe mertvyi chelovek] from whom nothing more
could be expected. The age of Kolokol had come to an end.[24]

Serno's assault on Herzen was devoid of any tribute to
Herzen's earlier years. He pronounced judgment on Herzen's entire career in the context of his present, fiery critique. For Serno,
Herzen's politics had always been bankrupt—he recalled Herzen's
willingness to support Alexander II's emancipation efforts (forget-
ting that, for a time, Chernyshevskii had done the same) as collaboration with the hated regime; he reminded Herzen of his calling
Karakozov a "fanatic"; he blamed Herzen for the demise of Zemlia
i Volia, which meant that he held Herzen indirectly responsible for
the arrest of his brother and for his own emigration; and he argued
that Kolokol had failed to provide the ideological leadership that
Chernyshevskii's Sovremennik had begun to exercise so effectively
before it was silenced by the autocracy. Serno's critique was merciless, vengeful, relentless, and uncompromising. He was seeking
to destroy not only Herzen's political credibility but also the legend
that surrounded him. In addition, Serno was looking beyond the
present impasse and issuing a call to arms for a new revolutionary
strategy to transcend Herzen's failures.

The last of this series of brochures was again occasioned by an
article to which Serno felt compelled to respond. This time it was a
piece on the Russian emigration written by N. Ia. Nikoladze and
published in 1868 in the third issue of the Geneva-based émigré
journal Sovremennost'.[25]

Nikoladze's article was highly critical of the Russian émigré community and included a number of insinuations about the motives and behavior of the Russians living in Europe. According to him, the émigrés were only semiliterate in political relationships, were devoid of firm conviction, lacked talent and skill in dealing with the serious matters in which they became involved abroad, and could not offer any well-conceived, convincing explanation for why they had chosen to flee their homeland. Under these circumstances, Nikoladze concluded, the émigrés had no alternatives other than to follow the example of Vasilii Kel'siev and return to Russia or to renounce political activity, remain abroad, and plunge into the narrow Philistine currents of ordinary, everyday life.[26]

Serno was enraged by what he considered a slanderous attack on the emigration and, by implication, on himself. Rather than issue a point-by-point refutation of Nikoladze's argument, he published a brochure, *Mikolka-Publitsist*,[27] in which he sought to discredit the author and to destroy his general portrait of the emigration. He did this by first asking a series of pointed questions. Since Nikoladze was not legally an émigré himself and could return freely to Russia, Serno wondered publicly why he would elect to publish an article abroad that could so easily have been published in Russia under the rules of the censor. Alternatively, why not publish in *Kolokol*, where, Serno believed, the criticism of the emigration in the article would have found acceptance and a wider readership. Moving one step further, Serno asked whether there might even be some connection between the *Sovremennost'* author and the tsarist Third Section.[28] The bulk of the brochure ridicules the viewpoint of Nikoladze's article. Serno makes his own preferences quite clear in mentioning Chernyshevskii's novel *What Is to Be Done?* as an antidote to what he calls the "social pathology" of the status quo, which his antagonist Nikoladze is prepared to accept.[29] Playing on the fact that both *Sovremennost'* and *Sovremennik* derive from the same root word, Serno belittles the former as a poor imitation of the latter. Further, he asserts that Chernyshevskii's journal displays "critical realism" in approaching questions of significance, while Nikoladze's journal exemplifies folly, collaboration with evil forces, and weakness.[30] Serno also mocks Herzen's memoir, *My Past and Thoughts*, as if it were a Richardson novel capable of little more than bringing tears to the eyes and passion to the heart.[31] While caricaturing Nikoladze as concerned solely with finding "a warm corner" on this earth to burrow into (here Serno quotes Marmeladov in Dostoevsky's *Crime and Punishment*),[32] Serno declares that he and all his émigré comrades have painfully renounced their "warm corners" to live abroad in discomfort for a higher purpose than the pursuit of the safe, secure careers they abandoned in Russia. "I am a man, I say, of lofty aspirations and bold ideals. I do not wish to be a shoemaker or a doctor [in an autocracy]; I want to be a social activist."[33]

Although it does not appear in these brochures, Serno was developing a political alternative as he moved away from Herzen's socialism. This alternative—the European workers' movement and the International—was never developed by Serno as a mature theoretical position, but there is little doubt that he was seriously committed to this new strategy, as his letters and activities clearly show. His involvement with the Geneva section of the International and the labor struggle in that city began in the winter of 1866–67, the same time that he was in the midst of his brochure campaign against Herzen. A personal tragedy of enormous significance for him also occurred at this time, and was at least partly responsible for his shift from warring against *Kolokol* to joining the International. In February 1866 he received the news that his brother, Nikolai, had died in an Irkutsk prison, and this he immediately translated into a motive for new action against the Russian autocracy. "I am tormented," he wrote of his comrades, "that I cannot go to Russia to avenge the death of my brother and his friends. But any individual revenge on my part would be insufficient and futile. By working here for the common cause, we will have our revenge on this cursed order, because the International holds the promise for the destruction of this entire system, everywhere!"[34] Thus, rather than turning away from Russia, he felt he was fighting the battle against autocracy from afar by aiding the efforts of the International.

Serno threw himself into the maelstrom of labor unrest in Geneva, working at a feverish pace reminiscent of his sleepless nights during the student upheavals in St. Petersburg in 1861. In the midst of his involvement in the 1868 Geneva builders strike, he wrote with enthusiasm of his new activities to his friend M. V. Trubnikova:

Here, in the last three to four weeks, the workers question has undergone a very serious revolution. As a member of the International Society of workers, I have written several articles that have been discussed in both camps. There is a huge amount of work, with the result that I am sleeping only two to three hours a night. Now the thunder is subsiding, but of course, it will soon revive with a new force. The International Society has selected me for a post in its statistical bureau, on a newspaper, and even in the local central committee.[35]

The newspaper Serno referred to was La Liberté, edited by Adolf Catalan, an independent radical who had close ties with the International and the labor movement in Geneva. Unfortunately, since the articles in La Liberté are all unsigned, it is impossible to determine how many and which ones were actually authored by Serno.[36] Nevertheless, from the evidence that has been identified with certainty during this period, it is clear that Serno was not entirely uncritical of the tactics of the International. While he admitted that the International was "the best creation of our age" and fully agreed with its ultimate objectives, he warned against adopting its position on "the economic question" as the dominant theme in the labor struggle to the exclusion of "the moral consideration of man."[37] Serno was also cautious about the timing of the strike tactic. The lesson of the 1868 Geneva strike for him was that the builders had been unable to choose the right moment to confront their employers successfully. This led him to call for a stronger organization of the International, which itself must become an independent force, bound and beholden to no political party or political leader.[38] Serno decided to take action on this himself. In the summer of 1868, after the demise of the Geneva strike, he began the process of creating an independent party of workers which, he hoped, would participate in the national elections on behalf of its own interests as well as in organizing strike movements designed to alter the existing relationship between labor and capital.[39]

As he became a prominent figure in the affairs of the labor movement and in the local organ of the International in Geneva, Serno came to the attention of Karl Marx. Serno, aware of Marx's role and reputation in the International, was both surprised and proud when Marx sent him a copy of the first volume of Das Kapital.[40] In a long letter that Serno sent to Marx in November 1868, he wrote that he "could not guess how you knew my name, all the more so since I am Russian." Serno had two main purposes in writing to Marx: to solicit Marx's participation in a new workers' paper Serno was planning to edit, and to apprise him of the local situation in Geneva in the aftermath of the spring strike. Serno told Marx that the workers' movement was strong in Switzerland and that its growth was intimately tied to the existence of the International—"the strength of the [labor] movement in the country is in direct relationship to the strength of the International." However, he added, "the International, like the country itself, is completely lacking in intellectual forces. With the exception of a few microscopic concentrations of people, all the rest understand nothing, absolutely nothing, and are led along by the vaguest and cloudiest aspirations. Consequently, the movement may collapse through the absence of any clear ideas, drowning as it is in a wave of catch phrases about brotherhood and solidarity, phrases that are contradicted by reality at every step."[41]

Serno's plan for counteracting this distressing state of affairs was to establish a weekly labor newspaper designed to reach a minimum of 2,000 subscribers under the aegis of the International Association. Serno was perfectly aware that for the newspaper to succeed in bringing the international labor movement to the attention of the local Swiss working-class population, it was necessary to recruit people who not only were socialist in thought but who also knew how to write. For this reason, he turned to Marx to ask him to participate in the newspaper as a contributor of "articles of theoretical questions." He also requested Marx to correspond with the newspaper on a regular basis on the workers' movement and on the history of the labor question, to indicate to Serno the best newspapers in English on the labor movement, and to send him a list of recent English brochures of interest to the International Association concerning strikes and trade unions.[42] Serno closed his letter to Marx by indicating that he was firmly convinced that "the workers' movement as it is presently developing here, despite all its defects, represents a genuinely impressive sight." However, because of the lack of preparation and the absence of a solid leadership, Serno confessed: "I have never been so afraid of a revolution as I am right now. I know that on this question I am in disagreement with many people who think that the main thing is to provoke a general upheaval as soon as possible. . . . The last strike revealed how few workers are capable of leading themselves." Nevertheless, Serno remained sanguine about conquering these difficulties, in the short run at least, if Marx would agree to aid in the newspaper effort.[43]

Serno's acceptance of the tactic of workers' participation in local elections and his rejection of the theory that a general insurrection was imminent brought him into direct conflict with Bakunin and the supporters of his Alliance of Socialist Democracy in Geneva. There was a good deal of ideological warfare between the

Bakuninists and the Internationalists on these issues, and Serno figured prominently in these battles.[44] One of the consequences of this conflict was that Serno was excluded from the constituency of the congress of the Italian and Spanish sections of the International, which was held 2–4 January 1869 in Geneva. This congress was dominated by the Bakuninists and the local paper *Egalité*, which supported them. In general, this was a period of rising Bakuninist influence that Serno was helpless to stop, in spite of all his efforts.[45]

All of Serno's activities were brought to a halt by the recurrence of a mental illness that finally incapacitated him in 1869. It is not clear how long Serno was afflicted by this disorder, nor is any specific diagnosis given in the materials on his career. Although there is some indication that Serno inherited the disorder from his mother, he managed to conceal it from his closest friends until it was quite advanced. Only his brother, Nikolai, really knew the seriousness of his problem: "My brother, Alexander, is a man who is very seriously disturbed. In the last two years [1862–63] he has been ill around thirteen times, and every time has feared for his life. He was sent abroad against his will, and because of the doctor's urgent demands, he remained abroad for the duration of a complete convalescence. He stubbornly wanted to return after one treatment. The illness has made him extremely anxious and nervous."[46]

There is no evidence of dysfunctionalism during Serno's transition from student agitator in Russia to revolutionary émigré in Switzerland. However, immediately after the January 1865 conference at which the émigrés confronted Herzen over the orientation of *Kolokol,* Serno suffered a nervous breakdown. In addition to working at a feverish pace, Serno had been terribly concerned about the condition of his brother, who was languishing in a tsarist prison, and about the fate of the child he had fathered during his affair with Lidia Shelgunova in Geneva shortly after his arrival from Russia in 1862.[47] In any case, Cherkesov, his closest friend abroad, arranged for his admission to a psychiatric hospital.[48] Serno lacked the means to pay for this hospitalization, and his bills were eventually paid by his self-declared enemies—Herzen, Ogarev, and Tuchkova-Ogareva. In spite of the antagonism between Serno and Herzen that had emerged at the 1865 conference and that would surface even more devastatingly in Serno's 1867 brochures, Herzen provided financial assistance to Serno at such critical moments. We do not know for sure whether Serno was even made aware of this generosity, since Cherkesov handled the arrangements and may have chosen not to anger Serno by revealing the identity of his benefactors. But Herzen went ever further by calling on Serno during a later hospitalization to discuss the future of *Kolokol*.[49] By this time Serno was gravely ill, and Herzen was showing compassion for a dying man.

We have already noted how Serno was affected by his brother's death in 1866, which he mourned deeply for a long period.[50] Even before his brother's death, however, Serno was writing to friends about suicidal urges and fears of insanity. In September 1865, while hospitalized, he wrote Tuchkova-Ogareva that he was losing his mind, that he had decided to drink himself into unconsciousness in order to be able to drown himself, and that he was profoundly depressed over his illness. The following month he again threatened suicide in a letter to Tuchkova-Ogareva. He also mentioned that he was slipping closer to a state of insanity as a result of all that he had lost, especially his son and his brother. Although both were alive at that moment, they were lost to him forever, as was his homeland, where they existed and to which he could never return.[51] When his brother died, Serno became even more depressed, but at the same time he gained a new purpose. As one of his comrades noted at the time, he now dedicated himself to the workers' movement, in part to avenge the death of his brother.[52]

Serno drove himself furiously, carelessly, with no regard for his health. During the builders' strike in Geneva, as we have already seen, he slept only a few hours each night for several months. In January 1869, after he was excluded from the editorial committee of the Bakuninist-oriented *Egalité* and from attending the congress of the Bakuninist sections of the International, Serno again suffered a breakdown. At the hospital, he asked for the truth about his condition. His doctor told him he had an incurable mental disturbance that would progressively deprive him of his powers of reasoning, and that increasing amounts of pain would accompany the deterioration. Serno decided not to endure this destiny, and on the night of 16 August 1869 he committed the act of suicide he had spoken about so often. In a note discovered later by friends, he wrote: "I love life and people, and I am sorry to have to leave them. But death is not the greatest evil. Far more terrifying is to be a living death."[53]

9

On the Eve: Toward the Development
of Ideology

With the death of Alexander Serno-Solov'evich in 1869, the Russian émigré community stood on the eve of an entirely new phase in its evolution. The work of the Heidelberg colony, of the Kel'siev brothers, and especially that of Serno had clearly established the framework for radical collective action abroad and had ended the search for a solution to Russia's political problems by isolated individuals like Nikolai Turgenev, Golovin, Sazonov, and Dolgorukov. As the 1870s dawned, bringing with it a whole new world of social and political protest, the Russian émigrés in Western Europe were swept into a maelstrom of ideological currents and political groups. Collective action became affiliated with charismatic leaders, mass organizations, and ideological commitments. In the process, a certain measure of independence and unpredictability, which Serno, for example, had cherished, was lost. Even before the advent of the Zurich Russian colony in 1872 and the dominance of Bakunin and Lavrov among the Russian émigrés at that time, it became increasingly difficult for autonomous collective activity to survive. As the theory and practice of engineering a revolutionary transformation in Russia from the vantage point of Western Europe grew stronger and more sophisticated, the spectrum of alternatives to the tsarist order narrowed.

Although the historical moment of this change can be identified, the reasons for it remain difficult to pinpoint. Herzen's death in 1870 was more of an anticlimax than a direct factor in causing the shift. By this time, Herzen's ideas, his position of authority in the opposition movement, and the influence of his pioneering and inspiring newspaper *Kolokol* had all been shattered and transcended by new forces abroad. The populist movement cannot explain the change either, since the émigrés had already been divided by the new political forces before Lavrov and Bakunin began to attract and influence Russian followers in the early 1870s. In many respects, the new politics that was to take hold of the Russian emigration emerged from the European milieu in which the émigrés lived and worked. Though they refused to assimilate and continued to function in a transported world of Russian culture, they could not help but be influenced by certain developments abroad. Thus, while the Nechaev trial—a very Russian event—was dominating the lives of the emerging populist revolutionaries at home,[1] the International— a very European event—was playing a similar role in the lives of the Russian revolutionaries abroad.

Before turning to the relationship between the International and the Russian emigration at the turn of the decade, and to the individual who epitomized this new trend, we must first briefly examine the careers of several émigrés whose activities and ideas formed the foundation for this new current.

N. V. Sokolov

The career of Nikolai Vasilevich Sokolov (1835–89) in many respects is a microcosmic reflection of the evolution of the Russian emigration as a whole. A prominent figure of the 1860s and 1870s, and the author of two books and several interesting articles on rebellion, Sokolov today has been almost completely forgotten by historians of this period.[2] Sokolov was born into an established military family and along with his brothers was educated for a military career.[3] He served as a military officer in the 1850s and was sent on a diplomatic mission to Peking in 1859. For reasons that are unclear even from his own autobiography, Sokolov went to London in 1860 after his return to St. Petersburg from China. It is possible that the intellectual ferment of the time surrounding the impending emancipation of the peasants affected Sokolov as it did so many other Russians of his generation, but there is no concrete evidence for the dramatic and rapid change that took place at this point in his life.[4]

In London, Sokolov contacted Herzen, who gave him a letter of introduction to Proudhon. Sokolov then journeyed to Brussels to see Proudhon and met with him on a daily basis for what appears to be a two-month period.[5] In the fall of 1860, Sokolov returned to St. Petersburg to work in the Statistical Bureau of the General Staff. In 1862 he resigned from military service and became the economic editor for *Russkoe slovo*. This transition was facilitated by several of his friends in the military who had become followers of Cherny-shevskii.[6] Sokolov's articles in *Russkoe slovo* were unabashedly Proudhonist, highly critical of capitalism, and full of information on the exploitation of the agricultural and industrial labor force.[7] In the summer of 1863, Sokolov again went to Europe, living mainly in Dresden and Paris. He remained on cordial terms with Herzen (whom he visited in February 1865) and received 100 francs "from the fund"—presumably the contested Bakhmetov fund—to carry on his work. In January 1865, Sokolov was with Proudhon when the French anarchist died. He delivered one of the eulogies at Proudhon's funeral, confessing his own adherence to the ideology of anarchism.[8] Then, in July 1865, he returned to St. Petersburg, where he worked on the two books for which he deserves to be best known. In April 1866, during the "white terror" that followed Ka-rakozov's attempt on the tsar's life, Sokolov was arrested for his involvement with the Nozhin circle.

Sokolov's *The Social Revolution*, which he wrote in German, was published in Bern in 1868, but the date on the final page of the book (25 October 1864) indicates that it may have been completed by the author while he was still abroad.[9] This book, perhaps the most explicitly revolutionary study ever written by a Russian before the advent of populism in the 1870s, is, as one historian has correctly noted, "without parallel in the contemporary Russian press, whether official or illegal."[10] The book clearly shows not only Sokolov's acceptance of Proudhonist ideology but also his familiarity with Lassalle's writings and with Engels' *Condition of the Working Class*. Just as scholars have failed to recognize Sazonov as the first Russian to embrace Marx's early political writings, they have neglected to point out that Sokolov was the first Russian to become a disciple of Proudhon. Interestingly, Sokolov's anarchism, as expressed for the first time in *The Social Revolution,* appears to have developed entirely apart from the influence of Bakunin.

In *The Social Revolution,* Sokolov argues that the central problem facing the Western world is "the social question." By this he means the increasing exploitation of the fourth estate—the proletariat—by the ruling forces of bourgeois Europe and the resulting threat of civil war and revolution. He speaks in Proudhonian terms of property ownership as the forceful theft of the possessions of workers by the ruling class, and defines capital as the new religion of contemporary society. It is too late, Sokolov states, for a peaceful resolution of the social question. Ruling-class entrenchment, with all its attendant privileges, is too long-standing on the one hand, while on the other the situation of misery and hopelessness among the workers is irreversible under the existing capitalist economic system. Sokolov views the state as the institutionalization of the oppressive organs of power used by the European bourgeoisie to maintain its position of authority. The state, therefore, is the organization of exploitation for the ruling class as well as the means of demoralizing society. Since no solution is possible under existing conditions, Sokolov predicts that there will be a violent social revolution by the workers of Europe to usher in a wholly new form of society. According to Sokolov, the postrevolutionary order will not resemble any previous situation. He discusses Lassalle's theory of "state communism" as merely a shift from one form of state exploitation to another. Property in the hands of the state remains property, government in the name of the people remains government. Political freedom and equality will remain illusions so long as human relations, social values, and economic processes are not themselves fundamentally altered: "Under contemporary political conditions, every political constitution is a veiled form of slavery and social murder against which the poor worker is unable to defend himself. A state constitution leaves him the freedom of choice—to gradually die of hunger or to more quickly commit suicide."[11]

In attempting to clarify the nature of the revolution that would finally transcend these difficulties, Sokolov wrote: "I am preaching revolution, yes, but what kind of revolution? It is a revolution of ideas, i.e., an intellectual transformation, a transition to a form of thinking, conceptualizations, and convictions on the basis of science and conscience."[12] Thus he distinguished previous *political* upheavals from the more general, comprehensive, and transcendent *social* revolution of the future: "We stand on the eve of a general revolution by comparison with which the French Revolution of the eighteenth century and also 1848 will appear as child's games. . . . The time for purely political movements has passed. If in the last century one *estate* of the people rose up against the *state*, then now there is a *class* which thinks about the overturning of *society*. This is why the coming revolution can only be a social one."[13] Sokolov chose his words carefully here. Whereas previous political revolutions had involved only minority sectors of the people (estates) directed against the controlling center of the government (the state) in order to form a new political government, the social revolution would involve all the people (social classes) and would create change in the widest possible sphere (society), making future governments unnecessary.

The last component of Sokolov's vision of social transformation has been referred to by commentators as "evangelical socialism"[14] or "Christian communism."[15] Although this theme was developed in greater depth in Sokolov's next book, *Otshchepentsy* (Heretics), he began in *The Social Revolution* to trace the origins of modern revolutionary movements back to Biblical and medieval religious rebels. In particular, he interpreted Jesus Christ "not only as a communist but moreover as an anarchist." The essence of Christ's rebellion was not directed against the existing government in order to establish a new government; rather, his teachings eroded the power of the state's institutions and laws in order to transcend political authority completely and to approach a new moral basis for society. This, for Sokolov, was the primal revolutionary act from which all modern radical activity had evolved.[16]

In *Otshchepentsy,*[17] Sokolov developed a theoretical prototype of the historical rebel, the man who stands against the institutions and values of his time, inspires others to follow him toward a better future, and in many cases sacrifices himself in the process.[18] Sokolov concentrated on the rebellious actions of the early Christians and on the Anabaptist Thomas Müntzer in the premodern era, and he devoted chapters to the utopian socialists of the nineteenth century. He reserved his greatest example for the book's end, where he described Proudhon as the ancestor of these earlier rebel-apostles and the harbinger of the coming social revolution that would abolish governments, politics, and class oppression forever.[19]

Sokolov was first arrested on 28 April 1866 as a result of his connection with the members of Nikolai Nozhin's circle who were involved in translating Proudhon's writings.[20] He was freed but later rearrested in 1867. After a period of Siberian exile, he managed to escape abroad in 1872 with the help of some members of the Chaikovskii circle. The rest of Sokolov's career extends beyond our framework, but it should be noted that he joined the Bakuninist camp in 1874 amid the Bakunin-Lavrov conflict in Zurich, after his meeting with the Russian anarchist leader. In the 1880s he was active in the Geneva Russian émigré community. During the 1870s and 1880s, Sokolov helped establish a Russian library in Paris, but in his last years he sank into destitution and demoralization, according to contemporary accounts.[21] Nevertheless, after his death on 5 March 1889, he attracted the largest crowd ever to attend a Russian émigré funeral in Paris—a tribute to his reputation among his comrades.

L. I. Mechnikov

Although the *dominant* trend in the late 1860s in the Russian émigré community was toward ideological commitment, as we have already seen with Sokolov this was by no means the *exclusive* trend. One of the more significant members of the Russian émigré community who tried at this time to remain above partisan involvements was Lev Il'ich Mechnikov. That he ultimately failed in this effort is itself a comment on the contemporary political atmosphere. Mechnikov was on friendly terms with Herzen and Bakunin at various times, but he nevertheless remained at a critical distance from both men. He maintained ties with editors of the legal press in Russia while he was abroad working in revolutionary movements, and at one time his writing was published simultaneously by Katkov and Chernyshevskii. An individualist who traversed most of the known world on personal missions before the age of forty-five, he was also involved in the collective activities of radical organizations in Western Europe at the rank-and-file level. Mechnikov was, after his years in the émigré underground, a geographer-orientalist with an outstanding reputation as a scholar and teacher who was fluent in ten languages. In spite of all these achievements, however, Mechnikov has never been the subject of a serious biography, and he remains virtually unknown to students of revolutionary Russia.[22]

Mechnikov was born on 18 (30) May 1838 in St. Petersburg, where his father served in an Imperial Guard regiment. In 1852 Mechnikov was admitted to the Kharkov gymnasium, and in 1856 he entered the medical faculty at Kharkov University. After only seven months, however, he was expelled from the university for reasons that have not been clarified. According to one account, he was expelled because of his "liberal orientation."[23] This may be an oblique reference to the likelihood that he was a member of the secret student organization that was formed in 1856 at Kharkov University.[24] In any event, Mechnikov then returned to St. Petersburg, where he enrolled in the Medical-Surgical Academy and also studied foreign languages in the evenings. He eventually transferred to St. Petersburg University and graduated in 1859 in the physical mathematics faculty with a specialization in the natural sciences. Immediately after graduation, because of his linguistic skills in Turkish and Arabic (and his father's connections with St. Petersburg officialdom), Mechnikov was selected to serve as a government translator on an official diplomatic mission to the Middle East. The mission, led by Gen. B. P. Mansurov, was designed to counter French and British influence there. However, Mechnikov was dismissed from this post for reasons of disobedience. He then abruptly abandoned state service and traveled to Venice, where he joined the struggle for the liberation of Venice and Lombardy from Austrian control. Mechnikov became more involved with the Italian struggle in the summer of 1860 when he joined the Italian volunteer army formed in Florence under Garibaldi. The reasons for this seeming lurch from state service to nationalistic revolutionary service have not been convincingly explained. Perhaps he was captivated by Garibaldi's charismatic appeal; perhaps for him the Italian war of independence served as a model for the Russian upheaval he wished to see in the future. In any case, temporarily without a cause, rootless, adventurous, and somewhat confused as to his political orientation, Mechnikov threw himself into the Italian struggle. Appointed to an artillery officer's post, he commanded troops at the front before being seriously wounded.[25]

In 1861 Mechnikov began his career as a publicist. From abroad he submitted articles about the Italian independence struggle, and these were published, usually under a nom de plume, in some of Russia's leading journals.[26] In 1864 Mechnikov moved from Italy to Geneva, where he became involved in the growing conflict between Herzen and the younger émigrés. The motive for this shift had emerged during the fall of 1863, when Herzen attended a banquet held in his honor in Florence. Mechnikov was present at the banquet, and he discussed with Herzen the various ways in which the London-based Russian émigré literature could be transported to Russia.[27] For a while, at least, Mechnikov organized a clandestine route for Herzen's publications via Constantinople to Odessa and then to the Russian interior.

Mechnikov was also present at the December 1864 congress of émigrés in Geneva at which Herzen was confronted directly by the opposition and resentment harbored against him by the younger émigrés. Mechnikov's position at the congress is not clear, a fact that distinguishes him from all the others present.[28] Certainly Mechnikov was not an uncritical supporter of Herzen (as was Kasatkin, whom the émigrés named "Herzen's watchdog"), in spite of his willingness to contribute articles to *Kolokol*.[29] Similarly, Herzen had mixed feelings about Mechnikov, whom he both criticized and praised in private letters.[30]

In 1868 Mechnikov again went off in an unorthodox direction. He managed to obtain an assignment from the editors of the *St. Petersburg Vedomosti* to be their correspondent in Spain. However, while in Barcelona and Madrid, he spent much of his time establishing ties between the Russian émigrés and Spanish revolutionaries.[31] Also in 1868, Mechnikov, in collaboration with N. Ia. Nikoladze, launched a new émigré periodical that was intended to remain independent of the growing factionalism in the émigré communities. The journal, *Sovremennost'*, survived for seven issues before closing down. We have already noted how one of the articles in *Sovremennost'* provoked Serno-Solov'evich to write his denunciatory pamphlet *Mikolka-Publitsist,* and we shall return to Mechnikov's journal in the discussion of émigré journalism during the 1860s.

Mechnikov's career does not end here, although his later activities fall outside the scope of this study.[32] He continued to maintain a life-style that permitted him to do serious geographical research and teaching without renouncing his deep commitment to social change in Russia. He accepted teaching positions in Japan and later in Switzerland, collaborated with Elisée Reclus, the anarchist geographer, on a major study,[33] and at the time of his death on 30 June 1888 was writing his memoirs.[34] He also worked closely with Plekhanov, Zasulich, Aksel'rod, and Kravchinskii abroad, while corresponding with G. E. Blagosvetlov and K. M. Staniukovich about the political orientation of the liberal St. Petersburg journal *Delo*.[35] Mechnikov clearly was an individualist who refused to adopt the reigning political currents of his time as many of his contemporaries did. He remains a fascinating figure in the Russian emigration, and his contributions merit a definitive study in their own right.

N. I. Zhukovskii

Another influential émigré of the 1860s who represents the turning toward ideology at this time is Nikolai Ivanovich Zhukovskii. Although a revolutionary of the next generation who knew Zhukovskii called him "one of the most original individual types among the emigration,"[36] very little is available in any language on Zhu-kovskii's career. He was born in 1842 to a gentry family and was given a traditional aristocratic education. He attended the exclusive Corps of Pages in St. Petersburg, spoke French fluently, was talented on the forte-piano, and was a habitué of the lavish balls given by the upper class during his formative years. After graduating from Moscow University, Zhukovskii worked in the Ministry of Foreign Affairs for a few years. He came of age during the emancipation of the peasantry and the ensuing response in society. Following the lead of his two older brothers, he joined the student upheaval of 1861 and was arrested in connection with his involvement with an underground printing press organized by the radical student P. D. Ballod.[37] Zhukovskii escaped arrest by fleeing the country, and in 1862 he arrived in London, where he met Herzen and began a lifelong career as a revolutionary émigré. Herzen received Zhukovskii warmly, and immediately gave him the job of ensuring the clandestine transportation of the publications of the Free Russian Press into Russia. To accomplish this, Zhukovskii moved to Dresden, where he could monitor the smuggling of the literature across the Russian border. It is highly likely that Zhukovskii contributed pseudonymously to *Kolokol* at this time, given his later work on a number of émigré journals, but apart from a letter to the editor, no concrete evidence has been found of any other contributions.[38]

In 1864 Zhukovskii became a legal émigré when he was sentenced *in absentia* by the Russian Senate "to eternal exile outside the borders of Russia" and was deprived of his rights as a citizen of the empire.[39] That same year he moved to Switzerland, joined the anti-Herzen "young émigrés," and began to associate with Bakunin's supporters. He was present at the 1864–65 émigré congress in Geneva, but did not break off relations entirely with *Kolokol,* even though he voted with the majority seeking a change in the editorial policy of Herzen's publication. Zhukovskii corresponded with Ogarev through the remainder of the 1860s, and together with Mechnikov and Utin, prodded him to change the orientation of *Poliarnaia zvezda.* In the fall of 1867, Zhukovskii wrote Ogarev a long letter in which he discussed in some detail his differences with Ogarev. The letter is also important because it reveals the evolution in Zhukovskii's thinking from an undefined radical outlook to a convinced Bakuninist orientation.

In his letter, Zhukovskii elaborated on a number of themes of concern to the emigration, including an evaluation of the possibility of a future peasant revolution in Russia and the roles to be played by the participants in that struggle. Zhukovskii argued that the coming revolution in Russia would have to be a peasant upheaval: "In this there is not, nor can there be, the slightest doubt."[40] Predictably he ruled out any hope for a government-initiated reform program that would resolve the profound inequities in rural Russia, citing the recent experience of the terms of the Emancipation Decree. More interesting and less expected, however, is his belief that the age of peasant leadership in rural rebellions had ended and that a new leadership from the masses would have to be found to ensure a successful revolution in the future. Razin and Pugachev could not translate their temporary military victories into a permanent social triumph because they could not bring the elements of science and politics—crucial tools in the modern world—to their constituencies. Without these elements, a new social structure could not be maintained. From what segment of society, then, would the new leadership of the masses emerge? Zhukovskii's answer, unique in the theoretical debates among the émigrés, was that the successors to the traditional peasant leaders would come from "the urban intelligentsia-proletariat, who are accumulating more and more in Petersburg and Moscow."[41] These people would not be aristocrats or graduates of higher educational institutions as Ogarev had presumed. They would be the new raznochintsy, radicalized seminary students joining with representatives of the gentry, the officialdom, and the workers in the cities to, in turn, fuse with the discontented masses in the countryside. Zhukovskii stated that attention must be turned to the proletariat, whose members form the country's urban artisanal associations and manufacturing artels. Their discontent must be channeled into constructive revolutionary activities. They must learn about socialist theory and practice, and then take these lessons back to the countryside.

Zhukovskii tried to convince Ogarev that his journal Poliarnaia zvezda should be transformed into an organ propagating these concepts. He gave specific advice. The journal would contain three sections, the first of which would expound in a readable manner the historical development of socialism in the West. The second section would then relate this Western socialist theory (by which he had in mind mainly the writings of socialists like Fourier, Considérant, Proudhon and Saint-Simon) directly to Russian conditions—to the urban artels and rural communes of Russia. The third section of Ogarev's journal, according to Zhukovskii, ought to be devoted to the actual experiments in the West with socialist institutions (Fourier's phalansteries, Owen's farms, etc.). Zhukovskii was convinced that "only the émigré press" could accomplish these tasks of bringing socialism to the urban proletariat for eventual transmission to the peasantry.[42]

Although Zhukovskii failed to convince Ogarev to alter the format of *Poliarnaia zvezda* along the lines suggested in his letter, some of his ideas did find their way into a series of articles written by Ogarev for *Kolokol*.[43] After this, Zhukovskii, with the collaboration of Mechnikov, negotiated with Herzen to create a new émigré journal. Ogarev was sympathetic, but Herzen refused to finance the venture.[44] Meanwhile, at the end of 1867, Zhukovskii met Bakunin, and the anarchist made a great impression on him. Working with Bakunin and Utin, Zhukovskii at last realized his dream of establishing a journal in which he could express his point of view on the Russian political situation. The new émigré journal *Narodnoe delo* began to appear in 1868.[45] Zhukovskii's commitment to Bakuninism deepened as he joined and became a leading member of Bakunin's Alliance for Socialist Democracy. Later, during the 1870s, Zhukovskii continued to propagate Bakunin's ideology through his work on the editorial boards of *Rabotnik* and *Obshchina*. Still later, in the 1880s, Zhukovskii strenuously opposed the formation of the *Osvobozhdenie truda* group, seeing in this the revival of the battle between the ideas of Marx and those of Bakunin in the First International.

In one of the few extant personal reminiscences of Zhukovskii, the Bakuninist is described as a man capable of endless conversation on the "burning questions of the day," but one who is at the same time incapable of being systematic and thorough. He virtually lived in the cafés of Geneva, talking far into the night over large quantities of alcohol with whoever would stay to listen and argue with him. He prepared his lectures for meetings and his journal articles at these cafés, but often he squandered his time and left most of his work unfinished as he collapsed in the night hours. When asked to lecture to groups of émigrés or workers, he could not be relied upon either to appear or, if he did come, to finish his assigned topic (usually on the International or the Paris Commune). He was a brilliant polemicist, full of sarcasm and wit. When he did appear before an émigré audience, he was so impressive that few people would attempt to stand up to him. However, in his last years, he came to be regarded as a "living relic of a past age."[46] His deterioration, the result of his pessimism about Russia and his despair over the obsolescence of his own role in the emigration, led him to absinthe addiction, a factor that contributed to his death in 1895.

V. A. Zaitsev

Yet another influential émigré from this period is Varfolomei Zaitsev. In spite of the fact that Zaitsev was one of Russia's most prolific and interesting journalists both before and during the period of his emigration, it is extremely difficult to find information about him.[47]

Zaitsev was born on 30 August 1842 in Kostroma. His father, a minor government official, was frequently transferred from one service post to another, and as a child, Zaitsev was periodically uprooted as the family moved from Kostroma to Warsaw, then to Riazan and Zhitomir. These frequent moves meant that young Zaitsev was never in a place long enough to attend the local gymnasium. Consequently, he was educated at home, where it became evident that he was extraordinarily gifted, particularly in reading and in languages, from an early age. When he was sixteen, with a reading knowledge of six languages, he applied for admission to Moscow University, but was refused because he was too young. With the help of his father, however, he succeeded in being admitted to the juridical faculty of St. Petersburg University. Then, one year later, he had to interrupt his studies, at the request of his family. Further moves rapidly followed, almost in imitation of his father's service-post transfers. Zaitsev studied for a brief period at the medical faculty of Moscow University, but in 1862 his father abandoned the family, and Zaitsev, now twenty, was forced to seek ways of supporting his mother and sister. In December 1862 he returned to the capital, earning money by translating and editing on a freelance basis while trying to continue his medical studies at the Medical-Surgical Academy.[48]

It was at this time, apparently through his sister's connections to the literary world in St. Petersburg, that Zaitsev met Dmitrii Pisarev and began an entirely new career.[49] Between 1863 and 1866 Zaitsev published a series of articles on literature and society for *Russkoe slovo;* these articles were widely read by followers of the "thick journals." With the closing of *Sovremennik* and the arrest of Chernyshevskii, *Russkoe slovo* became the most influential journal of its time for the Russian intelligentsia. On Zaitsev's articles for

Russkoe slovo, we have Shelgunov's statement that Zaitsev's work was "vibrant, passionate, combative, written with the blood of his heart and the juice of his nerves. Each separate review contains in itself a whole, conclusive thought, and all these separate thoughts compose one conclusive overarching, penetrating idea."[50] At the end of 1865, Zaitsev and Nikolai Sokolov left *Russkoe slovo* after an irreconcilable argument with the journal's publisher, G. E. Blagosvetlov.[51] Zaitsev worked closely with Sokolov on the writing of *Otshchepentsy* (which we have already discussed), and was involved with the circle that formed around Nikolai Nozhin in 1866, after Nozhin's return from abroad.[52]

Zaitsev was arrested in May 1866 in the aftermath of the Karakozov affair, and was kept in the dungeons of the notorious Peter and Paul Fortress for over four months while his case was reviewed by the authorities. He was finally released when no evidence was found linking him to Karakozov, but he was kept under close surveillance and was forbidden to publish his writings. Worse, he developed rheumatism, heart trouble, and poor eyesight as a result of his imprisonment. The period of his incarceration left him depressed about politics. In a letter to his sister, he wrote that he had "ceased to dream about social reforms and political transformations."[53] Realizing that his career as a radical journalist was at an end in Russia, he applied for permission to leave the country. According to his wife, whom he married in 1867, the main reason it took nearly two years for him to receive permission to go abroad was the persistent opposition of the former chief of police Mezentsev, who vowed that he would never allow Zaitsev to get a passport.[54] Only after the intervention of Professor S. P. Botkin, who testified to Zaitsev's critical need to go abroad for his health, did the authorities permit Zaitsev to leave. On 9 March 1869, forced to leave his wife and young daughter behind, Zaitsev went directly to Paris.

Zaitsev experienced both emotional and material difficulties in coping with his new environment. From his wife's memoir we have evidence of Zaitsev's personal feelings during his adjustment and we can speak with more certainty about his problems. However, much of what Zaitsev went through after his arrival abroad was experienced by most of his émigré comrades as well. In letters to his wife, whom he had been forced to leave behind against his will in order to get his passport, Zaitsev continually complained about his financial problems. For the first few months, he was barely able to eat because of his lack of money.[55] He finally managed to earn a modest income by doing original translations in Russian for two Russian publishers of the works of Lassalle, Voltaire, Diderot, Hobbes, and others. He also became a regular contributor to *Otechestvennye zapiski* in the 1870s after working out an arrangement with N. A. Nekrasov, the journal's editor.[56]

Worse than the financial problems was the emotional crisis Zaitsev underwent. He wrote to his wife of the sense of utter despair he felt as he realized, more so with each passing day, that he was irreparably cut off from all that he had known and loved. He began to realize what it meant to know that there was no hope of returning to his homeland, his culture, and his friends. He was not even certain, at this point in 1869, if or when he would see his wife and child again. He admitted that he felt "complete powerlessness," cut off as he was from the roots of his existence— "the heavy soil," as he put it, of Russia.[57] He suffered from migraine headaches, one of which lasted for two terrifying days without relief about a month after he left Russia. Of that transition into emigration, he wrote his wife: "I think that if I have to go through again what I did this February, I will ultimately go insane."[58] He felt trapped, caught between two worlds—one from which he had essentially been banished, and the other which he feared because his survival depended on an accommodation he was not certain he could make. Perhaps his most desperate moment came when, in a masochistic mood, he fantasized that only his wife, who was impossibly removed from him back in Russia, could save him from his fears. "If you do not rescue me in the course of this week, I'm telling you, you may never see me again; I am rotting away here now, which is not hard to do so long as one wishes it."[59]

Ironically, one of the sources of his anxiety became a factor of support and strength upon which he began to build a new vision. Paris was exploding into political and social chaos literally directly outside his apartment. In one of his letters, he wrote: "Paris is up in arms; every day brings the barricades and the slaughters. The people cry 'Down with Napoleon' and 'Long live the Republic.' We live in the most aroused quarter, St. Jacques, where barricades are being erected beneath our window. Napoleon sent in fierce troops and there was violence."[60]

Although he did not at first understand the emerging battle that was in fact to lead to the outbreak of the Paris Commune, Zaitsev soon turned his attention to comprehending the nature of the struggle. As he made interpretive sense of the turmoil on the streets of

Paris, he conquered some of his fears in the process. One means of accomplishing this was to write about the events he was witnessing. He was given this opportunity by Nekrasov, who invited him to write an article on the politics of the Second Empire for *Otechestvennye zapiski*.[61]

In the winter of 1870, Zaitsev's situation began to improve. Not only did he reap the material benefits of more translating and writing, but he was reunited with his wife and daughter. After traveling through Europe, he settled in Geneva and became intimately involved with the affairs of the Russian émigré community there. Meeting Zhukovskii, Mechnikov, and the other members of the Russian emigration who were then in Geneva, Zaitsev realized he had to make make a choice between ideological positions. The debate between followers of both Marx and Bakunin for control of the International had superseded the other important issue, control of *Kolokol*. Zaitsev gravitated to the Bakuninists, but left Geneva for Turin to live more economically with his sister and her husband, P. I. Iakobi.

Although Zaitsev was soon to become much closer to Bakunin himself, it is a measure of his effort to remain committed to a broader radicalism that he was interested in writing an article on Marx at this time. Collaborating with his brother-in-law, Iakobi, Zaitsev composed and managed to publish in a legal journal in Russia an article based on material from Marx's first volume of *Kapital*.[62] However, Zaitsev's ideological shift toward Bakunin was the more pronounced trend. While in Turin during 1870–71, he participated in the organization of the Italian section of the International, which was more sympathetic to Bakunin than to Marx.[63] More important, in November 1871 Zaitsev went to visit Bakunin. He returned again in the fall of the following year, and this time he lived in Bakunin's house and spent many evenings writing notes as the anarchist patriarch dictated to him.[64]

There is a large lacuna in Zaitsev's biographical materials between this point and the end of the 1870s. The omission is especially glaring since when the details of his life resume, Zaitsev has abandoned Bakuninism and has begun yet another shift in his career. During his last years, Zaitsev returned to journalism. He became a regular contributor to the liberal émigré newspaper *Obshchee delo*, edited by A. Kh. Khristoforov and N. Belogolovyi. More than eighty of his articles appeared in virtually every issue of the paper between 1877 and 1882.[65] Indeed, on the occasion of Zaitsev's death on 20 January 1882, the editors of the paper devoted the front page and a series of commemorative articles to him.[66] Elsewhere, little notice was taken of his death.

N. I. Utin: Emigré Internationalism

With the career of Nikolai Utin, we arrive at the end of the beginning. Utin's activities in the revolutionary underground represent
the culmination of many of the themes we have discussed. He grew
up, as he admitted freely, on Herzen, then found it necessary to turn
against Herzen in the context of a "young émigré" follower of
Chernyshevskii, and finally became a leader of the Russian section
of the First International, standing solidly with Marx against
Bakunin in that arena of combat. In many respects, as we shall see,
Utin carried the notion of collective action to new dimensions. On
the one hand, his activities marked the close of the period of the
emigration's origins, and on the other, they established a model of
revolutionary involvement that would characterize the next generation of Russian émigrés. That next stage in the evolution of the
emigration was the era of political party formulation, which first
reflected varieties of populism, and later, varieties of social democracy. Utin, then, was the precursor of the generation of émigré party
functionaries for whom ideology rather than ideas became so attrac-
tive. Although Sokolov, Mechnikov, Zhukovskii, and Zaitsev reflected aspects of this growing trend toward involvement in political
party formation, submission to charismatic political leaders, and the
development of revolutionary ideology, none was as deeply sub-
merged in these currents as Utin.

Utin, like most of the figures discussed in this study, lies buried
under historical neglect and distortion. Whenever he is mentioned
in the West, the imagery seems to emanate from a prejudiced account of Utin written by Bakunin in the heat of the battle over
control of the International. Venturi, for instance, quotes Bakunin
directly in evaluating Utin: "One cannot say that he doesn't work
seriously or that he takes a frivolous view of things. On the contrary,

I have met few Russians who work as hard. He is a martyr to the study of political and social problems . . . but he is gifted with a remarkable lack of ability to understand, to seize the essence, the real nature of the problem. . . . He runs along behind the thought and the thought scampers on ahead without ever letting itself be caught."[1]

A more recent and less balanced opinion of Utin can be traced to the same Bakunin tract: "Short, small and intense, Utin had a quick tongue and manner. Basically petty by nature, his judgment was often faulty, his sentiments frequently ungenerous. He had few fixed principles. Nevertheless, he was a talented man who was to play a crucial role in the émigré revolutionary movement."[2] Paradoxically, this same historian admits that "after Bakunin, [Utin was] the most prominent of the active Russian revolutionaries in Switzerland,"[3] though the claim is not substantiated in his account of the émigré movement. The facts of the situation are, in reality, quite clear in establishing Utin's significance. As a prelude to the material presented below, suffice it to mention here that there was adequate justification for the Third Section's view of Utin:

This man Utin is extremely dangerous to Russia, and before him in this respect the Bakuninist party (which broke with him) pales. . . . We repeat that Utin is a very influential person in the International revolutionary organization; he is one of the main pillars of the International; he knows all the ins and outs, and he, as one of the main members of the Comité du groupe de propagande, knows everything pertaining to the Russian revolutionary intelligentsia in the International.[4]

Another indication of Utin's prominence at this time can be found in a letter written by Dostoevsky in 1867 in which he compares Utin with Turgenev, Herzen, and Chernyshevskii in the same breath. While Dostoevsky was hardly approving of these individuals' efforts to create what he considered to be a materialist purgatory on earth, there is no doubt that he regarded Utin as a serious political figure of his era.[5]

Nikolai Isaakovich Utin was born in either 1840 or 1841; the date is uncertain.[6] He was born into substantial bourgeois wealth as a result of his father's career as a highly successful wine merchant. It is not clear exactly where Utin was born, since his father frequently moved from town to town in the northwestern sector of the empire while building his business. Sometime during the mid-1850s, the family settled in St. Petersburg, where they bought an elaborate town house and an equally luxurious dacha on the outskirts of the capital. The Utins were quite prominent socially and were often mentioned in newspapers in this capacity. Nikolai grew up in a house whose guests included members of the government, established businessmen, young writers, and scientists as well.[7]

Utin's path to St. Petersburg University was paved by his four older brothers. Significantly, his eldest brother, Boris, was arrested in 1849 in connection with the *Petrashevtsy*, but later became a professor at the university. The other three brothers all attended the university en route to their chosen careers in publishing, law, and government.[8] To encourage this array of brilliant careers, Utin's father hired cultured private tutors for his children and took the family abroad on summer vacations.

It was far from obvious during Nikolai Utin's school years that he would be the first and only member of his family to depart from the socially prominent roles of his siblings and parents. In 1858 he entered the historical-philological faculty of St. Petersburg University and in the following three years demonstrated that he was an outstanding student. Apart from the testimony of his teachers celebrating his abilities as a student, Utin won the gold medal in the spring of 1861 for his superior senior thesis. It is interesting to note that the second-place silver medal that year was awarded to Dmitrii Pisarev, the future nihilist.[9]

That, however, was the last honor tsarist Russia was to grant Utin. Utin's final year at the university coincided with the student upheavals that followed the Emancipation Proclamation. That spring in St. Petersburg, students established autonomous cooperative institutions, mutual-aid funds, libraries of forbidden literature, and mock courts designed to issue decisions to correct government abuses. Utin threw himself into these activities with abandon and commitment, finding, as he admitted, a new purpose for his life in this upsurge of student activism.[10] He quickly became a popular leader among the students as he tirelessly involved himself in many of the emerging organizations. Because of his skill as an effective orator, he was frequently asked to deliver speeches at meetings. He was selected as one of the editors of a collection of student papers and served on the student court. He was also chosen to serve as a student representative on the Kavelin commission, which was set up by a number of professors to publicize the students' grievances.[11]

Utin's political views shifted dramatically toward Cherny-shevskian radicalism in the spring, summer, and fall of 1861. He spoke openly in favor of Polish freedom and independence, and criticized the Russian government as an enemy against which he urged students to fight on behalf of Poland.[12] He continued to play a leading role in the student movement in the fall of 1861 up until his arrest on 26 September. He was released on 4 December as a result of his father's intercession with the authorities, but he returned to the student opposition movement immediately. In the spring of 1862, Utin's energies were devoted to two main endeavors. The first was organizing support to have P. V. Pavlov, a popular professor of history, reinstated at the university; Pavlov had been dismissed from his post by the administration because of his support for the student organizations. The second was working with the leadership of Zemlia i Volia.[13] Utin was of course closely watched by the agents of the police, who reported on his "criminal purposes" and who considered him to be Chernyshevskii's "right arm."[14] Utin did see Chernyshevskii on a number of occasions in 1862 prior to the *Sovremennik* editor's arrest, and discussed with him several anti-autocratic proclamations he had written.[15] Finally, in the spring of 1863, the police decided to seize Utin. They searched his apartment on the night of 18 May, but discovered that Utin had already fled. Actually, he had gone underground on 2 May, hiding out in the home of a friend outside the city before making his way abroad clandestinely. In a letter to his father dated 5 (17) July 1863, Utin explained that his departure from Russia had been decided upon quickly once he had learned from an informer that he was under constant surveillance and that the government "intended to arrest me" in the very near future.[16]

Utin's flight from St. Petersburg actually had been arranged by the Central Committee of Zemlia i Volia, of which Utin had recently been selected a member. Utin claimed that he had to be persuaded to leave the country by the Zemlia i Volia leadership because he "did not consider the danger to be so serious."[17] Nevertheless, there is no doubt that the police were preparing to seize him. The Zemlia i Volia leaders were aware of this, and decided that emigration was preferable to arrest in Utin's case. Utin was tried *in absentia* on 27 November 1865 for his involvement with the student rebellion, the Polish cause, Chernyshevskii, and Zemlia i Volia, and was sentenced to death by firing squad, with deprivation of all rights of property and citizenship until that time.[18]

Utin went immediately to London, where he was warmly welcomed by Herzen in August 1863. Herzen hoped to continue his
contacts with the surviving members of Zemlia i Volia who had
escaped arrest, and he enlisted Utin's aid to this end. He published a
letter by Utin to the Central Committee of Zemlia i Volia in *Kolokol*
in which Utin thanked the organization for his successful escape.[19]
Utin's relationship with Herzen remained friendly through the fall
of 1863 but soon began to sour. As Utin became more familiar with
the émigré milieu, he began to make his own proposals for revolutionary action. As early as November 1863, he was beginning to
conceptualize the notion of a unified emigration with its own united
émigré organ to promote the cause of political and social transformation in Russia.[20] He traveled to Switzerland to view the situation
firsthand and was disturbed by the isolation he found in the émigré
communities. While Herzen had devoted a good deal of effort to
establishing links between his London center and the Zemlia i Volia
leadership in St. Petersburg, he had, Utin felt, ignored the growing
divisions within the emigration itself. No émigré had emerged on
the Continent who could either rival Herzen's prestige by creating a
new émigré center, or find ways to fuse the geographically and
politically separate émigré communities in London, Paris, and Geneva. Utin assumed the latter task. The unification of émigré forces in
Europe was necessary to combat tsarism in Russia, Utin believed.
The problem that soon surfaced as Utin pressed his concerns upon
Herzen and Ogarev was what role *Kolokol* would play in the context
of a unified emigration. In another letter, Utin argued that in order
for the émigrés to accomplish their mission—which he defined at
this point as the "discrediting" and "paralyzing" of the Russian
government—it would be necessary to talk seriously "about reform-
ing the publication and content of *Kolokol*."[21] The suggestion to
reorganize *Kolokol* worried its editors, for both Herzen and Ogarev
saw this as a threat to their independence and control over the
journal.

Utin's idea was for Herzen and Ogarev to head a center around
which all émigrés could unite for the purpose of fighting tsarism. In
the wake of the Russian government's successful crushing of Zemlia
i Volia, it was hoped that a new revolutionary center would emerge
in Russia. To galvanize this opposition force abroad and to solidify it
on a permanent, ongoing basis, *Kolokol* would act as the theoretical
and practical organ of the movement. Thus, it was crucial for
Kolokol to adopt a programmatic format.[22] Utin developed this con-

cept more concretely in another proposal directed to the editors of *Kolokol*. As the theoretical organ of a united revolutionary emigration, he argued, the journal should contain an economic section with articles criticizing bourgeois theory, advancing European socialist economic concepts, and raising related crucial political and social questions. Utin also called for a section dedicated to "the elaboration of problems in historical context" in order to provide readers with a sense of continuity between past, present, and future. Finally, he urged that the new *Kolokol* include a section devoted exclusively to Russian internal affairs, a section in which the emphasis would be placed on the conflict between state and society.[23]

Herzen remained unconvinced and criticized Utin and his colleagues for their continuing efforts to involve him and his press in their affairs. Herzen, moreover, was somewhat puzzled that Utin expressed such militant opposition to him at the 1864 émigré congress, on the one hand, while, on the other, he went on corresponding with Herzen and Ogarev in a most respectful manner after the congress. Herzen may have overlooked a factor that could explain this apparently contradictory behavior—his own powerful influence over this generation of "sons" who, in spite of their rebellion against him, could not easily let go of him. Even Serno-Solov'evich, whose public criticism of Herzen was more devastating than Utin's, spoke on more than one occasion of his deep respect for his political antagonist.[24] In any case, Utin waited for more than two years from the time of his last letter to either of the editors of *Kolokol* before writing to them again. It was a period of transition for him as he began to search for new alliances among the émigré communities.[25] In February 1867, in response to a letter from Ogarev, Utin wrote once again about a new effort at collaboration to found a journal that could unify the émigrés on a common political platform. This time he was speaking not only for himself but also on behalf of Mechnikov and Zhukovskii, both of whom were willing to devote themselves to such a project. Utin reviewed the areas of disagreement between himself and the *Kolokol* editors, citing Herzen's calling Karakozov "a fanatic," his earlier "liberalist" position on the 1861 reforms and on the Polish Question, and his lack of a concrete revolutionary program. Nevertheless, Utin extended the olive branch to Ogarev.[26] The offer was rejected, however, as Ogarev stated that he saw no need for an explicit program.

There was one final exchange in 1869, when Utin, Zhukovskii, and Mechnikov were already publishing a new Bakuninist paper,

Narodnoe delo, in which they explored the possibility of linking
their paper with the Herzen press. Because problems had developed with Bakunin, Utin's attitude toward Herzen was once more
quite respectful. Again, however, nothing developed between them,
and the attempt to create a joint force collapsed.[27]

It is not entirely clear how Utin came to work directly with
Bakunin, who was in a short time to become his archenemy on the
left. Most likely it was through his friends Zhukovskii and
Mechnikov, who were genuinely sympathetic to Bakunin's ideas,
that Utin was asked to help establish *Narodnoe delo.*[28] There is
reason to believe that Bakunin hoped to organize the "young émigrés" in Switzerland, with whom Herzen had had difficulties, into
his own party. Regardless, the collaboration was short-lived. After
the initial issue in the fall of 1868, which consisted almost entirely of
Bakunin's work, disagreements emerged. Bakunin and Zhukovskii
resigned, leaving Utin in editorial control. Departing sharply from
the anarchist orientation of the first issue, the next issues of the
paper were dominated by a combination of Chernyshevskian socialism and strong attacks on Bakunin's *buntarstvo.* Within another
year, Utin had moved in an entirely new direction, as the main
organizer of the Russian section of the International.

The shift made by Utin from a vague radicalism influenced
mainly by Herzen and Chernyshevskii to the more concrete socialism of Marx was not as rapid and dramatic as it may appear. In
1868 Utin may have already been in touch with Marx.[29] A year later
he attended the Basel congress of the International, during which
time he befriended Anton Trusov. Prior to joining the International,
Trusov had emigrated from Russia after participating in the 1863
Polish uprising. In 1870 Utin and Trusov became coeditors of
Narodnoe delo, which they converted into an organ of Marx's wing
of the International. Utin, unable earlier to achieve an all-émigré
journal under Herzen's leadership, now published an internationalist paper under Marx's guidance.[30]

Utin's articles in *Narodnoe delo* between 1868 and 1870 are
not original, but they are faithful adaptations of the vocabulary and
content of Marx's ideas. There is no doubt that he steeped himself in
the literature of the International during these years. His essays
from this period reflect an almost obsessional concern for "the Russian proletariat," which would soon emerge to join the ranks of the
European and American proletariat in the global struggle against
capitalism. Instead of the political struggle against tsarism and au-

tocracy, which informed his earlier writings, Utin now wrote about "the socioeconomic conflicts" that lay beneath the political crises. The "class character" of the conflicts stood at the core of all existing problems, according to Utin. He also wrote about the liberating mission of the working class in its war against archaic "bourgeois forms," and the eventual transcendence of these "structures" by "a new mode of existence" dominated by the triumphant proletariat. He celebrated the International as the institutional center for the dissemination and organization of these new proletarian "modes of existence." He envisioned the growth of International sections in Russia in the near future, which would begin "to dismantle . . . the [bourgeois] institutions of the state, the church, trade, and industry." On the Russian peasantry, Utin combined Chernyshevskii's ideas on the socialist nature of the rural commune with Marx's conceptions of the struggle against capitalism. He foresaw a process of peasant nationalization of the countryside jointly proceeding alongside the proletariat's nationalization of state and private properties in the cities. It was a bold vision, simultaneously derivative and prophetic.[31]

Utin's ideological commitment was matched by his organizational work in setting up in Geneva the Russian section of the International in what was in fact a Marxist political party of Russian émigrés. He was joined by a number of newly arrived émigrés from Russia, Viktor and Ekaternia Bartenev, and Elizaveta Tomanovskaia (Dmitrieva) in addition to Trusov.[32] On 12 March 1870 Utin, Trusov, and Bartenev composed a formal document establishing the political program and constituency of the newly formed Russian section and sent it to the office of the General Council of the International for approval. The group also wrote a collective letter to Marx regarding permission to be the "official representatives" of the International for the Russian working class.[33] Two other letters from Utin, Trusov, and Bartenev were sent to Marx that year. One was a statement condemning Bakunin in general, and his relationship with Nechaev in particular; the other was a letter of recommendation for Tomanovskaia to join the Russian section.[34]

Utin's first personal letter to Marx was sent a year later, and it underscores the fact that no Russian émigré since Nikolai Sazonov in the 1840s had become so involved with Marx. After speaking about Tomanovskaia's virtues as a revolutionary and about the events in Paris concerning the establishing of the Commune, Utin tells Marx how much and how deeply he admires and respects

Marx's "mind and political acumen," and how determined he is to serve under Marx's banner.[35]

In the summer of 1871, Marx notified Utin that instead of a general congress that year, there would instead be a closed conference in London which would consider a resolution to expel Bakunin's Alliance for Social Democracy from the International.[36] It was at this point, judging from this letter and those which followed it, that Marx decided to call upon Utin to wage a systematic campaign on Marx's behalf against the Bakuninist wing of the International. At the London conference, Utin presented information about Nechaev's activities with the obvious intention of embarrassing Bakunin. Utin published a short report on this matter, which forms part of the stenographic account of the conference.[37] Utin continued this work after the conference, reporting to Marx on the attacks directed against the Marxist wing by the Bakuninists. At one point, Utin complained that "this filthy atmosphere of intrigue and disgusting slander" is a waste of valuable time which only weakens the real work of the International. He blamed this on his former comrades "the drunkard Zhukovskii" and "the idiot-schemer Elpidin," now identified with the Bakuninists.[38]

Utin's battle against the anarchist influence in the International continued into the next year as he helped prepare the brief that Marx used to expel Bakunin's delegations from the International at the 1872 Hague congress.[39] After the Hague congress, Utin drifted away from the movement, burned out by the exhaustive campaign against Bakunin. Although Marx referred to Utin as "one of my dearest friends,"[40] there was no further task for Utin to perform in the International, which was already beginning to disintegrate after Marx's pyrrhic victory at the Hague congress. At the same time, returning to Geneva after that congress, Utin found himself alienated from the many émigrés there who were sympathetic to Bakunin.[41] The Russian section remained a small group and declined rapidly after the Hague congress. Nevertheless, Utin clearly had awakened Marx to the possibilities of a Russian revolutionary movement years before the latter's contacts with Vera Zasulich and the Executive Committee of the People's Will. At the 1871 London conference, Marx paid tribute to Utin's efforts in this regard when he said: "[Utin] had great hopes for the Russian student movement. There the students, most of whom are quite poor, are very close to the people and will give a strong impetus to the working class. In Russia, secret societies are not necessary; one could perfectly well create there an organization of the International. Among the workers, the spirit of cooperation and solidarity is very strong."[42]

Regardless of the exaggeration in Marx's interpretation of the Russian situation, his interest in Russia as a result of his association with Utin was real. Utin, however, did not remain part of the socialist movement that had been so important to him. Having moved away from the milieu of the Russian émigré community concerned with Russia, he also did not maintain contact with the West European Internationalist movement. Thus, in the mid-1870s, Utin ended up in complete isolation. At the very moment when the Russian émigré community was becoming a truly revolutionary movement, with the elements of organization and ideology that he himself helped spawn, Utin abandoned the entire political struggle. Instead, he returned to school in London and earned an engineering license, then went to Rumania to work on a railway project. There he wrote a rather obsequious letter to the Third Section requesting a pardon and permission to return to his homeland. The request was granted in 1880 and he immediately went back to Russia. Lavrov called this "one of the earliest cases of renegadism in the ranks of Russian socialists, but alas, not the last."[43] Once in Russia, Utin worked for a short time as an engineer, with no further involvement in politics. He did not, as Kel'siev had tried to do (and as Tikhomirov was to do a few years later), turn against his former comrades and become an apologist for the autocracy. He did return to Europe in 1878 and remained abroad with his wife (mainly in Brussels) until the end of 1881, when they went back to Russia. Utin worked in the Ural mines as an engineer until his death in December 1883, which passed without notice among the representatives of both official Russia at home and revolutionary Russia abroad.

THE TURNING POINT

*To go into exile is to lose
your place in the world.*

JEAN-PAUL SARTRE

The Russian Emigré Press: In the Shadows
of *Kolokol*

Although we have considered aspects of émigré journalism in the
context of the individual émigrés who edited or contributed to Russian publications abroad, we have not as yet examined the evolution
of the Russian émigré press as a whole. The general trend of this
evolution, as will shortly become evident, is very much a reflection
of the currents that dominated the development of the émigré
communities.

The Russian émigré press was at first inspired by Herzen's Free
Press in London, then competed with it, and ultimately succeeded
it. Always, however, particularly during the height of *Kolokol*'s influence, the émigré press functioned in the shadow of Herzen's
paper. Most of the newspapers, journals, and other periodicals initiated by Russian émigrés in Europe were ephemeral; none lasted
nearly as long as *Kolokol,* nor did any single émigré publication
achieve either the immediate or the enduring influence of Herzen's
paper. Nevertheless, it would be historically inaccurate to assume
that Herzen's paper *was* the émigré press. Yet, because so little has
been known about Russian émigré journalism during this period,
this is exactly what historians have tended to do—to equate *Kolokol*
and Herzen's other publications with the entirety of the émigré
press. The reality of the situation was actually quite different. The
journalistic endeavors of the Russian émigrés were rich, varied, and
a permanent feature of émigré life.

Before turning to an analysis of the émigré press, however, we
must first review the origins of Russian journalism in Europe. In this
book, we have disputed many of the claims made by Herzen and by
historians of Herzen regarding the emigration, but one achievement
is indisputably his: Herzen founded émigré journalism. He was
actively involved with journalism almost from the moment of his

arrival in Western Europe. Undoubtedly he was influenced by the deluge of political journals and newspapers that flooded Paris during the revolutionary year of 1848.[1] Alongside these periodicals were the political clubs that in some cases published the radical journals and newspapers. Herzen was briefly associated with one of these groups, the Club de la Fraternité des Peuples, which had an international membership that also included Sazonov and Golovin among its Russian constituents.[2]

Herzen seemed somewhat torn at this time over whether to associate with a European-international kind of journalism or to launch a publication dealing exclusively with Russian affairs. On the one hand, he was asked to involve himself in journalistic projects by supporters of European intellectuals as diverse as Mazzini, Proudhon, and Fazy.[3] On the other hand, he wrote that he had been considering a Russian-language publication and printing press as early as 1849, and was in touch with his "friends in Russia" about this venture.[4] Nothing concrete was realized in this period, however, in part because of Herzen's peripatetic existence. Between 1849 and 1852 he moved from Paris to Fribourg and to Nice before settling in London. Once in London, he began to prepare for a series of Russian émigré publications in 1853. He announced to one of his friends in a letter in the spring of that year that "there will be a printing press," which he was certain would be "the best thing I've done in my life."[5] He was very conscious of the necessity for individuals in Russia to support this émigré press both by contributing and by subscribing. Without this active involvement from the homeland, the venture could not succeed. The choice, as Herzen saw it, was between silence and the continuation of autocratic oppression, or the possibility of freedom through uncensored politics as expressed in his émigré press. In this way, he inaugurated the Russian Free Press in 1853 and the first émigré periodical, *Poliarnaia zvezda,* in 1855. Explicitly linked with the Decembrist tradition, Herzen declared in the introduction to this new journal that his press would be "dedicated to the question of Russian liberation, and the spreading throughout Russia of a free form of thought," unfettered by political restrictions.[6] It was a formulation that would generate a great deal of activity abroad in addition to the contributions from Russia that he called for.

Herzen filled the pages of his new journal with an impressive variety of documents, all of which were intended to demonstrate the necessity of social change. In the first issue, he published an open letter to the new emperor, Alexander II, in which he made clear his concerns for the immediate future. The main goal was to bring about conditions of freedom for the intelligentsia and land for the peasantry. He stated that his journal would have "no system, no doctrine" to propound, and he issued an invitation to all sectors of Russian society, to Westerners as well as Slavophiles, "to the moderate and the extreme," to join in a united effort to realize a free Russia. Concerning the means to that end, he wrote, "We open our doors wide, we summon all arguments."[7]

In addition, beginning in the first issue of *Poliarnaia zvezda,* Herzen published his magnificent memoir, *My Past and Thoughts,* in serialized form. He also printed the 1847 correspondence between Gogol and Belinskii, which included Belinskii's famous attack on Gogol's *Correspondence with Friends,* and an abstract treatise, "What is the State?" written by his émigré friend V. A. Engel'son, with whom, however, he had serious disagreements. This was followed in future issues by the poetry of Pushkin, Lermontov, and Ryleev, contributions by his closest colleague, Ogarev, on the emancipation question, and the memoirs of the Decembrist I. D. Iakushkin, to mention only a small portion of the overall contributions.[8] Herzen's main objectives were to provide a forum for discussion of Russia's path from autocracy to political liberty, and to connect these contemporary problems to the developments that had spawned them since the 1825 Decembrist uprising. For Herzen, the thirty-year reign of Nicholas I was no longer to be seen as the apogee of autocracy, but rather as the prelude to the age of freedom he believed was now dawning in Russia.

In an effort to present the views of such prominent liberals as Boris Chicherin and Konstantin Kavelin, Herzen started a separate publication, *Golosa iz Rossii* (Voices from Russia). Many of his own concepts about the *obshchina* (commune) and Russian socialism emerged from his debate with these liberals, for whom Herzen had genuine respect in spite of disagreements with them.

Within two years, Herzen sensed the need for a new émigré organ with a different format. With the death of Nicholas I, followed by Alexander II's accession to the throne, Herzen perceived that the mood in Russia had switched dramatically from the fatalistic, albeit reluctant, acceptance of the oppressive existing order of things, to an emotionally charged optimism in which all manner of reform seemed possible. The arrival in London of Herzen's oldest and most trusted friend, Nikolai Ogarev, also spurred Herzen to respond to the challenge of the times by providing a new voice of change from abroad. The development that made the new organ a reality was Herzen's success in negotiating with the Trubner publishing house in London, which granted him vastly improved conditions for printing abroad in Russian.[9] The result was the appearance of the first issue of *Kolokol* on 1 July 1857.

The new publication resembled a newspaper more than a journal (to which *Poliarnaia zvezda* was more similar); it could appear more frequently and thus with more immediate information and opinion on the crucial questions of the day. Herzen announced that *Kolokol* would be dedicated to the same principles of freedom that had been proclaimed in *Poliarnaia zvezda*, but that the new publication would concentrate primarily on the problem of liberating the serfs with land, peacefully if possible. He warned his countrymen that unless emancipation was announced soon, with favorable conditions for the freed peasants, "the muzhiks will decide for themselves. Streams of blood will flow and who will be responsible for that? The government. Wake up. . . . Let us work while there is still time."[10]

Herzen's achievement with the creation of *Kolokol* was supreme. He fused the tradition of Russian critical journalism as practiced by Belinskii in his very last years with the tradition of European radical journalism, which particularly influenced Herzen at the time of the 1848 revolutions. Through this synthesis, he created an entirely new journalistic genre in the Russian context with a distinctive and personal idiom for its expression. Herzen's prose was elegant, complex, appropriately urgent in tone, and extremely relevant. In announcing his reform program—freedom of the word from censorship, freedom of the peasants with land from landlords, and the freedom of all Russians (not only the gentry) from corporal punishment—Herzen accelerated the emerging debate that was to lead to the Great Reforms of the early 1860s. In addition to printing his theoretical articles on the nature of the coming transformation in Russia, he devoted a good deal of space to the "unmasking" (as he called it) of official abuses in the government and the capricious everyday tyranny of landlords. He frequently included statistics and other forms of documentary evidence to illustrate forms of injustice. As Venturi has said, "The paper so widened its sources of information (which often included government offices) that it was able to publish secret documents of such importance that even today, after the archives have been opened, the *Kolokol* provides information on Russian life of the period which is not obtainable elsewhere."[11]

Herzen rang his "bell" for Russian contributors, and they appeared in numbers that exceeded his wildest expectations.[12] What he did not seem to anticipate at all, however, was that his publications would become an inspiring and competitive example to other émigrés. In this way, the concept of an opposition press, which Herzen had experienced firsthand during the 1848 revolution in Paris, was passed on to other Russian émigrés. The initial efforts that were made tended to be to Herzen's right, politically, but by the end of the 1860s, as the emigration itself became increasingly critical of Herzen and also more radical in its political orientation, the émigré press began to produce publications far to Herzen's left.

The first émigré periodical to appear after *Kolokol* was *Blagonamerennyi*, published in Leipzig in 1859 and edited by Ivan Golovin. Golovin camouflaged himself not only with a nom de plume but also with a title—Prince Khovry—in his capacity as editor and contributor. Some articles are signed with his real name, giving the impression that at least two people were responsible for the content of the journal. A total of twelve issues were published, each consisting of a lengthy essay by Golovin followed by five to ten pages of miscellany such as letters, book reviews, and brief notices about people or events. The themes of the lead essays are eclectic, ranging from trade and finance to European history and culture. Russia's role is not placed in any clear focus, nor is any political program to be found in Golovin's essays. Indeed, here he may have been reacting against Herzen's explicitly political orientation in *Kolokol*. Nevertheless, a brief survey of these essays reveals Golovin's concern for Russia and his own political ideas as well.

In the first issue of the journal, Golovin's essay "Leadership in Trade" combined some of his economic ideas with instructions to Russians on how to improve their business skills in commercial relations. He argued strongly for the advantages of free trade and commercial legislation while criticizing governments like Russia, where there was less commercial law and greater restriction on trade than in England or America. Recognizing the gap in business expertise between Russia and Europe, Golovin included in his essay examples of properly written business letters, billing forms, and procedures for account-charging for purchased goods. He also discussed bankruptcy and guidelines for speculative investments.[13]

In the second issue, Golovin shifted ground sharply in an essay called "On the Political Upbringing of the Russian People," which was a response to a letter and an article in Herzen's *Golosa iz Rossii* in which Russia's development was interpreted in the context of Western Europe's. Golovin argued against this, claiming that Russia had evolved historically in its own manner, quite distinct from the situation in the West. He wrote that Russia had first to solve the serf question and then could move on to the administrative and judicial transformation of the country. These were problems, he went on, that the West did not face; they were peculiar to Russia. The ultimate consequence of solving these issues would be a political change in Russia in which civil liberties and individual rights could be achieved as they had been in England and France. Only then, when the Russian people were ready—that is, properly educated and experienced in citizenship responsibilities—could political freedom be introduced. In calling upon the new tsar, Alexander II, to initiate these changes with appropriate legislation, Golovin was in fact agreeing with Herzen's strategy and reflecting the similar mood that existed in Russia at that time in educated society.[14]

Golovin devoted several issues to an analysis of the French Revolution in a long essay that he dedicated to Alphonse Lamartine.[15] He also devoted some of his essays to descriptions of both the history and the contemporary culture of Western Europe, with the intention of providing Russians with firsthand knowledge of Europe while convincing them that Russia's past, present, and future were not similar to the Western pattern.[16]

In the last few issues before the journal ceased publication, Golovin became more overtly political. In the tenth issue, he included an editorial preface that is the closest he ever came to providing a programmatic statement. The journal, he wrote, desires for Russia "the general good, not merely the private good of individuals." By this he meant the realization of "freedom in order and order in freedom, which resides in a harmonious government." Viewing Russia from abroad, he continued, permitted a different perspective on the nation's problems and prospects. As an émigré, Golovin claimed he could analyze Russian politics and society from a "humanitarian and humanistic" perspective, thereby escaping the narrower, "nationalistic" focus of viewing the nation's problems from within. He believed that neither socialism nor autocracy offered real solutions to Russia's problems. He also made it clear that he opposed both militaristic and aristocratic governments as well as attempts at violence and conspiracies. What he proposed as an alternative was a monarchical government based on "popular representation." His hope was that the tsar would recognize the need to bring the nation into the political process and issue appropriate legislation for the establishment of a government of law. He did not, however, have in mind a republic based on Western models such as England, France, or Switzerland. This would only create havoc in Russia. Russia must, Golovin concluded, find its own proper governing structure in accordance with its history, its people, and its existing institutions.[17]

Following this issue, Golovin wrote an essay on the relationship between the judiciary and the government in an effort to amplify his political statement, and he also managed to secure an article by M. N. Granovskii on the Eastern Question for publication in his journal. He also printed some anonymous poetry in the last issue of *Blagonamerennyi*, which was dedicated to Vissarion Belinskii.[18] Clearly, Golovin was moving toward a more political orientation, but he closed the journal at this point because of the absence of any significant response to his ideas. This was the moment of *Kolokol*'s greatest influence, and Golovin was unable to offer coherent new perspectives that would attract a wide Russian readership in this situation.

At the same time that Golovin's journal was floundering, P. V. Dolgorukov attempted to launch another alternative to Herzen's press. Although he altered the name of his journal twice, the style and content of the successors did not change very much from the original numbers of his first title, *Budushchnost'*.[19] Dolgorukov was quite conscious of the need to present a forum for Russian émigrés who did not agree with Herzen's political orientations.

In September 1860, in the first issue of his journal, Dolgorukov set forth a political program. This program consisted of a critique of injustice in Russia and a proposal for reform. The critique centered on the problem of serfdom, the abuses of the autocrat, and the corruption of the bureaucracy. Dolgorukov made it clear that he was not seeking change from below but rather was pleading with Alexander II to initiate the necessary reforms himself. "We consider it the responsibility of all honest people," he wrote, "of all true Russians, to try to open the eyes of Alexander II" to the critical problems surrounding him from which his officialdom shields him every day.

Dolgorukov wanted his journal to reflect what he believed to be a substantial body of opinion that favored "a constitutional monarchy" based on specific principles. These principles included the following: First, legislative power must be divided among the sovereign and two legislative bodies, which he called the *Zemskaia Duma* and the *Boiarskaia Duma*. The former, or Council of the Land, was to be a purely elective body, with rotating, defined terms of office, while the latter, or Aristocratic Council, would consist of members selected by the sovereign and of elected constituents. Second, all government ministers must be responsible to the Council of the Land rather than exclusive appointees of the crown. The regulation of finances also was to be placed in the hands of the Council of the Land. Finally, there was to be a list of liberties that would be guaranteed regardless of the composition of the government. These liberties were equality before the law; freedom of worship; no arrests or detention without lawful trial, in which guilt was to be proven, not asserted; the abolition of corporal punishment; and freedom of the press without censorship.[20]

Dolgorukov made his competitive relationship with *Kolokol* explicit: "The political principles of the editors of *Kolokol* are entirely separate from ours; they are socialists." While admitting his respect for the integrity of their search for the truth, Dolgorukov believed that the effort to move away from the structure of a constitutional monarchy was an error, and a potentially dangerous one. *Budushchnost'* would monitor all known instances of abuses and illegalities in Russia, propose constitutional legislation for discussion, and promised to publish contributions from interested readers, particularly materials that could not be printed in the legal press in Russia.[21]

Future issues of the journal did publish such contributions, but it soon became obvious to Dolgorukov that the large response he hoped for would never materialize. The great majority of the articles and news items during the journal's three years of existence were by Dolgorukov—his views on Russia's politics, its international relations, and its history. He repeatedly criticized the "Asiatic administration," the "Tarterization of our secret police," and the "abusive encroachments of the senior Petersburg bureaucracy."[22] However, without a supporting readership for his moderate political program, he was forced, in 1864, to abandon his journal.

One of the most stimulating and original journals of the émigré press at this time was Leonid Bliummer's *Svobodnoe slovo*.[23]

Bliummer, a former law student at Moscow University, established his journal in 1862 with high hopes of providing a moderate alternative to Herzen's *Kolokol*. Bliummer's effort is interesting not only because of the content of his journal but also because it reflects the general opinion among the Russian émigrés that individuals could compete successfully with Herzen. Bliummer himself had become a disciple of John Stuart Mill's liberalism, and his journal thus represents one of the more unusual instances of European intellectual influences on members of the Russian émigré community. Bliummer's articles are incisive and broad-ranging and certainly do not merit the complete neglect they have received from both Soviet and Western historians.

In his editorial introduction to the first issue of *Svobodnoe slovo*, Bliummer indicated he was convinced that "not all shades of Russian thought, free of censorship, have as yet found independent expression." Although freedom of thought has been "ably served by *Kolokol* and *Budushchnost'*," there is a certain kind of thinking, characterized by "deliberation and restraint," which is absent in the organs of Herzen and Dolgorukov. By this Bliummer meant a profound sense of tolerance even of one's enemies, "whether he is a petty thief or a grand autocrat," a commitment to human dignity for all, and a compassionate recognition of the fact that Russia's difficulties are the fault not only of certain individuals' intentions but also of circumstances such as upbringing, education, and social values.[24]

Guided by the philosophic principles of John Stuart Mill, Bliummer continued, *Svobodnoe slovo* would seek to analyze Russia's critical problems. Bliummer wanted to find a new path toward this end. He was trying to move beyond choosing between accepting the autocratic regime or rejecting it and then being compelled to embrace revolutionary strategies. This would be made clear, Bliummer promised, in the journal's articles on international and domestic political problems.

Bliummer also showed a great capacity to empathize with the psychological plight of the Russian émigré in Western Europe in a way displayed by no other editor, Herzen included. In a separate essay in the journal's first issue, Bliummer explored the stages of adjustment for Russians abroad and the emotional difficulties that had to be experienced as part of the process of geographical transition. The initial phase is dominated by feelings of remorse as the homeland and loved ones are left behind, perhaps forever. This sadness is combined with a sense of guilt as the émigrés with political commitments realize that those who are left behind must continue to function in circumstances of suffering and oppression. These feelings engender "a terrible despair, an agonizing, tormenting pain," which is rooted in the clash between the "pangs for a dead past" full of meaning, and the new life that had once been a dream and is now incomprehensible, mysterious, and somewhat frightening.[25]

This is followed by a second stage, in which "life abroad begins." Life abroad, Bliummer continued, is characterized by inevitable comparisons. The former student from Moscow is overwhelmed by the wealth and variety of the curriculum in the West; the former official is astounded by the efficient methods and modes of specialization that exist in the bureaucracies of Europe. All Russians suddenly awake in a new way to the political horrors of the autocracy as they learn about the mechanics of parliaments and democratic institutions abroad, "and feel deeply ashamed" for having endured tsarist politics for so long.[26]

Then, in the third stage, the émigré decides to cease observing and starts to act. Realistic goals, with appropriate strategies, must be formulated. A conscious plan is required to clarify the nature of the struggle against the autocracy, according to the demands of the times. The émigrés remorse and shame is at last overcome only with this phase of action. "We seek," Bliummer concluded, speaking in the context of this need for action, "full freedom of conscience and thought, political and civil security of the individual, equality of all before the law, and electoral rule; for this to be realized, the autocracy [in Russia] must be dismantled and transformed into a constitutional monarchy." He also stated that he intended, according to Mill's principles, to speak to his opponents as equals, and wished to be treated similarly by them.[27]

In the political articles that he printed in Svobodnoe slovo, Bliummer tried to set a model for these principles and for the high degree of tolerance that he valued so strongly. On the Polish Question, he argued for independence. He believed that so long as Russia controlled Poland, neither country could be free. The same was true for the Ukraine, which he argued must be permitted to decide its own destiny.[28] In another article he took issue with Ogarev's celebrating the closing of Russian universities and calling Russian youth to go to the people to seek real knowledge and truth. Bliummer saw the shutting down of Russian higher education as a tragedy to mourn, not as an act to applaud. The universities should be reopened as soon as possible, since, in spite of the need for drastic reform, they were the only repositories of enlightenment and learning. Bliummer believed unequivocally in the progressive potential of higher education, attributing to it a kind of secular mission in bringing enlightenment to the illiterate lower orders of society.[29]

Bliummer was also a firm supporter of the need to develop a tradition of émigré Russian literature free of censorship. Citing Mill and Guizot on the definitions of individual liberty, Bliummer argued that the only result of literary censorship had been to drive Russian literature abroad, where it could be expressed freely. He cited figures on the growth of Russian books abroad as evidence of this trend. "Russia is spilling the blood of her own sons," he wrote, who produce literature that the government deems distasteful and threatening. Interestingly, Bliummer did not approve of all émigré literature uncritically, and warned writers and publishers abroad that they had a special responsibility to assess what was publishable by virtue of its quality and usefulness. Printing what Bliummer called "indecent writings" solely because they were critical of Russia and could not be published there would only damage the whole arsenal of literary weapons in the battle against the autocracy.[30]

One of Bliummer's most cherished projects was his proposal for a Russian constitution. In a series of articles in Svobodnoe slovo, he discussed both the specific terms of the proposal and its underlying philosophical justification. It is here that nineteenth-century Russian émigré liberalism may have received its classic formulation. Bliummer began by asserting that liberty was the highest political goal of the individual and that arbitrariness was liberty's primary enemy. Thus, the most fundamental purpose of a constitution was to secure liberty in the face of this pervasive evil. Bliummer then asked the important question, Liberty for whom? In answering this question, he perceived Russian society as being divided between two conflicting interests—those of the great majority, the narod, whose concerns were "not only varied but in contradiction and opposition," and those of a more homogeneous, educated minority. Citing Mill once again, Bliummer argued that freedom for the majority could become "slavery for the remainder" of society. Rather than compelling the minority to conform to the majority's interests (the reverse was worse), Bliummer suggested a governing structure that would be "balanced" in satisfying the interests of both groups. This required a delicate and carefully conceived distribution of power which could be initiated by the formulation of a program of basic freedoms that would be regulated by law to ensure justice. These guaranteed freedoms must include the categories of legal equality, religious worship, and expression of thought and opinion. Free elections were essential to a free citizenry, and a free citizenry was one in which no element was tyranized.[31]

The growth of a free society would have to take place gradually in Russia, Bliummer wrote. He proposed voting qualifications based on age and a payment of minimal fees not so much as means of exclusion but rather because he assumed many people initially would either not understand or not be interested in the new governing forms. For those willing to participate from the start, an obligation was to be assumed—to ensure that political participation would be available to the entire population. Political development on a national scale in an autocracy, where it had never existed, would be the greatest challenge of the new regime.[32]

Bliummer opened the pages of his journal to all political tendencies in this direction. For example, he published, with an enthusiastic introduction, the first *Velikoruss* proclamation. He underscored the commitment to balanced reform which he saw in the proclamation—particularly the proposal of balancing the freeing of peasants, with land, with adequate compensation for deprived landowners. No social group should be alienated in the new constitutional order, according to Bliummer. He also printed the Tver gubernia gentry reform proposals as well as a proposal submitted to the St. Petersburg gubernia gentry committee which suggested the need for an elected Assembly of the Land.[33]

Revolution, for Bliummer, was another way out of the dilemma of misrule in Russia, but one that was to be avoided. Rarely in history has revolution produced a strong organization of civic and moral order, he noted. Revolution is a "tragic historical phenomenom, although sometimes an entirely legal one." Nevertheless, because of the possibility of violence and of minorities seizing control amid the chaos of rapid upheaval, Bliummer warned against this alternative. He was even more opposed to the so-called revolution from above, in which a new order is imposed upon society by the rulers. This he considered "an entirely illegal phenomenom," having nothing to do with popular sovereignty and dominated instead by court cliques and intrigue. Thus, while Alexander II could not himself create a constitutional order, he must, if violent upheaval was to be avoided, establish conditions for democratic elements in the society to do so. Only the people can act lawfully in their own interests; the sovereign must cooperate with this expression of popular will.[34]

In one of his last articles in *Svobodnoe slovo,* Bliummer analyzed the political situation in Russia in terms of political parties. Although he was perfectly aware that there were no "parties" as such under the autocratic regime, he deliberately used the term in order to delineate political tendencies and the constituents who comprised the existing Russian analogues of European political parties. He indicated four political parties: the state-bureaucratic, the aristocratic, the constitutional, and the republican-socialist or radical. Having designated the fatal schism in Russian history as state versus people (*gosudarstvo protiv narod*), traceable to Peter the Great's restructuring of Russian society, Bliummer distinguished these four parties in terms of their connection to the general population. The first two, he concluded, could never be "parties for the people," that is, based on popular interests. The bureaucratic supporters of autocracy owed their existence to the current regime and had no reason to ally with the people. As for the gentry, Bliummer acknowledged Kavelin's position that the landed upper class would gradually lose its significance now that peasant emancipation was a reality. Although he predicted that eventually the gentry would be compelled to join a democratic polity in order to survive, Bliummer saw the upper class in the immediate future as unyielding in its effort to retain the last vestiges of its authority and privileges. The radical party, on the other hand, was "a party for the people, but not of the people." Bliummer described the radicals as a group wishing to grant economic equality and political liberty to the people, but noted that their understanding of the people's needs was their own. Their ideas of change were in fact very different from the values and attitudes of the Russian peasantry on important questions such as the land, authority, the family, and religion.

Bliummer's choice was the constitutional party, represented abroad by Dolgorukov's writings. His central argument was that only the constitutionalists refused to impose models of political change upon the Russian people; only they were willing to permit the free expression of needs from the whole population, exploiter and exploited alike, and to ultimately incorporate these needs into the new order. Constitutionalists, according to Bliummer, would seek to establish an elected body to solve the complex problems of Russian society in a political framework acceptable to all concerned. The major unresolved conflict, however, was how to bring such an institution into existence peacefully amid a polity that forbade it.[35]

In addition to its theoretical articles, *Svobodnoe slovo* also contained reports on arrests in Russia, lists of Third Section agents operating in Western Europe to monitor the activities of the émigrés, and reviews of leading books and articles appearing in the Russian press. Bliummer had no illusions about the role his journal could play in the unfolding political conflict between the emigration and the autocracy. The journal could never "assume the role of the lightning rod of the revolution or even the mentor of society." It certainly did not aspire "to resolve the passionate needs of humanity and turn men into angels." Bliummer sought the far more modest task of providing a forum "for the expression of social opinion in Russia," which was denied within the country and discouraged by the editors of the leading émigré organ, *Kolokol*.[36] However, even this proved impossible. Abruptly and without explanation, *Svobodnoe slovo* ceased publication after the eighth issue, at the end of 1862. Another political voice fell silent in the emigration.

Of Bliummer's fate, we know very little. The son of a retired captain from Voronezh, he originally went abroad on a legal passport in November 1861. After spending 1862 devoted exclusively to *Svobodnoe slovo,* he started another journal the following year, *Evropeets*. He was in contact with Dolgorukov, who wrote to a friend on one occasion that Bliummer's intelligence might make "a remarkable writer" of him.[37] The Third Section regarded him with great mistrust, and those émigrés who met with him were considered political suspects by the Russian government.[38]

On 14 July 1865 Bliummer was ordered to return to Russia, and government reports indicate his intention to do so. The last item on Bliummer in the police files mentions that because of "the harmful content of his two journals," he was sentenced by the State Council to "deprivation of all rights and property," and was to be "exiled for hard labor in prisons for twenty years ." Lastly, the report states that in consideration of his age (twenty-three) and other factors, an appeal of the sentence was being studied.[39]

There were other journalistic ventures by Russian émigrés during the 1860s, reflecting the changes in the political orientation of the emigration. In 1862, Bakst and several of his comrades in the Heidelberg colony published a volume called *Letuchie listki*. Although they had hoped to establish a continuing series of *listki,* only the first issue ever appeared, which was devoted largely to the three *Velikoruss* manifestoes.[40]

In the summer of 1866, Mikhail Elpidin published the first issue of *Podpol'noe slovo* in Geneva. Elpidin had fled from Russia after several arrests for his involvement in the 1861 student disorders, the Ishutin group, and the Kazan Cathedral demonstration.[41] In his introduction to this issue, Elpidin indicated he intended to publish a series of brochures and small studies under the new journal's imprint dealing with the emergence of mass unrest in Russia. He also issued a public appeal "to all who sympathize with the development of the masses" to send him contributions as well as money to carry out this project.

The entire first issue of *Podpol'noe slovo* was devoted to the significance of the Karakozov assassination attempt on the life of Alexander II. In what was clearly the most radical political orientation thus far in the Russian émigré press, Elpidin interpreted the Karakozov affair as the opening of a whole new epoch of upheaval directed against the autocracy. He related the Karakozov *attentat* to the traditional peasant rebellions led by Razin and Pugachev, choosing to see this as a modern, urban version of the former rural rebellions.[42]

In the second issue of his journal, Elpidin treated the Kazan demonstration, documenting the mass of arrests across the country and the closing of journals critical of the government. He continued to interpret these events as the start of a general civil war between society and state. However, the money and materials he had requested were not forthcoming, and the journal ceased publication after this issue.[43]

After a decade of unparalleled success in pioneering the terrain of Russian émigré journalism, Herzen's *Kolokol* began to falter. Already in 1866, subscriptions began to drop and contributions from Russia declined. Early in 1867, Herzen reported in a letter that he was being told by Russians that "no one in St. Petersburg is reading *Kolokol* any longer" and that booksellers who formerly stocked the journal and who always had it on hand, now no longer order it. When asked for current issues, "they shrug their shoulders and say: no one wants it."[44]

For some years, Herzen had managed to steer an independent course as the tsarist government committed itself to a broad-ranging series of reforms. For that historical moment, on the eve of the 1861

Emancipation, Herzen was able to appeal to the tsar and his entourage in open letters, to engage in a lively debate with liberals such as Kavelin and Chicherin, and to attract the sympathies of a new generation of youth whom he referred to as "Chernyshevskii's children." During that time, he published some of his most memorable articles in *Kolokol*. However, in these very articles, the turning tide against Herzen also is quite visible. In the article "Very Dangerous!" in 1859, he attacked the editors of *Sovremennik* for their tendency to pronounce judgments on past and present literature on the basis of its political value to the overall process of social and political transformation in Russia. Further, he defended the idea of a broad coalition in society to work toward basic reforms, a policy which Chernyshevskii and Dobroliubov were criticizing.[45] This was followed by an article in the fall of 1860 in which Herzen analyzed the conflict of values between the "superfluous men" of the previous generation and the "jaundiced" youth of the current decade. Once again, he tried to defend the older generation for its historical significance while recognizing that it was being superseded by representatives of a new generation who had no understanding of culture, idealism, and the complexity of the transitions necessary for permanent, progressive, and just change. Limited by the difficult political circumstances of their functioning within the confines of autocracy, Herzen felt that the young generation was rushing headlong toward simplistic solutions with impatience and intolerance.[46]

Then, after the Emancipation was a reality, Herzen issued his eloquent call to that very generation to "listen to the moan growing, the murmur rising, from every side of our enormous country, the first roar of the ocean's waves . . . to the people! to the people!"[47] He called them "warriors of the masses," but he had no program to present to them. During the next few years, he found himself attacked by all sides, whether from Katkov's pro-government press, the liberals, or the nihilists, those "children of Chernyshevskii" now being aggressively silenced by the tsar's "White Terror." No one was more aware of the problem of Herzen's political eclipse than Herzen himself: "Like knight-errants in the stories who have lost their way, we were hesitating at a crossroads. Go to the right, and you will lose your horse, but you will be safe yourself; go to the left, and your horse will be safe but you will perish; go forward and everyone will abandon you; go back—that was impossible."[48]

Finally, after agonizing over the continuing declining fortunes of his journal, Herzen made a decision that was very difficult for him. In issue number 244-45 of *Kolokol* (1 July 1867), in an essay celebrating the tenth anniversary of the journal, Herzen announced to his readers that *Kolokol* would soon cease publication. He phrased it in terms of an "interruption in publication'" a pause to see "how great or weak, living or dying, the interest in *Kolokol* really is." By November 1867 Herzen reluctantly admitted that "no one [was] shedding tears" over the demise of his journal.[49] Many reasons have been cited by historians for the failure of *Kolokol* at this historical moment. According to one recent study, Herzen lost two of his most important and sustaining audiences beginning in 1863. First, because of his support for the Polish rebellion and for an independent Poland, Herzen angered the liberal reformers and bureaucratic officials who had previously been interested in *Kolokol,* particularly during the Emancipation discussions. Second, as we have seen, because he did not take a stronger revolutionary position in his journal, the more radical young generation became increasingly disillusioned with Herzen's analysis of the rapidly changing events in Russia.[50]

At the moment when *Kolokol* was ending its existence, two émigré journals appeared which competed briefly with each other to take its place. In 1868 Lev Mechnikov and N. Ia. Nikoladze joined together to produce *Sovremennost'*. Its purpose, according to the editors, was "to be both a review and a reflection of contemporary life, and to present to readers a portrait not merely of its aspirations and ideals, but the actual situation of things and the course of social action in Russia and Europe."[51] This modest and somewhat vague statement, however, does not adequately indicate the real thrust of the journal's content. In its pages, a wide range of theoretical and practical problems confronting the opposition movement were explored. These included the role of the revolutionary in contemporary society, "the heightening of social contradictions in Russia" as a result of the reform program of the 1860s, the place of the zemstvos in postreform Russia, the historical significance of revolutions and their impact on societies, the role of personality in the historical process, and the importance of "economic necessity" in the process of social transformation.[52]

One of the topics the journal treated frequently and extensively was that of the tasks facing Russian revolutionaries. The editors believed that all revolutionaries had to study and understand the needs of the popular masses before any appropriate strategy for change could be implemented successfully. This was particularly important because it was the only way they could prepare for the historical moment when the "mechanisms of state control" would weaken and become vulnerable for "the seizure of power" by the revolutionary forces. Never before in an émigré periodical had such an open commitment been expressed in favor of the seizure of state power by the masses and the "authentic revolutionaries," as the editors of *Sovremennost'* referred to them.[53]

This distinction between what amounted to true and false revolutionaries lay at the heart of the article on the Russian emigration that had provoked Alexander Serno-Solov'evich to write his scathing attack on the *Sovremennost'* editors.[54] Actually, the article in question was not really a criticism of the Russian emigration but was a broader critique of ill-prepared, self-styled revolutionaries who were more likely to endanger the future revolution than to further it. The editors of *Sovremennost'* analyzed the motives and activities of the young generation of revolutionaries abroad and lamented the absence of a serious, constructive program of action and goals, without which, they argued, no revolution could triumph. They also pointed to the lack of a general theory of social change in a broad historical context, within which the tactics of radical action should be planned out, and to the young émigrés' seeming disregard of the significance of massive popular involvement in the revolutionary movement. Their article was not antirevolutionary or anti-émigré, as Serno interpreted it. Rather, it attempted to confront the country's essential problems, which had to be resolved if a successful revolution was to be ensured.[55]

The editors of *Sovremennost'* were as critical of the anarchist orientations of Proudhon and Bakunin as they were of liberal and reformist solutions. They spoke about the "processes of objective social development," which these political figures ignored. Although they were not entirely clear about what these processes were, it is evident that Mechnikov and Nikoladze certainly had in mind an awareness of the interaction between economic relationships and political power. They also wrote about the determining influence of certain theories at any given time in history, and noted that these, too, were affected by this interrelationship.[56] Until Russian revolutionaries turned their attention to these questions, their efforts to bring about political change were doomed to fail, the editors stated. In one of their most striking formulations, the editors wrote that at the foundation of the revolutionary movement lay not a struggle over principles but the simple fact of "the battle of people for their very existence."[57]

With the appearance of *Narodnoe delo, Sovremennost'* directed its criticisms against this competing journal. In addition to attacking *Narodnoe delo*'s initial anarchist orientation, with which the *Sovremennost'* editors strongly disagreed, *Sovremennost'* argued that *Narodnoe delo* had only the most superficial understanding of the larger philosophical and economic forces at work in their time. It charged that discussions about mass uprisings and social revolutions were isolated and distorted in the absence of consideration of these broader forces. Tactics that were blind to the main currents of economic and social development in Western Europe and Russia could not succeed, the editors concluded.[58]

In spite of their intentions to move the thinking and planning of émigré revolutionaries a step beyond the political paradigm in which these facets had become encased, the editors of *Sovremennost'* soon discovered that widespread support for their views did not exist. After seven issues—the last appearing in October 1867—*Sovremennost'* came to an end.

The other competing journal, *Narodnoe delo*, survived, however, and continued the process of radicalizing the émigré press. With the appearance of *Narodnoe delo* in Geneva, we enter a new era, that of a strident, revolutionary vocabulary, the logic of polemics, and appeals to ideological justification. Instead of individual editors or a collaboration of editors (whose names had frequently been announced on the mastheads of many of the previous journals), we now witness the formation of the editorial collective, which while remaining publicly anonymous, claimed to speak in the name of a mass constituency in Russia. The journal was actually primarily run by Nikolai Zhukovskii and Nikolai Utin, with the support of Bakunin in its initial phase, though it would soon take a dramatic turn away from its original platform.

In the journal's first issue, in September 1868, the editors published a statement indicating their political orientation. Their first point was that the journal was to be a Russian one, concerned with Russian problems. They would not be indifferent to the political and social questions of Western Europe, but treatment of those problems would essentially be part of an attempt to familiarize Russians with European social movements and their methods of struggle. Although the people of Europe and Russia were seeking a similar liberation "from the yoke of capital, private property, and the state," important distinctions in the historical and contemporary peculiarities of these two areas of the modern world justified treating Russia separately.

A second point that was emphasized was the distinction between science and revolution. *Narodnoe delo* was to be a journal of active and committed revolutionaries, not of scholars or theorists interested in speculative thought. Indeed, the editors promised to engage in struggle against all who supported the contemporary political order. They categorized scientists, bureaucratic officials, artists, writers, and men of industry and commerce as "doctrinnaires," individuals with an unyielding loyalty to the existing order despite their attempts at affecting certain aspects of limited change. Similarly, the editors included among the philosophic enemies of the coming revolution the followers of positivism and utilitarianism, who also were interested in change but solely from within the framework of things as they were. As justifiers of the present, which they had a deep interest in preserving, they were scornfully dubbed "the aristocratic intelligentsia" by the editors.[59]

Third, the editors identified the state as the supreme institutional enemy, and its "jurists, economists, and political publicists" as ideological representatives of this "bourgeois-statist civilization," which stands in the path of the masses as they strive to overthrow oppression and inaugurate the revolution.[60]

What kind of a revolution was this to be? The editors provided the answer (despite their denunciation of solutions imposed "from on high"): "the full intellectual, socioeconomic, and political liberation of the people." This meant, above all, that "all land must belong to those who work it with their tools in communes," and that "all capital of the tools of labor must reside in the hands of workers' associations." Linked to this economic reorganization was the necessary restructuring of political power. All political institutions must exist in the form of free federations of voluntary workers, both industrial and agricultural. Finally, for full liberation to occur in the revolution, the state itself must be destroyed, along with all its attending institutions, from the government's ministries to its churches, universities, and banks.[61]

After publishing four issues of the journal during 1868–69, and discussing these principles in a variety of articles on strategy and tactics, the editors of *Narodnoe delo* began their second year by shifting completely from Bakuninism to Marxism. This change in political orientation resulted from the dispute over control of the journal, a dispute eventually won by Utin at the moment in which he himself became a disciple of Marx and a founder of the Marxist-oriented Russian section of the First International.[62] Thus, the program set forth in the first issue of the second volume of *Narodnoe delo* differed so strongly from its predecessor in the first volume as to represent a different journal in everything except name.

Utin and his collaborator Anton Trusov tried to explain the change in world view in their editorial introduction to this issue. They admitted that they were still committed to the general goal of a social revolution as it was formulated in the journal's first issue in 1868. However, they were now convinced that Russia's destiny was inextricably tied to the fate of the nations of Western Europe and could not be analyzed as a separate phenomenon. Furthermore, they continued, the success of the revolution depended on "the overall unity of action of the entire proletariat of Europe and America as well as of the Russian proletariat."[63]

The social revolution, according to the editors, had as its fundamental task "the transformation of all conditions of production and exchange" from their current forms. Rather than look to rural communes and land redistribution (as the Bakuninist program had urged earlier), the revolutionary process would instead center on the activities of the proletariat. Thus, revolutionaries must concentrate their tactics on "conscious elements" among the working masses to organize and direct the struggle against capital. This issue of *Narodnoe delo* also no longer referred to the state as the supreme enemy; the enemy now was the machinery of capitalism. With its destruction, the edifice of political authority would crumble automatically, the editors argued.[64]

The remainder of this issue was devoted to Marx and the International. The editors included a report of the 22 March 1870 meeting of the General Council of the International, the program of the Russian section of the International, and a letter from Marx to the members of the Russian section welcoming them to the fold and thanking them for their support.[65]

Narodnoe delo was published only briefly in its revamped format. Most of the articles concentrated on problems such as strikes, workers associations, and international political currents, all of which were interpreted in a Marxist framework. Each issue also included some message, report, or communiqué from the General Council of the International. In the fall of 1870, the journal ceased publication. Although there was no public explanation for this action, it was evident that there was little support for the journal's position. However, because it presaged the kind of émigré journalism that was to dominate the 1870s and the decades beyond,

Narodnoe delo may be regarded as a journal ahead of its time.

In general, the émigré periodical press of the next decade bore a far stronger resemblance to the style, format, and, in some instances, even the content of *Narodnoe delo* and *Sovremennost'* than it did to any of the earlier journalistic experiments we have investigated in this chapter.[66] Furthermore, the situation that existed in the 1860s would reverse itself entirely in the coming decades. The effort of individuals to establish their own journalistic platforms in the hope of touching the critical mood of a larger sector of the Russian readership at home or abroad—the work of Golovin, Dolgorukov, and Bliummer, for instance—was to be the minority current.[67] The era of émigré individualism, so dear to Herzen as well, effectively came to an end in 1870, as new forces began to transform the émigré communities and the battle for an alternative to the Russian autocracy.

12

The Emigration and Revolution

Developments after Herzen

On 23 January 1870 Alexander Herzen died in Paris.[1] About five hundred people came to his funeral, most of them French, reported one Russian émigré who attended. The only speech given at the funeral, however, was by a Russian émigré, Herzen's close friend Grigorii Vyrubov.[2] This situation accurately reflects the dilemma of the entire emigration: being spoken for by a countryman in the midst of foreigners in an alien land. At the time of Herzen's death, two generations of Russian émigrés had experienced this problem in one way or another, and the next generation of populist émigrés from Russia was about to arrive in the capitals of Western Europe. The growth of the émigré communities had reached a new level, and the emigration would soon swell to even greater numbers. Institutions had been established and became permanent features of the émigré landscape—certain neighborhoods to live in, selected cafés for discussions and planning, specific halls for larger meetings, and perhaps most important of all, reliable publishers and personally controlled printing presses to disseminate the voice of a free, uncensored Russia.

Herzen's death came at a critical moment in the history of the Russian emigration. Herzen himself had become concerned about the viability of the whole emigration as a political force during his last years. Before his death, he confessed to his daughter that he had come to feel like "a foreigner in our foreign circle, a perpetual outsider." Sadly he came to the realization that "we have become so tightly knit" that both the European left and the young Russians "regard us as outsiders."[3] He compared his life abroad to his earlier exile in Viatka, "a kind of second exile," not only because of the separation from Russia but also because of the schism between himself and the young generation of émigrés.[4] Herzen's pervasive sadness over his disintegrating career was noticed by friends who spent time at his home in London.[5] Beyond, or perhaps beneath, the sadness was another quality of émigré life, one that was noted by Herzen's friend Vyrubov when he visited the Russian community in Geneva in 1865: "They lived—survived would be a better way to put it—in a fog of bitter disappointments and unrealized hopes. Having no realistic soil on which to stand, externally irritated and angry at everything and everyone, they quarreled among themselves needlessly, without any reason."[6]

This senseless animosity and savage quarreling within the émigré milieu has been described by P. L. Lavrov as "a pathology endemic to any emigration, torn by the roots from its homeland and living with dreams about returning there." And while the country of the émigrés' birth, which has nourished their hopes, becomes more and more a "creation of their imagination," in reality it undergoes "a fatal transformation under the influence of events" with which they are no longer in touch. This, Lavrov adds, causes a form of suffering itself once the unbridgeable nature of the chasm between these two disparate worlds becomes a conscious part of the émigré mentality.[7]

This "émigré dilemma" is evident from numerous testimonies. Vasilii Kel'siev, of whom we have already spoken, wrote of the immense unhappiness he experienced abroad. He could not forget the world he had left behind, and felt that as an émigré "no one respected" him. Thus, the apartness and isolation he experienced were due not only to a natural longing for Russia but also to the disdainful attitude he encountered among Europeans in England, France, and Switzerland. Even when a Russian émigré wanted to assimilate, a wall of prejudice against him had to be overcome. It was impossible to both be Russian and be in Europe; one could either become a European (and renounce Russian culture) or live in a sequestered émigré community sealed off from both Russia and Europe. This, Kel'siev wrote, was the hardest thing to endure.[8]

In addition to this dilemma, a more serious issue confronting the emigration was the problem of leadership. During the era of the first generation, prior to the emergence of an authentic opposition movement abroad, there was no reason to raise this issue. However, during the 1860s, the second generation could not avoid confronting the problem of leadership. Many observers were of the opinion that, with Herzen's death, there was no single individual capable of providing an overall leadership. Hence, according to this view, the emigration was doomed to fall into disarray, to function only in internecine competing factions that tended to weaken the entire movement.[9] A number of émigrés were aware of this problem before Herzen's death and tried to fill the void with a new, collective leadership. Utin, most notably, dedicated several years to this task, as we have seen, but did not succeed.

There was one effort at establishing a post-Herzen leadership which we have not yet mentioned, one which was at once utterly logical and hopelessly impossible. In 1870, after Herzen's death, the revolutionary populist German Lopatin began devising a fantastic plan to unite the disparate factions of the demoralized emigration which he witnessed in his visits to the London, Paris, and Geneva émigré communities. As he wrote at the time, "There was only one person living at that time who could fire the imagination of an entire young émigré generation," who could be accepted by the great majority of the emigration as an authority. This was Nikolai Gavrilovich Chernyshevskii.[10] After all, it was in Chernyshevskii's name that most of the younger generation had opposed Herzen ever since the 1864–65 émigré congress. He had been the symbol of the revolt that Serno-Solov'evich had attempted to generate when he wrote his pamphlet attacks on Herzen. Lopatin's plan, however sensible it might seem in theory, was not one that could easily be realized. He did return to Russia to organize the freeing of Chernyshevskii, but the authorities made certain that their prisoner would not escape.[11] One can only imagine what changes might have occurred in the history of the opposition movement abroad and at home had this plan ever succeeded, with Chernyshevskii surfacing in Geneva to take command at that crucial moment, on the eve of the emergence of revolutionary populism.

Another vexing problem for the emigration was the difficulty of creating and sustaining abroad a permanent organization dedicated to the overthrow of the Russian autocracy. By 1870, émigré communities existed or were in the process of forming in London, Paris, Geneva, and several lesser cities in Western Europe. There was no clearly established center on the Continent or in England to plan strategy and tactics for the whole emigration, however. It was a problem analagous to the one facing Russian revolutionaries working inside the borders of the empire, where separated centers of radical activity had to be coordinated in order to move effectively against the government. The difference was that the émigrés faced

the seemingly insurmountable conflicts engendered by their peculiar circumstances as exiles rather than the confining restrictions
and repressive measures confronting the underground revolutionaries at home. First, they were burdened by the very conditions of
freedom which made it possible for them to carry on their work.
They were now at liberty to communicate as freely with one another
as they wished, but without an organizational framework, they were
in danger of setting up a vacuous network for themselves without
the force to affect the political situation inside Russia. Second, they
were essentially devoid of a natural constituency; this they had left
behind when they emigrated. The Russian people, in whose name
they were beginning to speak in louder voices, were far off, and the
lines of communication were too tenuous, too distant, between the
emigration and the empire.

To some extent, efforts to overcome these two formidable problems of leadership and organization were initiated during the 1870s.
The emigration was simultaneously weakened and strengthened at
this time as a result of a series of events. The decade began with the
revelations of the Nechaev affair, which tied together the new student generation (many of whose members were questioned in 1869
at the well-publicized trial in St. Petersburg of the Nechaev circle's
role in the death of the student Ivanov), and the emigration (where
Nechaev's association with Bakunin ultimately damaged the prestige of the whole opposition abroad for a time.) In addition, the
struggle between the followers of Marx and Bakunin for control of
the First International also made the emigration vulnerable to
charges from the established order and from bourgeois society, both
in Europe as well as in Russia, that the émigrés were hopelessly
doomed to internal factionalism. On the other hand, the arrival of a
large number of new students from Russia to study in Switzerland
during the early 1870s, including for the first time a significant
number of women, provided a burst of energy for the emigration as a
whole. Bakunin and Lavrov came to Zurich to compete for the
attention of this new generation of youth from their homeland which
stimulated some of the most original and enduring theories and
tactics for revolutionary activity that had been produced abroad by
the Russian emigration to date. This "Zurich colony," in a sense,
picked up where the Heidelberg colony had left off a decade ago.
This time, with changed conditions both in Russia and in the evolution of the emigration, matters intensified. For the moment,
Bakunin and Lavrov provided the desperately needed leadership

for the emerging émigré communities abroad, and the colony in Zurich similarly provided a model for Russian émigrés on the realities of revolutionary organization outside the country.

The rise to "power" of the émigré leadership in this manner fed directly back to Russia. Never before had such an effective linkage been established between the émigrés in Western Europe and revolutionaries in the empire. Rather than the very loose and unorganized affiliations that had existed between Herzen and the first Zemlia i Volia group in the early 1860s, the new connections forged between the populists in the Chaikovskii circle, the main populist revolutionary organization in Russia at this time, and the groups around Bakunin and Lavrov in Zurich were far stronger and more consistent.[12] As hordes of populists, many of whom had been in Zurich themselves, fanned out into the Russian countryside to carry out the tactics they had learned either from Bakunin and Lavrov, or from their followers and publications, they were at the same time acting on the slogan of Herzen, who years before, from his émigré vantage point in London, had called on Russia "to go to the people."

Despite efforts by the Russian government and the legitimate press to portray the activities of the emigration in unflattering terms and to minimize their impact, the fact was that illegal émigré publications hostile to the regime found their way into all the provinces of the empire west of the Urals. Privately, however, the government and the police did admit that the influence of the radical emigration in Russia had grown to unacceptably threatening proportions, as the official reports of this period carefully record.[13]

The articles that did appear in the Russian press contained information on the growth of the emigration as a center of political opposition in spite of their critical interpretation of the émigrés' political intentions and moral integrity (which was the reason they were permitted to be published in the first place). The émigrés were referred to as self-appointed "leaders of the people and decision-makers of Russia's destiny" whose efforts to undermine the existing order required conscious resistance, especially on the part of the university-age population in Russia. It was there, in that milieu, one article warned, that the émigrés' influence could spawn "various Nechaevs," who could conceivably emerge with hopes of applying these "misguided notions" from abroad.[14]

In another article, a correspondent admitted that "large numbers of gullible people" in Russia had contributed sizable amounts of money, in addition to moral support, to the Russian émigrés in

Europe. Although the article sought to show that this money was only being squandered by irresponsible and manipulative émigrés, it nevertheless concluded with a stern warning that unless these "generous donations" of support were halted, the emigration might be strengthened at the expense of the stability of the government and public order in Russia.[15]

The police eventually broke down this "movement to the people" and severed the links that had been built to the émigré centers in Europe. For a time, the émigrés lost their vital connection to the emerging sectors of critical and radical opinion in Russia. During the late 1870s, funds were sent abroad to them in smaller amounts, and evidence of smuggled publications from the émigrés into Russia fell to insignificant levels. According to one study of this period, by around 1880 "the population of Russian political émigrés was fragmented and the sense of community that had prevailed in the mid-seventies had vanished."[16]

However, the connections were revived during the next two decades when another generation of radical figures from the Russian underground fled abroad and rebuilt the émigré communities in Europe. Plekhanov, Aksel'rod, Deich, Zasulich, and others assumed positions of leadership for the next generation of émigrés as they developed new strategies for political and social change in Russia and became an inspiration for younger revolutionaries like Lenin and Trotsky. Continuity with the émigré past was reestablished. A wide range of émigré politics flourished again around the turn of the century, especially in the pages of the Russian press abroad, and this would ultimately have a salient impact on the transformation the Russian empire was undergoing in these years.[17] Among the most important of these influences was the formation abroad of many aspects of the political parties that were legalized during the 1905 upheaval when for the first time in Russian history the tsar was forced to grant a national Duma with elected parties. Twelve years later, when the Bolsheviks came to power in the October Revolution, the man who headed the new Soviet government was an émigré who had arrived in Russia only six months earlier, after spending nearly two decades in Europe. During those years of exile, Lenin and his followers had developed the theoretical strategy and organizational tactics that would serve as the foundation for the policies he adopted when he was catapulted to national leadership on the wings of the successful revolution in 1917.[18]

A Quantitative Portrait of the Emigration

Having cursorily explored these broad trends in the history of the Russian emigration after Herzen's death, we shall now turn to the more objective realm of quantification for the emigration during its formative period. The essential question is, How many people comprised the Russian emigration from its origins, when Nikolai Turgenev became the first émigré by refusing tsarist orders to return to Russia in 1825, through the evolution we have traced up to the death of Herzen in 1870?

To try to answer this question, we must examine the existing data on the Russian emigration. The most striking fact that is immediately discovered is that there are no specific data on the number of émigrés in Western Europe. This lacuna was recognized as early as 1904, when the scholar assigned to write the article on "emigration" for the Brockhaus-Efron encyclopedia admitted that figures on the Russian emigration were not published by the government. He also indicated that the only estimates possible under these circumstances had to be based on passport statistics for Russian citizens at ports of disembarkation, such as Hamburg and Bremen in Germany. Even with these figures, however, one still had to separate the politically motivated émigrés from the general population of departing Russians, which included many people who were abroad temporarily for vacations or for diplomatic or commercial purposes, as well as economic refugees seeking permanent assimilation abroad.[19]

Another source of data on Russians abroad can be found in the French National Archives. The French government began keeping lists of Russians entering France in 1849, with brief descriptions of age, position, and intentions. For the year 1840, for example, 75 Russians are listed as having entered the country for visits of varying purposes and durations. Most appear to be aristocrats, military officers, and merchants. There are some short reports on specific Russians who were targeted by the government to be monitored by the police, but these materials are of only limited use in analyzing the Russian émigrés in particular.[20]

In fact, the Russian government was compiling statistics on people leaving the country, in spite of the fact that they were never published. Every year, the Third Section was required to file a lengthy report on its activities to the government. Starting in the 1850s, when "political crimes against the Empire" spread to West

European cities, the Third Section's agents devoted a good deal of attention to these activities in their annual reports. The trials and tribulations of Herzen's press in London were meticulously described, often by agents who managed to gain access to Herzen's home, his meetings, and his *Kolokol* staff. The publications of Herzen's press were analyzed, and copies of the actual pamphlets and brochures were sent back to St. Petersburg for perusal.[21] The Third Section's annual reports also include statistics on Russians abroad, with breakdowns according to social class and official reasons for leaving the country. Unfortunately, it is impossible to tell from this material how many of those accounted for were political émigrés.[22]

Recently, a Soviet researcher investigated yet another source of data on the emigration, the names of individuals going abroad which were published in Russian newspapers. In this case, three prominent newspapers were selected (two in the capital, one in Moscow), and a collective accounting was created from the separate listings in the newspapers for the period of 1857–61. Of the total of 213 names, 39 individuals left the country in 1857, 46 in 1858, 70 in 1859, 34 in 1860, and 24 in 1861. The overall record generated by the newspaper listings includes the names of many of the émigrés we have discussed (Dolgorukov, Bliummer, Utin, among others), some we have not analyzed (V. I. Kasatkin, A. I. Evropeus, N. M. Satin), and some who would play a role in émigré politics much later (A. Kh. Khristoforov, for example). It also includes, however, the names of writers like Ivan Turgenev and Tolstoy, publicists and critics like Annenkov and Katkov, and a wide variety of other Russian citizens, some of whose names would be familiar to students of Russian history (A. V. Tretiakov, A. N. Pypin, V. P. Botkin, T. P. Passek, etc.). Yet, as interesting as this information is from the standpoint of a social history of prominent travelers abroad, it is not a useful guide to greater knowledge of the Russian émigrés—that is, those individuals who left for strictly *political* reasons. Moreover, the list does not reflect the illegal journeys out of Russia taken by many émigrés. The newspaper listings are also repetitious from year to year, since many of the people named vacationed abroad every summer (like the Utin family) or traveled to Europe for artistic, business, or diplomatic purposes each year.[23]

Some work has been done on a slightly later period than our own in trying to account for the numbers of Russian émigrés in Western Europe, but here too the results are not satisfactory. It is clear that most Russian émigrés congregated in Geneva, Paris, and London. Geneva was geographically the closest, Paris the cheapest, and London the most distant and most expensive city to live in. It has been estimated from police reports that in 1881 around 50 émigrés were involved in Russian revolutionary activities in Geneva; for Paris and London the numbers were 96 and between 7 and 10, respectively. There were, to be sure, additional émigrés in other cities of Switzerland, France, and England, just as there were still others living in Germany, Italy, Rumania, and other European countries. The data are very inconsistent, however. In the case of France, for instance, while the police counted 91 émigrés in Paris in 1880, another government list categorizes 181 Russian families as "nihilists" or "nihilist sympathizers." According to a separate list compiled by the reactionary Russian organization responsible for counteragitation against Russian émigrés in Europe, there were only 31 militant exiles abroad in 1881. Meanwhile, the French press claimed there were at least 2,000 Russian nihilists in the country![24]

According to an unpublished Soviet dissertation on the emigration movement of a somewhat later era, 104 émigrés arrived from Russia during the 1860s and 1870s in Western Europe. This list, compiled from both published and unpublished Russian materials (i.e., no data from European sources were included), extends for twenty years from the time of the first Zemlia i Volia group in 1861 up to, but not including, the collapse of Narodnaia Volia in 1881. It does not, however, include émigrés who came earlier than 1861. An additional 9 Russians emigrated in 1881, according to this material, and another 24 arrived in Europe during 1882–83 in the aftermath of the breakup of Narodnaia Volia.[25] Among other available studies are two contemporary sources commissioned by the Russian government. According to one, there were 200 "socialist and anarchist" émigrés in West European countries in 1881,[26] while in the other, a list of 112 Russian émigré activists in Switzerland alone was compiled for the period 1870–74. The latter list, which includes biographical sketches on each of the 112 individuals, is based primarily on Swiss archival and government records, supplemented by Russian data. There are also several statistical tables on the nationality, social class, and educational background of the émigrés in this particular study.[27]

Taking these varied and contradictory pieces of evidence together, the most reliable estimate we can make is that there were between 200 and 225 active Russian revolutionary émigrés in Western Europe during the early 1880s—about 37 percent in Switzerland, 25 percent in France, and 6 percent in England. The numbers changed frequently as political conditions in Russia changed (there were marked increases in the number abroad, for example, following the student disorders of 1861–62, after the Nechaev trial in 1869, and again in the wake of the arrests at the time of the assassination of Alexander II in 1881). There seem to have been fluctuations in the numbers for other reasons as well, reasons that relate more to individuals or to the internal development of the emigration itself. Furthermore, since the émigrés moved from city to city so frequently, it would not be surprising to learn that some of them were counted by the police in several different countries during the same year.[28] In any event, allowing for some reduction in these figures, which were compiled for the early 1880s, it would seem accurate to assume that slightly less than 200–225 émigrés were politically active in the 1860s.

The Significance of the Russian Emigration: Intelligentsia in Exile

By the time of Herzen's death in 1870, the emigration had become a permanent force in the evolution of prerevolutionary Russia. In spite of his acerbic and sometimes inaccurate rendering of his émigré contemporaries in his memoir, Herzen prophetically conceptualized the crucial role the emigration was to play in Russian history in his 1851 essay, *Du développement des idées révolutionnaires en Russie,* as we have noted.[29] Herzen was clearly aware of the profound transformation Russia was undergoing, and understood that, because of this, the emigration's significance would become even more vital with the passing of his generation. He clung to this faith in spite of opinion to the contrary from close and respected friends. In one instance, A. A. Chumikov, a fellow émigré, told him: "Our emigration becomes estranged from anything native and it loses its support and becomes incomprehensible for the masses." Moreover, Proudhon wrote to him at about the same time that "exile, like prison, derails the judgment." To these skeptics, Herzen replied with confidence that the Russians abroad form the ranks of a growing army that "protests vigorously against the despotism of St. Petersburg" and continues "to work toward the common liberation. Far from becoming foreigners, they make themselves the free organs of young Russia, her interpreters."[30]

Herzen's conviction about the significance of the Russian emigration was shared by most of his contemporaries abroad. To be sure, they had serious differences over tactics, and they all experienced some sense of disorientation from the shock of adapting themselves to their new milieu far beyond the familiar borders of the homeland. As we have seen, Leonid Bliummer was so acutely aware of these problems of adjustment that he wrote a sensitive article in his journal on the stages of the adjustment process experienced by Russian émigrés. Also, we know that in some cases the adjustment became intolerable or was deemed not worth the sacrifice; Vasilii Kel'siev's decision to return to Russia and to renounce the revolutionary cause abroad was to a large extent a result of his inability to cope with these enormous problems over an extended period of time which appeared to have no boundaries. In addition, instances of periodic or complete breakdown occurred: our discussion of Zhukovskii's disintegration into alcoholic dysfunctionalism and Alexander Serno-Solov'evich's suicide can be interpreted in this context. Sazonov's spending sprees and his accumulation of enormous gambling debts are indications of insecurity and unresolved conflicts concerning his changed life as an émigré.

Nevertheless, for most of the Russian émigrés we have discussed, anxiety was overcome through activity and commitment. For them the external enemy was a greater threat than the enemy within. They managed to transcend the despair and guilt of leaving behind their country and its battlefield, no longer "envying the sufferings" of their victimized comrades at the mercy of tsarist jailers in the Peter and Paul Fortress or in Siberian exile labor camps.[31] Europe became the new staging area for the continuation of the struggle against the autocracy, which legitimized their very existence. They gradually established a separate community abroad for this purpose, and it assumed its own historical evolution. In the framework of this unusual society-in-exile, they made constructive use of their own crises, faced as they were with the dilemma of functioning in a situation of extreme alienation. On the one hand, while they refused to assimilate into either bourgeois European society or the radical European social movement, they were dependent on European liberties and tolerance to carry on their work; on the other hand, while they could not return to Russia without risking arrest, they were dependent on forces of protest and on a favorable response to their ideas in Russia in order to sustain their work. Disconnected from the realities of both Russia and Europe in this way, they fashioned new political orientations and new concepts of ideology concerning the role of the intelligentsia, the nature of workers' movements, and the strategy of revolution.

Among the most important questions concerning these new political currents is the degree to which they were reflections of Russian or European political conceptualizations. The émigrés themselves, at least those of the first two generations, reveal a variety of interests in this regard. All of them, in one way or another, believed there was something vital about the West, something of significance in Europe, that would be useful for a transformed Russia. In some instances, the search for European tools and methods to solve Russian political problems was quite explicit. For Sazonov and Utin, the answer seemed to lie in the theories being developed by Karl Marx; as a result, they proclaimed themselves his disciples at opposite ends of Marx's long career. For Dolgorukov, Golovin, and Turgenev, the solution resided in determining how to apply appropriately the variations of European constitutional monarchy to the Russian empire.[32] Bliummer was an outspoken follower of the ideas of John Stuart Mill, and Sokolov considered himself a Proudhonist. Serno-Solov'evich was an exception in that he saw the most promising strategy to bring about the downfall of the autocracy not in any theory, but in the day-to-day struggle of the Swiss labor movement. However, the attraction of theory continued to dominate most of his émigré comrades.

Yet, not all of the émigrés looked so completely to Europe to find an alternative to Russia's political system. Zhukovskii, Zaitsev, and, for a time, Mechnikov, all turned to Bakunin, whom they believed embodied a Russian understanding of their country's problems. Vasilii Kel'siev thought he had located the future of Russia in the dissenting religious sects of Old Believers. Serno-Solov'evich, in spite of his attraction to the workers' movement in Switzerland, was an ardent disciple of Chernyshevskii, and was highly suspicious of European socialist theory as a means of resolving political problems in Russia. In addition, émigrés like Nozhin, Bakst, and Mechnikov, though they were very Russian in their political orientations, remained independent critics who never really reached the stage of deciding on the side of any theory or theorist.

The backgrounds of the émigrés were also rather varied, the general shift from an aristocratic, wealthy first generation to a somewhat less privileged second generation notwithstanding. Still, these differences were of little concern when compared to the overriding sense of outrage and envy which united the younger émigrés in their criticism of Herzen's elegant life-style and his financial security. Similarly, once abroad, the distinctions in educational background dissolved into insignificance. The fact that Dolgorukov, Sazonov, and Utin had won prestigious prizes at school and had been highly regarded for their intelligence before leaving Russia did not influence their choice of comrades, organizations, or ideas once abroad; neither was it powerful enough to affect their widely contrasting politics.[33]

The émigrés, it should be recalled, were only one of a number of groups of Russians abroad. There were also increasing numbers of university students and research scholars, vacationers, businessmen, and literary critics (like Annenkov) visiting for personal or professional reasons, religious dissenters (of whom Ivan Gagarin and Vladimir Pechorin are the best known), and the aristocrats and diplomats who comprised the Russian salon culture of the capitals of Europe. The last group was by far the largest of the Russian communities abroad. Some of its members assumed the responsibility of acting as a counter-emigration on behalf of the regime at home. In an era before the Okhrana was established in Europe to combat émigré revolutionary activities, several prominent Russian aristocratic salons became active defenders of tsarist politics abroad, extolling the autocracy and agitating against the émigrés. It is not certain how deeply this influence penetrated the public consciousness of European society, but in Paris, at least, there was a measurable impact upon those who wished to prevent the undermining of monarchical values.[34]

The émigrés' battles, however, were directed elsewhere. The struggle to alter the political system in Russia was paramount. Not only was it their "cause" but it was the sole way in which, if they were successful, they could realize their dream of returning home, of ending exile and healing the wounds of years of banishment. This dream drove them forward, kept them alive, and infused their agonized existence with a meaning and a purpose that would otherwise have been impossible to achieve. To accomplish all this, they created what one historian has called, in speaking of a later period, an "intelligentsia in exile."[35] Through the first two generations of its existence, the emigration assumed many of the characteristics associated with the development of the Russian intelligentsia within the borders of the empire. The émigrés began as disconnected individuals and gradually moved toward establishing groups, circles, and organizations galvanized by their intense opposition to tsarism and their passionate commitment to inaugurate a new form of social and political existence for Russia. They came to see themselves as possessing a special consciousness because of their freedom from the restricting pressures of Russian politics at home. Conditions abroad also made it possible for them to become aware of themselves as a kind of collective conscience for their homeland, bearers of new values, with an inspired vision of the future and a realistic knowledge of the evolution of history, in which they felt themselves to be important participants. Above all, they believed they had to take action to bring about the desired changes.

From the perspective of the revolutionary intelligentsia, the foundation for the political and social changes that would later move Russia closer to the abolition of autocracy was built by the emigration. Those who went abroad to do battle were considered indispensable to the upheavals that came later. Looking back across the decades from the vantage point of the ashes of the 1905 revolution, one sympathizer wrote that the pioneers of the Russian emigration were heroes "who knew no compromise, who knew no other happiness on this earth other than service to the lofty ideals of the whole of humanity. They carried out the struggle for freedom with such commitment that the ability of the contemporary intelligentsia to wage its war would be unthinkable without them."[36]

Perhaps it takes a visionary poet to comprehend the necessity, the complexity, and the tragedy involved in the relationship between the émigré and his government. At a time when the world seemed to be collapsing around him in this century, W. H. Auden wrote:

> Exiled Thucydides knew
> All that a speech can say
> About Democracy
> And what dictators do,
> The elderly rubbish they talk
> To an apathetic grave; . . .[37]

And because those who know this in any age cannot be tolerated and must be driven out as exiles, we—society—end up enduring the agony of oppression:

> The enlightenment driven away,
> The habit-forming pain,
> Mismanagement and grief:
> We must suffer them all again.[38]

APPENDIXES

Regulations for the Aid of Political Exiles
from Russia, 13 December 1855 (Geneva)

The following document, which forms part of the Dragomanov collection in the Central State Archives for Literature and Art (Moscow), reflects an effort by some émigrés to establish a society to aid political exiles from Russia. The document was written near the end of 1855. Although the authorship is uncertain, the document is evidence of the earliest known aid society for the Russian émigré communities in Western Europe. Many of the tendencies characteristic of the émigrés at this time, particularly the shift toward a collective organizational structure, are reflected in these statutes. It is interesting to note the realization on the part of these émigrés of the necessity to cooperate openly with the federal authorities abroad (see clause VI).

    I. The purpose of the Society is mutual aid for its members. In extreme cases, the Council may decide to distribute aid from the treasury of the Society to persons who are not members of the Society.

    II. Only political exiles may be members of the Society, e.g., people who, as a consequence of acts directed against the political and social order in Russia, have been subjected to persecution by the [Russian] government.

    III. Persons wishing to become members of the Society submit their names to the Council two weeks before a meeting. The persons recommending candidates morally guarantee the individuals whom they are representing.

Source: Tsentral'nyi Gosudarstvennyi Arkhiv Literatury i Isskustva, *fond* 1065, *opis'* 4, *ed. khran.* 55.

IV. Membership of new and prospective members is decided by secret ballot.

V. The Council's term is to last six months, and is elected by secret ballot.

VI. These statutes must be submitted for confirmation to the State Council of the Geneva Republic.

Police Surveillance at Herzen's House
in London, 1862

The document discussed below highlights one of the most difficult problems confronting the émigrés in their political activities: how to find methods of secrecy in order to avoid infiltration of their operations by the tsarist police agents stationed in Europe for this purpose. This particular police report has been selected because it shows that the tsarist agents were able to gain access to émigré meetings in Herzen's own house:

On 24 June (6 July) 1862, on the eve of the departure of Vetoshnikov from London, a meeting was held at Herzen's home. Attending were: Ogarev, Bakunin, Vetoshnikov, [Vasilii] Kel'siev, Perets, Stasov, Albertini, Kovalevskii, the Suzdal'tsev brothers, Chernetskii, Tkhorchievskii, Count Branitskii, the Plautin brothers, Ogarev's relatives, plus 2 [unidentified] Poles and 3 [unidentified] Russians.

Vetoshnikov spoke a long time with Bakunin in another room. Herzen read to us an article about the fires [in St. Petersburg] and the proclamation "Young Russia."

On 5 July 1862, Pavel Aleksandrovich Vetoshnikov was interrogated upon his return to St. Petersburg. The police report states that he was "quite cooperative" in giving details of the meeting at Herzen's house. He claimed he himself ended up at Herzen's meeting "by chance" through Kel'siev, who took him there "for reasons he claims were not clear to him at the time." Among the materials found in the possession of Vetoshnikov at the time of his apprehension were 57 copies of various issues of *Kolokol* (nos. 118 through 138), an essay by Ogarev in French, an anthology on the *raskolniki* by Kel'siev, a brochure by Nikolai Serno-Solov'evich, and 3 photo-

Source: TsGAOR, *fond* 112, *opis'* 1, *ed. khran.* 50.

portraits of Bakunin. As a result of these pieces of incriminating evidence, Vetoshnikov, Serno-Solov'evich, and Chernyshevskii were placed under arrest, which ended the careers of the latter two significant activists in the opposition movement.

―――――――――――***C***―――――――――――

The League of Peace and Freedom,
1867–1868

In 1867 and 1868, two international congresses were held in Switzerland under the sponsorship of the League of Peace and Freedom. The first meeting took place in Geneva and the second in Bern. It was estimated that 6,000 delegates from many countries of Europe attended these two meetings, although the first was by far the largest. The Russian emigration was represented by Bakunin, Dolgorukov, and Vyrubov; Herzen and Ogarev also were invited but chose not to attend. One of the original organizers was Jules Barni (1818–78), a French political philosopher, teacher, and activist who emigrated to Geneva after the coup d'état of Louis Napoleon.

Initially, a great deal of euphoria surrounded the League's potential to form an organizational base for a wide spectrum of dissenters from all countries on the Continent. In the name of "free democ-

Sources: The article by Dolgorukov in a Geneva newspaper, dated 28 September 1867, is preserved in the Nicolaevskii Collection, no. 191, #20, in the Hoover Institute at Stanford University. The name of the newspaper is not included in the file. The meeting of the League actually took place 9–12 September.

For Herzen's assessment of the League of Peace and Freedom, see his article, "Les Russes au Congres de Berne," *Sobranie sochinenii*, 30 vols. (Moscow: Akademiia nauk, 1954–65), 20:380–82.

On Vyrubov, see his "Revoliutsionnyia vospominaniia," *Vestnik Evropy*, 1913, no. 1:66–75.

For a lively discussion of the League's meetings, see E. H. Carr, *Michael Bakunin* (London: Macmillan, 1937), pp. 327–44.

Another contemporary account of the second League meeting in Bern, which includes unflattering and critical portraits of Bakunin and Utin, can be found in P. D. Boborykin, *Vospominaniia* (Moscow: Khudozh. lit., 1965), 2:15–22.

racy," the League's organizers nobly hoped to rise above parochial nationalistic interests to create a "United States of Europe," free of war and ruled by principles of justice for all peoples. There was a call for unity between moderate and more militant socialists and émigrés under the banner of "the destruction of the Old Regimes and the dawn of the New Society," as Vyrubov stated it. Ten thousand signatures in support of the League's vague goals were collected across Europe; some of the leading intellectuals and political figures of the age (such as Mazzini, Hugo, and Mill) were among the signatories.

The unity that was hoped for proved to be an impossibility. Not only were there conflicts among the various nationalities, but, to treat the one case that is of concern to us, the Russians themselves could not ally with one another at the congresses. Bakunin's impassioned and aggressive oratory in favor of international socialism, nihilism, and federalism proved to be the most divisive aspect from this perspective.

Dolgorukov, who was active in organizing the first congress in Geneva, publicly disaffiliated himself from the congress proceedings because he felt Bakunin was actually "organizing a European revolutionary committee for the propagation of his own ideas . . . which aspire for the dismemberment of his country." According to Dolgorukov, the purpose of the congress had been "to disseminate information to foster economic rapprochement between nations, to establish cooperative societies, to seek to reduce permanent armies and replace them gradually with local militias, and to organize journals to formulate and propagate these goals." The "communism" and "nihilism" of Bakunin's ideas were, Dolgorukov continued, efforts at sabotaging these goals. He accused Bakunin of seeking war on governments, not rapprochement, the destruction of armies, not their transformation into bodies of local defense, and of urging the lower classes to attack private property, which would only "compel capital to emigrate and, as a result, [would] lead to even greater poverty." Furthermore, "by having the congress declare that peace and progress are compatible exclusively with a Republican form of government," Bakunin was not only "violating Swiss neutrality" but setting conditions that automatically condemned most existing governments.

Herzen also was critical of the League, and he too centered his discontent on Bakunin. At the same time, he was perfectly aware that the League "had no means to render its resolutions binding" upon the delegates and had neither the authority nor the power "to diminish armaments, dissolve armies, and halt warfare." As "a European tribune," the League could bring some influence to bear, but only if ways were found to prevent certain theories from becoming dominant over all others. Herzen pointed an accusing finger at "Bakunin, Vyrubov, and the small group of their friends," who style themselves as "men of the new world," trying to be representatives of both "the golden mean and Jacobinism, who in spite of the best of intentions, support the old ediface with one hand while pulling it down with the other."

Finally, Vyrubov himself expressed doubts about the very notions being attributed to him. He was not certain that he could support a platform proclaiming a nihilist Russia as a goal of the League, and objected to being associated with Bakunin as one of the "men of the new world," as Herzen had called them.

The Geneva congress of the League formed a central committee, with Bakunin among its members, and held a second congress, in Bern, in 1868, but it never reconvened after that. Bakunin hoped to merge the League with the International Workingmen's Association, in spite of his growing differences with Marx, but this too was never accomplished. With the passing of the ephemeral League of Peace and Freedom, two things became clear. First, conflicts over political ideology and nationality were too severe to be resolved within the bland and general framework of the League's platform. Second, hopes for creating a unified émigré political program also could not be realized within the context of this moderate forum. New structures had to be created to deal with these forces.

Natalie Herzen's Dream, 1869

The pages of Natalie Herzen's diaries are filled with passages expressing fear, despair, and insecurity over her tenuous existence as a perpetual stranger, wandering without roots, far from home. There is perhaps no better metaphor to express the strain of émigré anxiety than a dream recorded by Herzen's daughter. In her letter to Ogarev describing the dream, she first mentions the great "confusion in my brain at times," her realization of the brevity of life, and the consequent need to "make use of every minute, *do* something for others . . . but there is always something that prevents me." Then she tries to understand why she is unable to do what she feels she ought to do. "It's so hard for me, everything is incoherent, much is muddled and I want to put it all in order. I'm searching for a conclusion. It's a kind of madness." Following this, she begins to make sense of a fantastic image that possessed her in her dream:

Imagine that I had lost myself; I was seeking myself in all the ages, throughout all the centuries, in all the elements; in short, I was everything in the world, starting from gases and ether, I was fire, water, light, granite, chaos, all kinds of religions. . . . I know little about historical facts but all the same I saw a great deal, and dreadfully vividly. It was extremely interesting, and I do not regret being ill. There were times when I suffered greatly, first for the others; they tortured all of them, and then set upon myself; and the countless times they killed me! And guillotined me, and hanged me, and shot me, carved me to pieces and poisoned me. I felt it all; that is what it means to have an imagination, a sick one. . . . I took myself to be the personification of all phenomena—electricity, phosphorescence, au-

Source: Natalie Herzen to Nikolai Ogarev, 7 December 1869, in Michael Confino, ed., *Daughter of a Revolutionary: Natalie Herzen and the Bakunin-Nechaev Circle* (La Salle, Ill.: Library Press, 1973), pp. 146–47.

topsy, harmony, stupidity, everything good and evil, and it all came
out as a *pot-pourri*—and I was a coward of the first order. *Je suis
l'univers personnifié*, such was my conclusion. And indeed, every man
is a little world unto himself and understands the world after his own
fashion. Sometimes I kept hearing: "*Nichts ist drinnen nichts ist
draussen, dann was innen das ist aussen!*" And everything grew dark,
I thought that the end of the world had come, everything vanished,
the globe and the solar system and all history with it. And far, far in
the distance there was a tiny star, a new world was beginning. I
wanted to rescue everyone and take them there with me. But it's
impossible to tell the whole story, and then, I do not wish to think
about it any more.

Although many of Natalie Herzen's own conflicts are expressed
here, these difficulties have a greater meaning because they also
contain echoes of the conflicts facing many émigrés of her generation. There is the overwhelming feeling of living in an alien world,
and of being lost in its utter vastness and infinitude. To cope with
this fear, she imagines that she and the vastness are one, that she
embodies the very elements of existence from the beginning of time.
By doing this, she is attempting to eclipse time and space in order to
counteract the unacceptable concrete reality of being geographically away from Russia for an undetermined period. The other
important aspect of the dream is her conflict over saving and rescuing others. Those she feels obligated to save were subjected to oppression, a symbolic representation of the Russian people suffering
under the yoke of the tsarist autocracy. However, she not only fails to
save the oppressed others but becomes herself the victim of a violent assault until she is killed. Her death is imagined repeatedly and
terrifyingly. This must refer to the enormous guilt she and so many
émigrés felt about their position of relative freedom abroad while
their comrades continued to suffer at home. Though few émigrés
openly admitted this, we know from Sazonov, Serno-Solov'evich,
and especially Bliummer how pervasive this feeling was. Also by
imagining herself to be "the personification of all phenomena," especially elements of power like electricity, Natalie Herzen is seeking a source of strength to accomplish her task. But she cannot
succeed. Finally, in her dream, she witnesses the end of the world
and of history, signifying the futility of the émigré cause and its
inevitable doom. Yet there is a renewal at the end, and a recurrence
of her need to serve others, to rescue them and transport them to the
new world of the future illuminated by the star she describes—the

postrevolutionary order, the society of justice in Russia which the émigrés had committed their lives to realizing and for which they had abandoned their homeland. Only this would bring an end to the exile and release the émigrés from their stressful and troubled life abroad.

Notes

1. The World of Emigration in Nineteenth-Century Europe

1. J. H. Rosny, "Nihilists in Paris," *Harper's New Monthly Magazine,* August 1891, p. 430.
2. See, e.g., the two-part article by A. W. Benni, "Russian Society," *Fortnightly Review* 6 (1866) : 549–66, 728–44, and the response by P. D. Boborykin, "Nihilism in Russia," ibid. 10 (1868) : 117–38.
3. George Haupt, "Rôle de l'exil dans la diffusion de l'image de l'intelligentsia revolutionnaire," *Cahiers du monde russe et soviétique* 19, no. 3 (1978) : 237.
4. See the detailed account of the response of the British authorities to the émigrés by Bernard Porter, "The British Government and Political Refugees, c. 1880–1914," in *From the Other Shore: Russian Political Emigrants in Britain, 1880–1917,* ed. John Slatter (London: Frank Cass, 1984), pp. 23–45.
5. [O. V. Aptekman], "Iz istorii osvoboditel'nogo dvizheniia v Rossi. Pavel Borisovich Aksel'rod. Ego zhizn', literaturnaia i prakticheskaia deiatel'nost'" (typed MS), Russian Archive, Columbia University, p. 154. Aptekman's point was that because of the restrictions placed on political activity in Russia by the tsarist regime, Europe became "by necessity" the only milieu where such political education could take place. The same argument has been advanced more recently by Alexander Solzhenitsyn to prove the opposite conclusion. Whereas Aptekman was trying to show the importance and relevance for Russia of these developments abroad, Solzhenitsyn now argues that the Russian revolution was prepared abroad by Lenin and his supporters according to a European ideology and in complete disregard for Russia's own history. See, *inter alia,* Solzhenitsyn's interview with C. L. Sulzberger, *New York Times,* 7 March 1976.
6. Although there is no monographic study in any language devoted to the prerevolutionary emigration as a whole, some works have appeared which, though falling outside the chronological boundaries

of this book, deserve mention. These include: A. Ia. Kiperman, "Glavnye tsentry russkoi revoliutsionnoi emigratsii 70-kh–80-kh godov XIX v.," *Istoricheskie zapiski*, no. 88 (1971): 257–95; James Hulse, *Revolutionists in London* (New York and London: Oxford University Press, 1970), has chapters on Stepniak and Kropotkin; L. Mysyrowocz, "Agents secrets tsaristes et révolutionnaires russes à Geneve, 1879–1903," *Revue suisse d'histoire*, no. 1 (1973): 29–72; A. E. Senn, *The Russian Revolution in Switzerland* (Madison: University of Wisconsin Press, 1971); Ye. Ia. Zazerskii and A. V. Liubarskii, *Lenin: Emigratsiia i Rossiia* (Moscow: Izdatel'stvo politicheskoi literatury, 1975); Robert Williams, *Culture in Exile: Russian Emigres in Germany, 1881–1941* (Ithaca, N.Y.: Cornell University Press, 1972). P. Kovalevskii, *Zarubezhnaia Rossiia* (Paris: Librarie des cinq continents, 1971), deals with the Soviet period, as does George Fischer, ed., *Russian Emigre Politics* (New York: East European Fund, 1951). Works relevant to the period under study here, including biographies of individual émigrés and unpublished dissertations on émigré themes, will be cited below in both the notes and the bibliography.

7. John Hope Simpson, *The Refugee Problem* (London: Oxford University Press, 1939); Donald R. Taft and Richard Robbins, *International Migrations* (New York: Ronald Press, 1955); E. P. Pletnev, *Mezhdunarodnaia migratsiia rabochei sily* (Moscow: Izdatel'stvo instituta mezhdunarodnykh otnoshenii, 1962). For a good recent study, see William H. McNeill and Ruth S. Adams, eds., *Human Migration* (Bloomington: Indiana University Press, 1978).

8. Mary McCarthy, "A Guide to Exiles, Expatriates, and Internal Emigres," *New York Review,* 9 March 1972, p. 8.

9. See the discussion in Margery Weiner, *The French Exiles* (London: Murray, 1960), particularly pp. 8–28. See also Donald Greer, *The Incidence of the Emigration during the French Revolution* (Cambridge: Harvard University Press, 1951).

10. See James Billington's recent study, *Fire in the Minds of Men* (New York: Basic Books, 1980).

11. Paul A. Ladame, *Le Role des migrations dans le monde libre* (Geneva: Droz, 1958); N. A. Citroen, *Les Migrations internationales* (Paris: Libraire de Medicis, 1948); Rene Gonnard, *Essai sur l'histoire de l'emigration* (Paris: Valois, 1927); Jules Duval, *Histoire de l'emigration* (Paris: Guillaumin, 1862); Andzhei Marianskii, *Sovremennye migratsii naseleniia* (Moscow: Statistika, 1969); V. V. Obolenskii, *Mezhdunarodnye i mezhdukontinental'nye migratsii v dovoennoi Rossii i SSSR* (Moscow, 1928).

12. The pioneering and still valuable study of the sociology of migration, particularly from the perspective of theory, is S. M. Eisenstadt, *The Absorption of Immigrants* (London: Routledge and Kegan Paul,

1954). There is a stimulating theoretical discussion relevant to the psychology of emigration in Erik Erikson, "Identity and Uprootedness in Our Time," *Insight and Responsibility* (New York: Norton, 1964), pp. 81–107. See also Paul Tabori, *The Anatomy of Exile* (London: Harrap, 1972), pp. 16–17, 29–37. On the phenomenon of immigrant mourning, see G. S. de Dellarossa, "The Immigrant of Professional Descent," *International Journal of Psychoanalysis* 57, pt. 1 (1978): 37–44. In recent years, psychiatric researchers and epidemiologists have become interested in the psychopathology of migrating groups. For examples of these studies, see H. B. M. Murphy, "Migration and the Major Mental Disorders," in *Mobility and Mental Health*, ed. M. Kantor (Springfield, Ill.: Charles C. Thomas, 1965), pp. 5–29; Victor D. Sanua, "Immigration, Migration and Mental Illness: A Review of the Literature," in *Behavior in New Environments*, ed. Eugene Brody (Beverly Hills, Calif.: Sage, 1969), pp. 291–352; Charles Zwingmann and Maria Pfister-Ammende, eds., *Uprooting and After* (Berlin: Springer-Verlag, 1973).

13. On this theme, see the discussion in Hans Speier, "The Social Conditions of the Intellectual Exile," *Social Order and the Risk of War* (New York: 1952), pp. 86–94.

14. Tabori, p. 43.

15. For a general treatment, see ibid., pp. 49–50. See also Franz Neumann, "Intelligentsia in Exile," in *Critical Sociology*, ed. Paul Connerton (Middlesex: Penguin Books, 1976), pp. 423–25.

16. Robert C. Williams, "European Political Emigrations: A Lost Subject," *Comparative Studies in Society and History* 12 (1970): 145.

17. See Margaret Wicks, *The Italian Exiles in London, 1816–1848* (Manchester: Manchester University Press, 1937), and, among the source materials, E. F. Richards, ed., *Mazzini's Letters to an English Family*, 3 vols. (London: John Lane Co., 1920), and the letters of Carlyle's wife on Mazzini in Lawrence and Elizabeth Hanson, *Necessary Evil: The Life of Jane Carlyle* (London: Constable, 1952), pp. 247–55.

18. For a recent discussion of Mazzini's importance in this context, see Billington, pp. 149–51, 165. Billington also discusses some of Mazzini's predecessors among the Italian exiles, such as Carlo Bianco and the followers of Buonarroti in Belgium during the early 1830s (ibid., pp. 168–69).

19. Ibid., p. 184. The League of Outlaws, which claimed a membership of about one hundred people, could also be translated as "the Exiles' League" (*Bund for Geächteten*). See also A. Muller Lehning, "The International Association, 1855–59," *International Review for Social History* 3 (1938): 194. This comprehensive article contains a wealth

of information on the socialist movements of this period, and includes much data on the various emigrations as well.

20. Also in Paris during the 1840s were Moses Hess, Heinrich Heine, Arnold Ruge, and many more German émigrés who were establishing their reputations as exiles from their homeland. On the German emigration in general, see Billington, pp. 261–79, and Lehning, pp. 192–200, both of which contain numerous references to the relevant literature on this subject.

21. See Peter Brock, "The Socialists of the Polish 'Great Emigration,'" in *Essays in Labour History,* ed. Asa Briggs and John Saville (London: Macmillan, 1967), p. 141. To gain a sense of this figure, the following comparison may be instructive: "Of the 4,380 political refugees who found themselves in England in 1853, according to the statistical data of the English government, 2,500 were Polish, 260 German and 1,000 French." Lehning, p. 201.

22. Brock, "The Socialists of the Polish 'Great Emigration,'" p. 169; see also the same author's "The Polish Revolutionary Commune in London," *Slavonic and East European Review* 35 (1956): 116–28.

23. Quoted in Franco Venturi, *Studies in Free Russia* (Chicago: University of Chicago Press, 1982), p. 173.

24. H. Payne and H. Grosshans, "The Exiled Revolutionaries and the French Political Police in the 1850s," *American Historical Review* 68 (July 1963): 954.

25. For a good study of this response in France, see ibid., pp. 955–73. For the situation in England at this time, see Alvin R. Calman, *Ledru-Rollin apres 1848 et les proscrits Français en Angleterre* (Paris: Rieder, 1921).

26. Herzen's statements are quoted in Venturi, *Studies in Free Russia,* pp. 142–43.

27. On this controversy, see Lehning, pp. 208–9, and on the activities of the Commune revolutionnaire in general, see ibid., pp. 201–12.

28. Ibid., pp. 214–15; A. I. Herzen, *My Past and Thoughts,* trans. Constance Garnett, 4 vols. (New York: Knopf, 1968), 3:1169ff.

29. For the most damning attack on Mazzini by the International Association, see Lehning, pp. 232–33.

30. G. V. Plekhanov, "Gertsen-emigrant," *Sochineniia,* vol. 23 (Moscow-Leningrad: Gosizdat., 1926), p. 414.

31. M. Gershenzon, "Gertsen i zapad," *Obrazy proshlogo* (Moscow: Levenson, 1912), p. 176.

32. For Herzen's life during these years, see Martin Malia, *Alexander Herzen and the Birth of Russian Socialism* (Cambridge: Harvard University Press, 1961); Franco Venturi, *Roots of Revolution* (New York: Knopf, 1960), pp. 1–35; Isaiah Berlin, "Alexander Herzen," *Russian Thinkers* (New York: Viking Press, 1978), pp. 186–209.

33. See the recent analysis of these writings in Edward Acton, *Alex-*

ander Herzen and the Role of the Intellectual Revolutionary
(Cambridge: Cambridge University Press, 1979), pp. 40–82, and
also the discussion in Franco Venturi, "Russians, French, and
Italians in Nice, Genoa, and Turin after the Revolution of 1848,"
Studies in Free Russia, pp. 140–86.

34. One of the earliest and still eminently readable discussions of
Herzen's relationships with Western exiles is Gershenzon's essay,
"Gertsen i zapad," pp. 175–280. For a good treatment of the émigré
circles around Herzen in Nice, see Venturi, *Studies in Free Russia*,
pp. 148–76.

35. Gershenzon, pp. 180–81.

36. The quoted phrases are from ibid., p. 184.

37. Herzen, *My Past and Thoughts*, 2:684.

38. Ibid., p. 686.

39. As in the case of Karl Peter Heinzen; see ibid., pp. 688–93.

40. As with Saffi; see ibid., pp. 706–8.

41. Ibid., p. 733.

42. On this incident, see Venturi, *Studies in Free Russia*, pp. 158–61.

43. Herzen, *My Past and Thoughts*, 2:741–42. The kind of émigré
Herzen had in mind in this analysis was Arnold Ruge, who was
politically destroyed by the 1848 defeat. Herzen poignantly describes how the progressive Paris editor of the 1840s tried to regain
his place in London a decade later by giving a series of lectures on
contemporary German philosophical movements and their political
implications. Ruge stood before an empty hall, a lonely, embittered,
and forgotten man, delivering his prepared talks to only Herzen and
Worcell, who comprised the audience. Afterwards, he reacted in
anger and irrationally. Seeing nations instead of people before him,
he said: "Poland and Russia have come, but Italy is not here; I
shan't forgive Mazzini or Saffi for this when there's a new people's
rising" (ibid., 3:1157).

44. On this, see E. H. Carr, *The Romantic Exiles* (Boston: Beacon
Press, 1961), pp. 47–121, and also Acton, pp. 83–104.

45. Ibid., p. 1046.

46. Ibid., pp. 1023–24.

47. Ibid., p. 1044.

48. Ibid., p. 1140.

49. William James Linton, *Memoirs* (London: Lawrence and Bullen,
1895), p. 146. On Herzen's English relations, see Monica Partridge,
"Alexander Herzen and the English Press," *Slavonic and East
European Review* 36, no. 8 (1958): 453–70, and idem, "Aleksandr
Gertsen i ego angliiskie sviazi," in *Problemy izucheniia Gertsena*,
ed. B. P. Volgin (Moscow: Akademiia nauk, 1963), pp. 348–69. In
the latter article, Partridge argues with a wealth of evidence that
Herzen was not nearly as isolated from British society as he

suggests in his memoir. When he wrote his memoir, he did not mention individuals in politics whom he knew, such as Charles Bradlough and Joseph Cowan, for reasons that still remain unclear. Partridge suggests that he feared compromising their reputations by writing of them in his memoir, but there may have been other reasons. Isaiah Berlin argues that in spite of Herzen's wide contacts within British society—which included dining with Robert Owen, Charles Darwin, and the Carlyles, among others—he never had truly close friends in London. England provided Herzen with the liberty to operate as a successful émigré writer and thinker, but he never felt at home there in the way he did in Nice, for example, where he clearly developed warmer relationships. See Isaiah Berlin, "Herzen and His Memoirs," *Against the Current* (New York: Viking Press, 1980), pp. 199–200.

50. V. I. Kel'siev, "Ispoved," *Literaturnoe nasledstvo* 41–42 (1941): 273–74, quoted in Abbot Gleason, *Young Russia: The Genesis of Russian Radicalism in the 1860s* (New York: Viking Press, 1980), pp. 96–97.

51. A. I. Herzen, *Sobranie sochinenii,* 30 vols. (Moscow: Akademiia nauk, 1954–65), 12:64.

52. Boborykin, "Nihilism in Russia," p. 126. All of the major studies of Herzen have discussed his vast influence. For a recent analysis of one of the lesser-known areas of Herzen's impact in Russia, see T. S. Vlasenko, "O revoliutsionnoi deiatel'nosti 'Biblioteki Kazanskikh studentov'," in *Epokha Chernyshevskogo,* ed. M. V. Nechkina (Moscow: Nauka, 1978), pp. 89–90.

53. P. V. Annenkov, *Extraordinary Decade* (Ann Arbor: University of Michigan Press, 1968), p. 166; idem, *Literaturnye vospominaniia* (Moscow: Gosizdat, 1960), p. 300.

54. Annenkov, *Extraordinary Decade,* pp. 166–67.

55. Ibid., p. 165.

56. Ibid.

57. Ibid., p. 166.

58. Ibid., p. 173.

59. Ibid., p. 185.

60. Ibid., p. 176.

61. Ibid., p. 194.

62. Herzen, *My Past and Thoughts,* 2:850.

63. Annenkov, *Extraordinary Decade,* p. 178.

64. Ibid., p. 183.

65. Herzen, *My Past and Thoughts,* 2:959. On Sazonov, see ibid., pp. 951–68.

66. On Golovin, see ibid., 3:1397–1418.

67. Ibid., p. 1397.

68. Ibid., p. 1398.

69. Ibid.

70. Ibid., p. 1399.
71. Ibid., p. 1400.
72. Ibid., p. 1406. An example of Herzen's point here can be seen in a letter from Engels to Wiedemeyer dated 12 April 1853. Discussing Herzen's book *Du développement des idées révolutionnaires en Russie* (Paris, 1851), Engels mentions the "democratic social communist Russian republic under the leadership of the triumverate Bakunin, Herzen and Golovin"; quoted in Herzen, *Sobranie sochinenii*, 7:119.
73. Annenkov, *Extraordinary Decade*, p. 167.
74. Ibid., p. 169.
75. This section of Herzen's book *Du développement des idées révolutionnaires en Russie* was omitted from the editions of 1853 through 1858. Some reprintings of the book do not carry this section at all. It appears in the Soviet edition of Herzen's works in a note under "Variations," not in the text. See Herzen, *Sobranie sochinenii*, 7:404–6 (in the Russian translation), 401–4 (in the original French edition).

2. N. I. Turgenev: The First Political Emigré

1. V. Semevskii, "Nikolai Ivanovich Turgenev," *Entsiklopedicheskii slovar'* (St. Petersburg: Brockhaus-Efron, 1890–1904), 67:106–13. See also the obituary essay, I. S. Turgenev, "Nikolai Ivanovich Turgenev," *Polnoe sobranie sochinenii*, vol. 14 (Moscow: Nauka, 1967), pp. 214–23, 518–25.
2. E. I. Tarasov, *Dekabrist Nikolai Ivanovich Turgenev v Aleksandrovskuiu epokhu* (Samara: Izvestiia Samarskogo gosudarstvennogo universiteta, 1923).
3. A. N. Shebunin, *Nikolai Ivanovich Turgenev* (Moscow: Gosizdat, 1925).
4. P. Miliukov, "N. I. Turgenev v Londone," *Vremennik obshchestva druzei russkoi knig* (Paris, 1932), 3:61–78; Iu. G. Oksman, "Pis'ma N. I. Turgeneva k Gertsenu," *Literaturnoe nasledstvo* 62 (1955): 583–90; O. V. Orlik, *Peredovaia Rossiia i revoliutsionnaia frantsiia* (Moscow: Nauka, 1973); idem, *Rossiia i frantsuzskaia revoliutsiia 1830 goda* (Moscow: Mysl', 1968); Shebunin, *N. I. Turgenev*; *Istoriia russkoi ekonomicheskoi mysli* (Moscow: Akademiia nauk, 1955), vol. 1, pt. 2, pp. 165–92. The only article in English on Turgenev is B. Hollingsworth, "N. I. Turgenev and *Kolokol*," *Slavonic and East European Review* 41, no. 96 (1962): 89–100.
5. The following dissertation and articles are all by V. M. Tarasova: "Dekabrist N. I. Turgenev i ego mesto v istorii obshchestvennogo dvizheniia Rossii 20-60-kh godov XIX v." (Kandidat. diss., University of Leningrad, 1966); "Dekabrist N. I. Turgenev: Sotrudnik *Kolokola*," in *Problemy izucheniia Gertsena*, ed. Iu. G. Oksman et

al. (Moscow: Akademiia nauk, 1963), pp. 239–50; "Iz istorii izdaniia knigi N. I. Turgeneva *Rossiia i Russkie,*" in *Problemy istorii obshchestvennogo dvizheniia i istoriografii,* ed. N. M. Druzhinin et al. (Moscow: Nauka, 1971), pp. 93–101; "Iz istorii polemiki vokrug knigi N. I. Turgeneva *Rossiia i Russkie,*" in *Pushkin i ego vremia,* ed. M. M. Kalaushin, vol. 2 (Leningrad: Izdatel'stvo gosudarstven-nogo Ermitazh, 1966); "K voprosu ob obshchestvenno-politicheskikh svaziakh N. I. Turgeneva v gody revoliutsionnoi situatsii," in *Revoliutsionnaia situatsiia 1859–61 gg.,* ed. M. V. Nechkina (Moscow: Nauka, 1963), pp. 278–94; "N. I. Turgenev v 1861 g.," ibid., pp. 426–44; "N. I. Turgenev v zapadnoi Evrope v 30–50-kh godakh XIX veka i ego obshchestvenno-politicheskie sviazi," *Uchenye zapiski Mariiskogo gos. ped. instituta im N. K. Krupskoi, Kafedra istorii* (Ioshkar-Ola) 28 (1966): 45–136; "O vremeni znakomstva [Ivan] Turgeneva s N. I. Turgenevym," in *Turgenevskii sbornik,* ed. M. P. Alekseev (Moscow-Leningrad: Nauka, 1964), 1:276–78; "Rol' N. I. Turgeneva v obshchestvennom dvizhenii Rossii 20–70-kh godov XIX v.," in *Istoriia i istoriki,* ed. M. V. Nechkina (Moscow: Nauka, 1973), pp. 107–25; "*Rossiia i Russkie:* N. I. Turgenev o Rossii 30–50-kh godov XIX v.," *Uchenye zapiski Mariiskogo gos. ped. instituta, Kafedra istorii* (Ioshkar-Ola) 27 (1965).

6. N. I. Turgenev, *Opyt teorii nalogov* (St. Petersburg, 1818).
7. N. I. Turgenev, *La Russie et les Russes,* 3 vols. (Paris, 1847). A Russian edition was published in 1915 in Moscow as *Rossiia i Russkie.*
8. Tarasova, "N. I. Turgenev v 1861," p. 428.
9. Many of Turgenev's letters, particularly those written prior to his emigration, have been published in *Arkhiv brat'ev Turgenevykh,* ed. E. I. Tarasov, vols. 1–2 (St. Petersburg: Tipografiia Imperatorskoi Akademiia nauk, 1911–13) and vol. 3 (Petrograd: Gosudarstvennaia tipografiia, 1921). V. M. Tarasova, in her articles on Turgenev's émigré years, was the first to make extensive use of the huge unpublished Turgenev correspondence for the years after 1824.
10. G. A. Kuklin, *Materialy k izucheniiu istorii revoliutsionnogo dvizheniia v Rossii* (Geneva: Kuklin, 1905), p. 348. This work is the earliest to indicate Turgenev's significance as the first Russian émigré and also to devote serious attention to the Russian emigration as an integral part of the revolutionary movement. Chapter 5 is entitled "The Political Emigration under Nicholas I." Miliukov mentions Turgenev in a similar manner in "N. I. Turgenev v Londone," as does Tarasova in her articles.
11. At the beginning of this century, Semevskii called Turgenev's *La Russie* "the only study during the Nicholas era in which Russian political liberalism received sufficiently full expression" ("Nikolai

Ivanovich Turgenev," p. 110). More recently, a French scholar has classified Turgenev as the "doyen" of the "liberal emigration" in France in the period before the Crimean War. See M. Cadot, *La Russie dans la vie intellectuelle française* (Paris: Feyard, 1967), pp. 24–25.

12. Turgenev lived abroad "extremely secluded and maintained relations with practically no one" (Shebunin, p. 105). According to another view, Turgenev lived abroad as a "solitary and embittered emigre . . . having broken off totally and completely with the Decembrists, and utterly alienated from Russia" (I. G. Bliumin, Introduction to N. I. Turgenev, *Opyt teorii nalogov*, 3rd ed. [Moscow: Gosizdat, 1937], p. xvi).

13. Miliukov, "N. I. Turgenev v Londone," pp. 76–78; Tarasov, *Dekabrist Nikolai Ivanovich Turgenev*, pp. 395–96.

14. See especially Tarasova's articles and Oksman's article ("Pis'ma") on the relationship between Herzen and Turgenev. Tarasova, who pays more attention to Turgenev's articles than to his book *La Russie*, points to Turgenev's criticism of the English political system and concentrates on his militant concern for the liberation of the Russian peasantry not as an isolated period of his activity but rather as the defining feature of his career.

15. R. C. Howes and L. D. Orton, eds., *The Confession of Mikhail Bakunin* (Ithaca, N.Y.: Cornell University Press, 1977), p. 46.

16. Ibid., p. 61. Bakunin is, or course, referring here to the 1848 revolution.

17. The letter, dated 20 July 1862, can be found in I. Fetisov, "Iz perepiski N. I. Turgeneva v 40–60-ye gg.," *Pamiati dekabristov* (Leningrad: Akademiia nauk, 1926), 3:102–3.

18. Herzen, *Sobranie sochinenii*, 14:328–29; the article originally appeared in *Kolokol*, 15 October 1860.

19. I. S. Turgenev, "Nikolai Ivanovich Turgenev," p. 220.

20. Ibid., pp. 222–23.

21. For the published letters, see *Arkhiv brat'ev Turgenevykh;* the archival location of the unpublished letters can be found in Tarasova's articles.

22. See N. I. Turgenev, *La Russie*, 1:26–55, 295–301; and M. L. Vishnitser, "Baron Shtein i N. I. Turgenev," *Minuvshie gody*, July 1908, pp. 232–72, and October 1908, pp. 234–78.

23. The book quickly sold out and a second printing was ordered in May 1819. In 1826, as a consequence of the government's decision to prosecute Turgenev for his Decembrist involvement, all remaining copies of his book were confiscated and publication of further editions was forbidden. As a result, the book has become a bibliographic rarity. Since the revolution, it has been republished only once, in 1937, and has never been translated.

24. Semevskii, p. 107.
25. Ibid.
26. On Turgenev's activities in the Decembrist movement, see M. V. Nechkina, *Dvizhenie dekabristov*, 2 vols. (Moscow: Akademiia nauk, 1955).
27. Semevskii, p. 109.
28. See Kuklin, p. 351.
29. One of his children, Petr Nikolaevich, became a well-known sculptor who, upon his death in 1913, bequeathed the enormous archive of his father to the Russian Academy of Sciences.
30. See Tarasova, "K voprosu," pp. 284–87. Tarasova sees these visits to Russia as crucial in revising earlier views on Turgenev as moderate politically and isolated from Russian reality. Her argument is that Turgenev turned toward a "moderate liberal position" only after 1864, i.e., after he ceased his active contacts with Russia (ibid., p. 294).
31. Miliukov, p. 78.
32. Tarasova, "N. I. Turgenev v zapadnoi Evrope," p. 50.
33. Ibid., p. 51.
34. Ibid., p. 53.
35. Ibid., pp. 48–49.
36. Ibid., pp. 57–58.
37. Ibid., pp. 59–60.
38. Ibid., p. 69.
39. Ibid., p. 70. Nikolai Turgenev was concerned about his brother Alexander, who had left London for Paris at this time, where he remained for several months before returning to Russia in September.
40. Ibid., pp. 70, 71.
41. Orlik, 1968, p. 86. A number of other Russians in Paris participated in the July Revolution, including S. D. Poltaratskii, M. M. Kiriakov, and M. A. Kologrivov, all of whom are discussed by Orlik.
42. Ibid., p. 88.
43. Kuklin, p. 352; Orlik, 1973, pp. 216–17; Tarasova, "N. I. Turgenev v zapadnoi Evrope," pp. 126–30.
44. Oksman, p. 583.
45. N. I. Turgenev, *La Russie*, 3:214, 231, 234, 237–38.
46. "Viola en realite les seules victims qui sernot offertes en holocauste a la reforme!" (ibid., p. 242).
47. Ibid., p. 245.
48. Ibid., p. 248.
49. Ibid., p. 24.
50. Semevskii, p. 111.
51. The letter, written in 1843, is quoted by Semevskii (ibid.).

52. The article, "Pora!," appeared in *Russkii zagranichnyi sbornik,* 1858, pt. 2, bk. 1; quoted in Kuklin, p. 353.

53. For a detailed discussion of Turgenev's emancipation proposals, see his "Vopros osvobozhdeniia i vopros upravleniia krest'ian," in *Russkii zagranichnyi sbornik,* 1859, pt. 3, bk. 1, pp. 1–110.

54. For these criticisms and for material on Turgenev's own emancipation experiments on his family estates, which he arranged during his trips to Russia in the late 1850s, see N. I. Turgenev, "Economic Results of the Emancipation of Serfs in Russia," *Journal of Social Science,* no. 1 (1869): 147–49; and Tarasova, "N. I. Turgenev v 1861," pp. 432–34.

55. The exact number remains a matter of some dispute. See Hollingsworth, "N. I. Turgenev"; and Tarasova, "Dekabrist N. I. Turgenev."

56. Herzen, *Sobranie sochinenii,* 11:58–59 and 27:143. For additional information on Herzen's relationship with Turgenev, see Tarasova, "N. I. Turgenev v zapadnoi Evrope," pp. 110–11.

57. Letter dated 20 March 1861; see Oksman, p. 587.

58. Oksman, p. 586. This letter was also published in Fetisov's article in *Pamiati dekabristov,* 3:99–100.

59. See Fetisov's article in *Pamiati dekabristov,* 3:95. The letter is dated 1856, at the time of Alexander II's coronation.

60. Ibid., 3:91, n. 1. See also P. Shchegolev, "Pomilovanie N. I. Turgeneva," *Byloe,* 1907, no. 9:33–36.

61. *Pamiati dekabristov,* 3:101.

62. See Tarasova, "N. I. Turgenev v zapadnoi Evrope," pp. 85–111.

63. Letter dated 16 April 1860, TsGALI, *fond* 501, *opis'* 1, *ed. khran.* 301, *list* 1. Many similar letters expressing support can be found in the Turgenev collection, *fond* 501, in this archive. See also Tarasova, "K voprosu," pp. 278–94.

64. Tarasova, "N. I. Turgenev v 1861," pp. 428–32.

65. See, e.g., Tarasova, "N. I. Turgenev v zapadnoi Evrope," p. 97.

66. TsGALI, *fond* 101, *opis'* 1, *ed. khran.* 287, *listy* 1–2.

3. I. G. Golovin: Emigré Individualism

1. M. K. Lemke, "Emigrant Ivan Golovin," *Byloe,* no. 5 (1907): 24–52, and no. 6 (1907): 261–85 (referred to throughout this chapter as Lemke, pts. 1 and 2).

2. Cadot, pp. 27–31; W. Sliwowska, *W kręgu poprzedników Hercena* (Warsaw: Instytut Historii Polskiej Akademii nauk, 1971), pp. 144–201; idem, "Un émigré russe en France: Ivan Golovine, 1816–1890," *Cahiers du monde russe et soviétique* 11, no. 2 (1970): 221–43.

3. I. G. Golovin, *Zapiski Ivana Golovina* (Leipzig: Gerhardt, 1859), p. 9.
4. Lemke, pt. 1, p. 25.
5. Ibid., p. 26.
6. Golovin, *Russia under the Autocrat,* 1:25.
7. TsGAOR, Otchet o deistviiakh III Otdeleniia sobstvennoi ego imperatorskogo Velichestva kantseliarii i korpusa zhandarmov. These reports, compiled annually by the Third Section, include data on Russians going abroad. Virtually all are listed under "reasons of health."
8. I. G. Golovin, *L'Esprit de l'economie politique* (Paris, 1842).
9. I. G. Golovin, *Des Economistes et des socialistes* (Paris, 1845).
10. Golovin, *Russia under the Autocrat;* idem, *Types et caractères russes* (Paris, 1847).
11. G. Bakalov, "Pervaia revoliutsionnaia broshiura russkoi emigratsii: *Katekhizis russkogo naroda* I. G. Golovina, 1849 goda," *Zven'ia* 1 (1932): 195–217.
12. See TsGAOR, *fond* 109, *opis'* 1, *ed. khran.* 50, *chast'* 1/1843, *listy* 1–4; and Lemke, pt. 1, p. 27. All the materials from the police files used but not identified in citations by Lemke are in the TsGAOR dossier. Tolstoy managed to see parts of Golovin's manuscript before publication through literary acquaintances who had been asked to read it for evaluative purposes.
13. Golovin, *Russia under the Autocrat,* 1:9.
14. Ibid., p. 28; Lemke, pt. 1, p. 31.
15. Golovin, *Russia under the Autocrat,* p. 27.
16. See Cadot, p. 29.
17. Golovin, *Russia under the Autocrat,* 1:iii.
18. Ibid., p. v.
19. Ibid.
20. Ibid., pp. 42–43.
21. Ibid., p. 75.
22. Ibid., p. 136.
23. Ibid., p. 138.
24. Ibid., pp. 86–87.
25. Ibid., p. 87.
26. Ibid., pp. 161–62.
27. Ibid., 2:320. Golovin's vivid and realistic descriptions of the Russian military campaigns against the Circassians in the Caucasus resemble a sketch of modern guerilla warfare.
28. Ibid., 1:94–95.
29. Ibid., p. 99.
30. Some of the positive notices Golovin received in the French press are mentioned in his *Zapiski,* pp. 90–91.
31. Lemke, pt. 1, p. 33. Golovin inherited the equivalent of 40,000

francs at the time of the publication of his book on Nicholas I; the money came from his brothers in Russia as a result of a settlement on the family estate.

32. I. G. Golovin, "A Revolt of the Peasants," *A Russian Sketch-Book* (London: T. C. Newby, 1848), 2:105–70. For a discussion of the book as a whole, and a French review of it, see Sliwowska, "Un émigré russe," pp. 229–30.

33. Golovin, *Zapiski,* chaps. 15–16, pp. 106–29. Lemke interprets this material to show Golovin as frivolous; see Lemke, pt. 1, pp. 33–35.

34. See Orlik, 1973, p. 263.

35. See I. G. Golovin, *Quelques vérités à la France à propos de mon expulsion* (London, 1850). See also Sliwowska, "Un émigré russe," pp. 231–32, 241–43, which includes a letter written by Golovin on his expulsion from France.

36. Bakalov, p. 195. Bakalov seems to have been unaware that Golovin's "Catechism" had been previously published as he erroneously indicates he is publishing it for the first time. For the earlier publication, see Kuklin, pp. 369–80.

37. Bakalov, pp. 203–4.

38. Ibid., pp. 216–17.

39. Ibid., p. 217.

40. For the police and diplomatic documents, see ibid., pp. 197–203. Golovin admitted his authorship of the "Catechism" thirty years later in his *Russische Nihilismus* (Leipzig, 1880), p. 73. See also the discussion in Sliwowska, "Un émigré russe," p. 235, n. 1.

41. Sliwowska, "Un émigré russe," p. 235.

42. While still in school, Peter Kropotkin read Golovin's censored book, *Types et caractères russes* at the home of one of his relatives. See P. A. and A. A. Kropotkin, *Perepiska,* 2 vols. (Moscow-Leningrad: Academia, 1932), 1:61.

43. TsGAOR, III *otdelenie,* I *ekspeditsiia,* no. 15 (1851), *list* 30.

44. Sliwowska, "Un émigré russe," pp. 223–24.

45. On James Fazy in this period, see M. Veilleumier, ed., *Revolutionnaires et exiles du XIXᵉ siecle: Autour d'Alexandre Herzen* (Geneva: Droz, 1973), esp. pp. 14–30.

46. See Golovin, *Zapiski,* pp. 66–67.

47. Sliwowska writes of this brochure the following: "The tone of this brochure is without doubt in harmony with that of Herzen's book, *From the Other Shore.* It is easy to see the common features, not only in their critique of bourgeois France of that time, but also in their method of arguing their cases. Of course, Herzen's literary talent is in no way to be compared with that of Golovin, who lacks both fervor and authentic emotion" (Sliwowska, "Un émigré russe," p. 236).

48. Ibid., p. 237.

49. I. G. Golovin, *The Nations of Russia and Turkey* (London: Trubner, 1854).
50. I. G. Golovin, *Stars and Stripes* (London and New York, 1856), p. 1.
51. Lemke, pt. 2, p. 276.
52. Ibid., pt. 1, p. 40.
53. Ibid., p. 41.
54. Ibid., pp. 43–44.
55. Ibid., p. 45.
56. See Veilleumeir, p. 174.
57. Lemke, pt. 2, p. 280.
58. Ibid., pt. 1, pp. 48, 49.
59. Ibid., pt. 2, p. 275.
60. Ibid., p. 278.
61. Sliwowska, "Un émigré russe," p. 236.
62. See I. G. Golovin, "Chteniia ob ugolovnom prave," *Blagonameren-nyi,* no. 12 (1862). Golovin's journal is discussed in more detail in chapter 11 of the present volume.
63. See, for example, Golovin's letter to *L'Opinion nationale,* 26 July 1866, where he strongly criticizes the tsar's policies of driving Russians into exile merely because they express dissenting opinions. He hoped for a response, but none was forthcoming.
64. Golovin, *Russische Nihilismus,* p. 62. See also the discussion in Lemke, pt. 2, p. 282.
65. Golovin, *Russische Nihilismus,* pp. vi–vii, 59–91.
66. Kuklin, p. 368.
67. Sliwowska, "Un émigré russe," p. 239.

4. N. I. Sazonov: Marx's First Russian Follower

1. Carr, *The Romantic Exiles,* pp. 30–31. Recently, portions of Sazonov's career have been treated objectively in an article by Franco Venturi, "Sazonov and Italian Culture," *Studies in Free Russia,* pp. 187–215.
2. B. P. Koz'min, "Iz literaturnogo nasledstva N. I. Sazonova," *Literaturnoe nasledstvo* 41–42 (1941): 178–252; quote is on p. 187.
3. N. Ye. Zastenker, "N. I. Sazonov–Gertsenu," *Literaturnoe nasledstvo* 62 (1955): 530.
4. D. I. Riazanov (pseud. for D. I. Gol'dendakh), *Karl Marks i russkie liudi sorokovykh godov* (Petrograd: Izdanie Petrogradskogo Soveta, 1918). Riazanov discovered the correspondence between Sazonov and Marx and published the letters in his book. The letters have recently been republished in *K. Marks, F. Engel's i revoliutsionnaia Rossiia* (Moscow: Izdatel'stvo politicheskoi literatury, 1967), pp. 146–55. The only other scholarly article on Sazonov prior to Riazanov's book is B. Modzalevskii's entry "N. I. Sazonov" in

Russkii biograficheskii slovar' (St. Petersburg: Demakov, 1904), 18:56–58. Sazonov appears in the recent works by Cadot and Sliwowska in a more positive light, but he remains entirely unstudied in the United States.

5. Howes and Orton, *The Confession of Mikhail Bakunin*, p. 61.

6. P. Ia. Chaadaev, *Sochineniia i pis'ma*, ed. M. Gershenzon, 2 vols. (Moscow: Put', 1913–14), 1:240.

7. K. S. Aksakov, *Vospominaniia studentstva 1832–35 godov* (St. Petersburg, 1911), pp. 30–33; cited in Riazanov, p. 12, and Koz'min, pp. 178–79.

8. N. I. Sazonov, "Alexander Herzen," *Gazette du Nord*, no. 13 (26 May 1860), reprinted in *Literaturnoe nasledstvo* 41–42 (1941): 194–201; see esp. pp. 196–97. See also Herzen's discussion of this period in his *My Past and Thoughts*, vol. 2, pt. 4, pp. 389–638.

9. M. K. Lemke, "Ocherk zhizni i deiatel'nosti Gertsena, Ogareva i ikh druzei," *Sovremennyi Mir*, January 1906, pp. 67–69.

10. N. I. Sazonov, "Ob istoricheskikh trudakh Mullera," *Uchenye zapiski Moskovskogo universiteta* 60 (1833).

11. Sazonov to K. S. Aksakov, 2 February 1836 from Geneva, quoted in Koz'min, pp. 248–49.

12. See Zastenker, pp. 530–32.

13. Sazonov to N. Kh. Ketcher, 18 June 1837, quoted in Koz'min, pp. 249–50.

14. Riazanov, p. 14.

15. V. P. Botkin to P. V. Annenkov, 26 November 1846, in *P. V. Annenkov i ego druz'ia* (St. Petersburg, 1892), p. 525.

16. [Avdot'ia Iakovlevna Panaeva], "Vospominaniia A. Ia. Golovachevoi," *Istoricheskii vestnik*, March 1889, p. 555. Koz'min believes Sazonov adjusted to Parisian life "like a fish in water" (p. 181), while Riazanov sees him having more difficulty making the transition (pp. 14–15).

17. B. Nikolaevskii, ed., "Pis'mo N. I. Sazonova k Gervegu," *Letopis' marksizma* 6 (1928): 80.

18. Ibid., p. 81.

19. "Pis'mo N. I. Sazonova–N. P. Ogarevu," *Zven'ia* 6 (1936): 348–49.

20. Ibid., pp. 349–50.

21. Ibid., p. 351.

22. Ibid.

23. Ibid., p. 352.

24. Ibid. The quote is from *Henry VI*, pt. 2, act 4, sc. 2.

25. "Pis'mo N. I. Sazonova–N. P. Ogarevu," p. 353.

26. Riazanov (pp. 21–28) discusses Sazonov's radical journalism and activities during the 1848 revolution. See also Zastenker, p. 538.

27. Riazanov (pp. 28–29) suggests this, and also two possible later meetings between Marx and Sazonov in 1848 and 1849.

28. *K. Marks,* pp. 146–47.
29. Ibid., p. 148.
30. Ibid.
31. Ibid., p. 149.
32. Ibid., p. 150.
33. Ibid., p. 151.
34. Ibid., p. 152. Sazonov also included details on printing expenses, honoraria for contributors, and the potential readership for the journal.
35. Ibid., p. 153.
36. Ibid., p. 154.
37. Ibid., p. 155. This last letter from Sazonov to Marx was included in Marx's pamphlet *Herr Vogt* (London, 1860), in which Marx rebutted Carl Vogt's criticism of his work. Vogt's attack on Marx was the "polemic" referred to by Sazonov in his letter.
38. Koz'min, p. 183. Zastenker (p. 527) takes a similar position. Interestingly, neither of these historians even mentions Riazanov's book, where the claim of Sazonov's Marxism was first made. They cite instead P. N. Sakulin, *Russkaia literatura i sotsializm* (Moscow: Gosudarstvennoe izdatel'stvo, 1922), p. 253, in which Riazanov's thesis is repeated.
39. See Herzen's comments on Sazonov in Zastenker, p. 523; and Sazonov's ambivalent evaluation of Herzen in his 1850 letter to Marx, *K. Marks,* p. 151.
40. See Zastenker, pp. 532–39, for the letters of Sazonov to Herzen written in 1849.
41. Herzen to M. K. Reikhel', 20 June 1852, in "Pis'ma k M. K. Reikhel', 1850–52 gg.," *Literaturnoe nasledstvo* 61 (1953): 339. See also Herzen's letter to M. Hess, 29 May 1843, in which he explains his break with Sazonov in severe terms. He speaks of how Sazonov "wounded" him and of Sazonov's tendency to "spend a lot and work little" (Riazanov, pp. 43–44). On the affair between Herzen's wife and Herwegh, see Carr, pp. 47–121.
42. Sazonov to Herzen, 24 March 1852, quoted in Zastenker, pp. 540–41.
43. Sazonov to Herzen, 6 September 1852, ibid., p. 541.
44. N. I. Sazonov, *Rodnoi golos na chuzhbine. Russkim plennym vo Frantsii* (London: Free Russian Press, 1855).
45. Riazanov, pp. 45–46.
46. Ibid., pp. 46–47.
47. Ibid., p. 49.
48. Ibid., pp 49–50.
49. Ibid., p. 50.
50. See Sazonov's letter to Herzen, 20 August 1855, quoted in Zastenker, pp. 542–43.

51. Koz'min p. 185. Sazonov's authorship of the book was first revealed by Christian Ostrowski in his book *Lettres slaves* (Paris, 1857), p. 22. The text of the book was published for the first time in Russian in Koz'min, pp. 202–48.
52. Koz'min, p. 238.
53. Ibid., p. 225.
54. Ibid., p. 244.
55. Articles signed by Sazonov appeared in the following issues of *L'Athenaeum français* during 1855: no. 8 (24 February), pp. 145–46; no. 26 (30 June), pp. 544–46; no. 31 (4 August), pp. 648–51; no. 32 (11 August), pp. 685–87. There are, in addition, many other essays and reviews by Sazonov, but since they are signed with pseudonyms, it is more difficult to establish authorship for them. According to a recent study, Sazonov also knew Baudelaire at this time, who mentions him approvingly in his correspondence; see Cadot, p. 34.
56. Modzalevskii, p. 58.
57. Zastenker, p. 527.
58. Koz'min, p. 186, and especially Zastenker, pp. 527–30.
59. *Gazette du Nord,* no. 15 (14 April 1860).
60. Ibid., no. 4 (28 January 1860).
61. Ibid., no. 16 (21 April 1860).
62. See Riaznov, p. 52.
63. See Sazonov's articles on Russia, "De l'emancipation des serfs en Russie," in *Gazette du Nord,* no. 13 (31 December 1859), no. 1 (7 January 1860), no. 3 (21 January 1860), no. 4 (28 January 1860), no. 7 (18 February 1860), and no. 9 (3 March 1860).
64. Ibid., no. 9.
65. N. I. Sazonov, "A propos d'une soirée russe à Paris," ibid., no. 12 (24 December 1859).
66. Koz'min, pp. 188–94. The essay is entitled "Ivan Turgenev" and is ostensibly a review of the writer's book, *Nest of the Gentry,* which appeared in French translation in 1859 in *Revue contemporaine.* The review originally appeared in *Gazette du Nord,* no. 13 (31 March 1860).
67. Published as *La Revolution et le monde russe* in 1860 in Paris.
68. Sazonov, "Alexander Herzen," p. 197.
69. Ibid., pp. 197, 200.
70. See Zastenker, pp. 544–45, n. 6. Sazonov responded angrily to this scandal in his article "A propos d'une soirée russe à Paris ."
71. Sazonov to Herzen, May 1860, quoted in Zastenker, p. 543. The title of Dolgorukov's book was *La Vérité sur la Russie.* On Dolgorukov and his book, see chapter 5 of the present volume.
72. Sazonov's review of Dolgorukov's *La Vérité sur la Russie* was published in *Gazette du Nord,* no. 16 (21 April 1860).

73. Letter dated 16 September 1855 from Hamburg, TsGALI, *fond* 1283, *opis'* 1, *ed. khran.* 1, *list* 1.
74. For the remainder of this correspondence, see ibid., *listy* 3–47.
75. TsGAOR, III *otdel.*, III *eksped.*, *ed. khran.* 425/1849, *list* 1.
76. Ibid., *list* 14.
77. Report dated 14 (26) August 1857, ibid., *list* 31.
78. Ibid., *listy* 50–51.
79. Ministry of Foreign Affairs to Chief of III Section, 27 September 1858, ibid., *list* 57.
80. Ministry of Foreign Affairs to III Section, 30 October 1858, ibid., *list* 58.
81. Ministry of Foreign Affairs to III Section, 8 March 1861, ibid., *list* 60.
82. Ibid.
83. Riazanov, p. 55.
84. Ibid., p. 56.
85. Herzen, *My Past and Thoughts*, 2:968.

5. P. V. Dolgorukov: The Republican Prince

1. Quoted in S. B. Bakhrushin, "Respublikanets-kniaz' Petr Vladimirovich Dolgorukov," in P. V. Dolgorukov, *Peterburgskie ocherki* (Moscow: Academia, 1934), p. 51.
2. In addition to the Bakhrushin article cited above, Dolgorukov's bibliography consists mainly of the following items: M. K. Lemke, "Kniaz' P. V. Dolgorukov v Rossii," *Byloe,* 1907, no. 2 (14): 144–67; (referred to throughout this chapter as Lemke, pt. 1); M. K. Lemke, "Kniaz' P. V. Dologrukov—emigrant," *Byloe,* 1907, no. 3 (15): 153–99 (referred to throughout this chapter as Lemke, pt. 2); Carr, *The Romantic Exiles*, chap. 13; B. Hollingsworth, "The 'Republican Prince': The Reform projects of Prince P. V. Dolgorukov," *Slavonic and East European Review* 47 (1969): 447–68; D. Field, "P. V. Dolgorukov's Emigration from Russia," ibid. 48 (1970): 261–65 (a corrective note to Hollingsworth's article). In addition, Dolgorukov is mentioned briefly by Sliwowska (pp. 323–27), Cadot (pp. 62–64), and S. F. Starr, *Decentralization and Self-government in Russia, 1830–70* (Princeton: Princeton University Press, 1972), pp. 68–70, 266–70.
3. The Dolgorukov family occupies over eighty pages in the *Russkii biograficheskii slovar'* (St. Petersburg, 1905), 6:494–577. For the article on P. V. Dolgorukov, see pp. 554–55. The article on his father was written by Grand Prince Nikolai Mikhailovich.
4. Carr speculates that Dolgorukov was probably involved in homosexual relations at the time and that this may have been the cause of his demotion. See *The Romantic Exiles,* p. 276.
5. Hollingsworth, p. 449; Carr, p. 276; Bakhrushin, pp. 8–9.

6. In 1863 a pamphlet was published which claimed to have irrefutable evidence indicating Dolgorukov as the author of the lampoon. See A. Ammosov, *Poslednye dni i konchina A. S. Pushkina* (St. Petersburg, 1863). A Soviet scholar who subjected the original document to handwriting analysis concluded that Dolgorukov did indeed write the damaging lampoon. See P. E. Shchegolev, *Duel i smert' Pushkina* (Moscow: Zhurnal'no-gazetnoe ob'edinenie, 1936). See also M. I. Barsukov, "P. V. Dolgorukov o tsarskoi Rossii i o duele A. S. Pushkina s Dantesom," *Zven'ia* 1 (1932): 77–85.

7. P. V. Dolgorukov, *Rossiiskii rodoslovnyi sbornik,* 4 vols. (St. Petersburg, 1840–41).

8. Paris: Didot Frères, 1843. The title page indicates that proceeds from the sale of the book are "au profit des pauvres."

9. Iakov Tolstoi to Count Benckendorff, 22 January (3 February) 1843, TsGAOR, *fond* 109, *opis'* 1, *delo* 50, *chast'* 1/1843, *listy* 1–4.

10. Ibid., *list* 22 (Lemke, pt. 1, pp. 146–48).

11. Ibid., *listy* 36–40 (Lemke, pt. 1, pp. 148–50). The letter to Nicholas I, written in Berlin by Dolgorukov, is dated 10 (22) April 1843.

12. Ibid., *listy* 46–51, 69–70, 94–95.

13. Ibid., *listy* 146–47. The letter is dated 4 April 1844.

14. Ibid., *listy* 252, 255. Three further volumes followed in 1857.

15. Ibid., *listy* 295–295 verso. The letter, dated 2 February 1857, is to Prince Vasilii Andreevich Dolgorukov, a cousin, who had succeeded Benckendorff as chief of the Third Section.

16. *Dictionnaire historique de la noblesse russe* (Brussels, 1858).

17. The details of Dolgorukov's plan are discussed in Field, p. 261; Bakhrushin, p. 21; and V. N. Rosental', "Narastanie 'Krizisa verkhov' v seredine 50-kh godov XIX veka," in *Revoliutsionnaia situatsiia v Rossii v 1859–1861 gg.,* ed. M. V. Nechkina (Moscow: Nauka, 1962), pp. 56–57.

18. Field, p. 262. On the prohibited Russian-language publications that were appearing in Europe at this time, see the excellent bibliography, S. N. Valk and B. P. Koz'min, *Russkaia podpol'naia i zarubezhnaia pechat'* (Moscow: Politkatorzhan, 1935).

19. Field, pp. 262–63. The letter is dated 14 July 1858.

20. Bakhrushin, p. 20.

21. Quoted in Field, p. 264.

22. Hollingsworth, p. 451; Bakhrushin, pp. 22–23.

23. Field, p. 264.

24. Lemke, pt. 2, p. 154.

25. Bakhrushin, p. 26.

26. Hollingworth, p. 451.

27. Lemke, pt. 2, pp. 161–64.

28. TsGAOR, III otdel., 1 *eksped.,* no. 50, *chast'* 2/1843, *listy* 2–2 verso. The letter is dated 4 (16) April 1860.

29. Ibid., *listy* 7–8. The letter is dated 3 (15) April 1860. Amplifying

244 NOTES TO PAGES 95–98

this point elsewhere, Dolgorukov wrote: "Publicity is the medicine for Russia. . . . Publicity is the most efficacious remedy to extirpate the old abuses and to prevent the formation of new ones" (*La Vérité sur la Russie* [Paris, 1860], p. 2). Golovin, as we have seen, argued a similar position.

30. Lemke, pt. 2, p. 168.
31. Hollingsworth, p. 453; Bakhrushin, pp. 27–30, 35; Lemke, pt. 2, pp. 172–74.
32. Carr, p. 285; Hollingsworth, p. 453.
33. Bakhrushin, p. 25.
34. This was announced in *Kolokol*, no. 121 (1 February 1862): 1012. In all, twenty-five issues of *Budushchnost'* were published.
35. Six issues of *Pravdivyi* and four of *Le Véridique* appeared.
36. Twenty-two issues of *Listok* were published.
37. P. V. Dolgorukov, *La France sous le régime Bonapartiste*, 2 vols. (Brussels, 1864). This book, which was highly critical of Louis Napoleon, won the admiration of Victor Hugo. Hugo, himself in exile at the time on the island of Guernsey and a prominent opponent of Napoleon III, received Dolgorukov for a four-day visit in May 1865. In the words of a Soviet scholar: "In Dolgorukov, Hugo found a new ally in his struggle against the despised emperor of France" (M. P. Alekseev, "Viktor Giugo i ego russkie znakomstva," *Literaturnoe nasledstvo* 31–32 [1937]: 838). Echoes of Dolgorukov's critique of Napoleon III from this book designed for his Russian readers can be found in his articles in *Listok*, no. 12 (1863) and no. 19 (1864).
38. Mistitled *Memoires du prince Pierre Dolgorukoff*.
39. Dolgorukov to J. G. V. de Persigny, 31 July 1862, TsGALI, *fond* 1245, *opis'* 1, *ed. khran.* 7, *list* 1.
40. Ibid., *listy* 3–4.
41. Some of these essays have been reprinted in Dolgorukov, *Peter-burgskie ocherki*.
42. On Gagarin, see Sliwowska, pp. 301–37.
43. Dolgorukov to I. Gagarin, 10 September 1860, TsGALI, *fond* 1245, *opis'* 1, *ed. khran.* 3, *listy* 29–30. In this letter, Dolgorukov also repeated his intention to publish in the coming year biographies of individuals in Russia "occupying important positions or having influence on affairs." He intended to keep his "political biographies" above the level of matters dealing merely with "private life." Ibid., *list* 30.
44. Dolgorukov to Gagarin, 4 June 1862, ibid., *list* 38.
45. Ibid., *listy* 41–43.
46. Ibid., *listy* 44. On the Heidelberg colony, see chapter 7 of the present volume.
47. Dolgorukov to Gagarin, 18 (6) January 1863, ibid., *list* 46.

48. Bakhrushin, p. 31; Hollingsworth, p. 455.
49. Bakhrushin, p. 33. See also the critical evaluation of Dolgorukov at this time in G. N. Vyrubov, "Revoliutsionnyia vospominaniia (Gertsen, Bakunin, Lavrov)," *Vestnik Evropy*, 1913, no. 1:57–58.
50. See B. P. Koz'min, "Dolgorukov i Elpidin," *Krasnyi arkhiv* 3, no. 34 (1929): 231–32.
51. Lemke, pt. 2, pp. 187–91; Carr, p. 288.
52. Bakhrushin, p. 36; Carr, p. 288.
53. P. V. Dolgorukov, *Des reformes en Russie* (Paris, 1862), pp. 99–100, 105–6.
54. Dolgorukov, *La Vérité*, p. 7.
55. Dolgorukov, *Des reformes*, pp. 108–9.
56. Lemke, pt. 2, p. 177.
57. Bakhrushin, pp. 53–54.
58. Dolgorukov, *La Vérité*, p. 32.
59. *Budushchnost'*, no. 1 (15 September 1860): 2.
60. See *La Vérité*, chap. 6, pp. 89–133, and the discussion in Bakhrushin, pp. 58–65, and Hollingsworth, pp. 458–60.
61. Dolgorukov, *Des reformes*, p. 61. On Russian liberalism in this period, see V. A. Kitaev, *Ot frondy k okhranitel'stvu. Iz istorii russkoi liberal'noi mysli 50–60-kh godov XIX veka* (Moscow: Mysl', 1972), See also D. Field, "Kavelin and Russian Liberalism," *Slavic Review* 32, no. 1 (1973): 59–78.
62. Dolgorukov, *Des reformes*, pp. 50–51.
63. Ibid., pp. 171–98.
64. See ibid., pp. 139–70. It has been pointed out that Dolgorukov's proposed voting and election procedures resemble the system of elections which was instituted in Russia after the 1905 revolution. See Bakhrushin, p. 76.
65. Rosental', p. 57.
66. N. G. Sladkevich, *Ocherki istorii obshchestvennoi mysli Rossii v kontse 50-kh nachale 60-kh gg. XIX v.* (Leningrad: Izdat. univer-siteta, 1962), p. 118.
67. Starr (pp. 69–71) claims that among the Russians, Dolgorukov was the "least restrained disciple" of Odilon-Barrot and Regnault, and cites him as an example of Russian thinkers "importing a batch of ideological castoffs"—i.e., ideas already passé in France which Russians take back to St. Petersburg as the latest vogue.
68. *La Vérité*, p. 5.
69. See P. V. Dolgorukov, "O knizhke N. I. Turgeneva: Vzgliad na dela Rossii," *Pravdivyi* (Leipzig), no. 4 (31 May 1862): 28–30. See also the discussions in Sladkevich, pp. 115–16, and Hollingsworth, p. 463.
70. Dolgorukov, *Des reformes*, p. 70.
71. Among the figures who appear in this series of critical essays called

"Petersburg Sketches" are Grand Prince Konstantin, M. N. Murav'ev, D. N. Bludov (chairman of the State Council), V. V. Panin (minister of justice), A. F. Golitsyn (member of the State Council), A. M. Gorchakov (vice-chancellor), and V. A. Dolgorukov (head of the Third Section). This series, which originally appeared in Dolgorukov's journals, has been collected in *Peterburgskie ocherki.*

72. Carr, p. 275.

73. See I. S. Turgenev, "Pis'mo k redaktoru *S.-Peterburgskikh vedomostei,*" *Polnoe sobranie sochinenii i pisem,* 28 vols. (Moscow: Nauka, 1960–68), 15:147–48.

74. Dolgorukov to Alexander II, 4 (16) August 1863, *Listok,* no. 11; Lemke, pt. 2, p. 185.

75. P. V. Dolgorukov to V. A. Dolgorukov, chief of the Third Section, 14 February 1867, quoted in Lemke, pt. 2, p. 191.

6. Perspectives on the First Generation

1. Two recent books that examine these currents during the reign of Nicholas I are Nicholas Riasanovsky, *A Parting of Ways: Government and the Educated Public in Russia, 1801–1855* (Oxford: Oxford University Press, 1977); and Gleason, *Young Russia,* pp. 1–76.

2. Bakunin really lived through two separate émigré periods. The first, which chronologically corresponds to our discussion of the first generation, ended in 1849 when he was arrested during the Dresden uprising. The second follows his escape from Siberia. In 1861 he returned to Western Europe and remained deeply involved with both the revolutionary populist movement in Russia as well as with the struggle for control of the International Association of Workers until his death in 1876. On Bakunin's first émigré period, see E. H. Carr, *Michael Bakunin* (New York: Vintage Books, 1961), pp. 97–204, which remains the most readable and comprehensive account of his life and thought in English. For a more recent treatment, which tends to be tendentious in demonstrating its thesis, see Arthur Mendel, *Michael Bakunin: Roots of Apocalypse* (New York: Praeger, 1981), pp. 148–239.

3. Quoted from an unpublished letter in V. M. Tarasova, "Dekabrist N. I. Turgenev: Sotrudnik *Kolokola,*" in *Problemy izucheniia Gertsena,* ed. Iu. G. Oksman et al. (Moscow: Akademiia nauk, 1963), p. 250.

4. Franco Venturi believes that Turgenev's book *La Russie* "had no small influence on the formulation of Belinsky's 'minimum' program." See his "Russian Populism," *Studies in Free Russia,* pp. 252–53.

5. Martin A. Miller, *Kropotkin* (Chicago: University of Chicago Press, 1976), pp. 25–26.

6. See Z. P. Bazileva, *"Kolokol" Gertsena 1857–67 gg.* (Moscow: Gosizdat, 1949), pp. 152–53.

7. The Origins of Collective Action Abroad

1. On these developments, see Venturi, *Roots of Revolution*, pp. 220–84.

2. The term refers to Dostoevsky's characterization of the polemic between the two preeminent nihilist journals during the early 1860s, Chernyshevskii's *Sovremennik* and Pisarev's *Russkoe slovo*. See B. P. Koz'min, "Raskol v nigilistakh," *Iz istorii revoliutsionnoi mysli v Rossii* (Moscow: Akademiia nauk, 1961), pp. 20–67.

3. A. Ia. Kiperman, *Raznochinskaia revoliutsionnaia emigratsiia (1861–1895)* (Tambov: Tambovskii Gosudarstvennyi Pedagogicheskii Institut, 1980), p. 27.

4. I. S. Turgenev, *Fathers and Sons*, ed. R. E. Matlaw (New York: Norton, 1966), p. 53. There has been no scholarly discussion of the Heidelberg colony in Western historiography. Although Venturi gives an exhaustive treatment of the radical movements of this period, he mentions the colony only once in passing; see *Roots of Revolution*, p. 273.

5. TsGAOR, III *otdel.*, I *eksped.*, 1863, *delo* 2.

6. The term used was *delo emigratsii*. On the students from Russia in Heidelberg, see V. I. Modestov, "Zagranichnyia vospominaniia," *Istoricheskii vestnik* 11, no. 2 (1883), esp. pp. 397–406. See also L. I. Mechnikov, *Etiudy optimizma*, enl. ed. (Moscow: Nauchnoe slovo, 1913); and idem, "A. O. Kovalevskii: Ocherk iz istorii nauk v Rossii," *Vestnik Evropy*, 1902, no. 12:773–75. The distinction between Russian students and émigrés in Heidelberg was very clear at the time. On this, see S. Svatikov, "Russkie studenty v Geidel'berge," *Novyi zhurnal dlia vsekh*, 1912, no. 12:70–82. For a list of the members of the colony, see Ia. Z. Cherniak, "Ogarev–V. I. Bakstu i drugim organizatoram Geidel'bergskoi chital'ni," *Literaturnoe nasledstvo* 63 (1956): 108.

7. B. P. Koz'min, "Gertsen, Ogarev i 'molodaia emigratsiia,'" *Iz istorii*, p. 493. One of the Russians involved in this effort, Novitskii, was denounced as an agent of the Russian police by Bliummer and also by Dolgorukov (ibid., p. 494). Another colony member who was closely affiliated with the Herzen faction of the colony, A. F. Stuart, also was suspected of being an informer for the Third Section.

8. Examples of the extraordinary praise for Nozhin from his contemporaries can be found in the reminiscences of Lev Mechnikov and N.

K. Mikhailovskii, among others. See S. Svatikov, "Turgenev i russkaia molodezh' v Geidel'berge," *Novaia zhizn'*, 1912, no. 12:155-60; and E. L. Rudnitskaia, *Shestidesiatnik Nikolai Nozhin* (Moscow: Nauka, 1975), pp. 9-10.

9. See Rudnitskaia, *Nozhin,* pp. 60-64, on this meeting.

10. See Ogarev's correspondence with Bakst in Cherniak, pp. 122-25; and Ia. I. Linkov, *Revoliutsionnaia bor'ba A. I. Gertsena i N. P. Ogareva i tainoe obshchestvo "Zemlia i Volia" 1860-kh godov* (Moscow: Nauka, 1964), pp. 284-86.

11. See Cherniak, pp. 107-20. V. I. Kasatkin, an émigré in Geneva at this time, wrote to Herzen asking about money to support the Bern press. See B. F. Egorov et al., eds., *Letopis' zhizni i tvorchestva A. I. Gertsena, 1812-1870,* 3 vols. (Moscow: Nauka, 1974-83), 3:398.

12. Rudnitskaia, *Nozhin,* pp. 46-48; Koz'min, "Gertsen, Ogarev i 'molodaia emigratsiia,'" pp. 507-10. For a detailed account of Ogarev's involvement with the press in Bern, see I. Miller, "Propagandistskaia deiatel'nost' N. P. Ogareva v 1863 g. i Bernskaia tipografiia," in *Slavianskoe istochnikovedenie,* ed. S. A. Nikitin (Moscow: Nauka, 1965), pp. 53-81.

13. I. S. Turgenev, *Fathers and Sons,* p. 165.

14. For Turgenev's response to Sluchevskii, see ibid., pp. 185-87.

15. Svatikov, "Turgenev," p. 182.

16. Venturi, *Roots of Revolution,* p. 273; Koz'min, "Gertsen, Ogarev i 'molodaia emigratsiia,'" p. 495.

17. On the differences between Herzen and Chernyshevskii, see the discussion in William F. Woehrlin, *Chernyshevskii: The Man and the Journalist* (Cambridge: Harvard University Press, 1971), pp. 251-59; and B. P. Koz'min, "Vystuplenie Gertsena protiv 'Sovremennika' v 1859 godu," *Iz istorii,* pp. 606-37.

18. N. V. Shelgunov, *Vospominaniia* 2 vols. (Moscow: Khudozh. lit., 1967), 1:123.

19. N. A. Belogolovyi, *Vospominaniia* (Moscow: Aleksandrov Press, 1898), p. 116. Criticism of Herzen in Russia was accelerating at the same moment within the ranks of the opposition. Zainchnevskii, for example, once a disciple of Herzen's, now turned against him. See Venturi, pp. 293-96.

20. A. I. Herzen, "1865," *Kolokol,* no. 193 (1 January 1865): 1581. Although the article is signed by both Herzen and Ogarev, Herzen was the sole author. See E. L. Rudnitskaia, *N. P. Ogarev v russkom revoliutsionnom dvizhenii* (Moscow: Nauka, 1969), p. 356.

21. Utin to Herzen, 5 August 1864, in B. P. Koz'min, "N. I. Utin–Gertsenu i Ogarevu," *Literaturnoe nasledstvo* 62 (1955): 670.

22. Utin to Herzen, 16 December 1864, ibid., p. 676.

23. Ibid., p. 675.

24. Ibid., p. 676.
25. Herzen to Utin, 25 December 1864, in B. P. Koz'min, "Pred-staviteliam 'molodoi emigratsii,'" *Literaturnoe nasledstvo* 61 (1953): 276.
26. Koz'min, "Gertsen, Ogarev i 'molodaia emigratsiia,'" pp. 521–22. Herzen also mentioned his concerns about moving his press to the Continent as the younger émigrés wanted, in that general political conditions were unstable there. But his overriding concerns were his suspicion of the émigrés themselves and his fear of losing his independence in any cooperative venture with them.
27. Koz'min "Gertsen, Ogarev i 'molodaia emigratsiia,'" p. 530. On Luginin, see Cherniak, pp. 109–110.
28. B. P. Koz'min, "Aleksandr Serno-Solov'evich: Materialy dlia biog-rafii," *Literaturnoe nasledstvo* 67 (1959): 708. For an unflattering portrait of the young émigrés similar to Herzen's, written by Nikolai Belogolovyi during a visit to Geneva at this time, see S. A. Makashin, "*Obshchee delo* i ego zakulisnyi redaktor," ibid., 87 (1977): 433.
29. B. P. Koz'min, "A. A. Serno-Solov'evich v I Internatsionale i v Zhenevskom rabochem dvizhenii," *Istoricheskii sbornik* 5 (1936): 81; Koz'min, "Aleksandr Serno-Solov'evich," p. 701; M. V. Korochkin, *Russkie korrespondenty K. Marksa* (Moscow: Mysl', 1965), p. 55. On the Bakhmetev Fund, see N. P. Antsiferov, "Pis'mo P. A. Bakhmeteva Gertsenu," *Literaturnoe nasledstvo* 41–42 (1941): 526–28.
30. Quoted in Koz'min, "N. I. Utin–Gertsenu i Ogarevu," p. 621.
31. A. A. Serno-Solov'evich, *Nashi domashnie dela* (Vevey, 1867), quoted in Koz'min, "Gertsen, Ogarev i 'molodaia emigratsiia,'" p. 534.
32. Khudiakov's formative years are discussed in Venturi, *Roots of Revolution*, pp. 338–42. See also Gleason, *Young Russia*, pp. 311–32.
33. E. S. Vilenskaia, *Khudiakov* (Moscow: Molodaia gvardiia, 1969), pp. 92–93.
34. Ibid.; Venturi, *Roots of Revolution*, p. 342; E. S. Vilenskaia, *Revoliutsionnoe podpol'e v Rossii* (Moscow: Nauka, 1965), pp. 372–73.
35. On this episode, and for details on Khudiakov's later years, see Vilenskaia, *Khudiakov*, pp. 99–142.
36. Indeed, though no commentator seems to have noted it, if there is any parallel to Kel'siev inside Russia, it would most likely be Afanasy Shchapov. See Venturi, *Roots of Revolution*, pp. 196–203, and Gleason, *Young Russia*, pp. 180–225, for discussions of Shchapov.

37. For a recent interpretation of Bakunin's motives at this time, see the introduction by Lawrence Orton in Howes and Orton, *The Confession of Mikhail Bakunin,* pp. 11–28.

38. See J. A. Duran, "L. A. Tikhomirov and the End of the Age of Populism in Russia" (Ph.D. diss., University of Illinois, 1957); and Abbot Gleason, "The Emigration and Apostasy of Leo Tikhomirov," *Slavic Review* 26, no. 3 (1968): 414–29.

39. Herzen, *My Past and Thoughts,* 3:1328.

40. Ibid., p. 1329.

41. Ibid., p. 1330.

42. Ibid., pp. 1331–32.

43. Ibid., p. 1332.

44. Ibid., p. 1333.

45. Ibid., p. 1334.

46. M. Klevenskii, "*Ispoved'* V. I. Kel'sieva," *Literaturnoe nasledstvo* 41–42 (1941): 256.

47. Quoted in Venturi, p. 114.

48. Ibid., p. 115.

49. Herzen published the pamphlet *Narod i gosudarstvo* in 1863, and also published a letter by Mart'ianov in *Kolokol,* no. 132 (8 May 1862). Mart'ianov was arrested upon his voluntary return to Russia in 1863 and was condemned to hard labor and exile in Siberia for his association with Herzen and *Kolokol.* He died in Siberia in 1865. The best source material on this interesting and utterly neglected individual dissenter can be found in M. K. Lemke, *Ocherki osvoboditel'nogo dvizheniia "shestidesiatykh godov"* (St. Petersburg: Popova, 1908), pp. 333–56. The Third Section's unpublished file on Mart'ianov is in TsGAOR, *fond* 112, *opis'* 1, *ed. khran.* 35 and 36.

50. These talks are recorded by Kel'siev in his article "Iz razskazov ob emigrantakh," *Zaria* (St. Petersburg), 1869, no. 3:95–97.

51. Quoted in Klevenskii, p. 259.

52. Kel'siev "Iz razskazov," p. 98.

53. Klevenskii, p. 268.

54. Lemke, *Ocherki,* pp. 35, 111; Linkov, p. 266. A good memoir account of Kel'siev's stay in St. Petersburg is in Shelgunov, "Iz proshlogo i nastoiashchego," *Vospominaniia,* 1:171–80.

55. Klevenskii, p. 312. Some doubt has been cast on the veracity and accuracy of Kel'siev's reporting of his talks with Nikolai Serno-Solov'evich. For this, see Linkov, p. 267.

56. Klevenskii, p. 325.

57. Lemke, *Ocherki,* pp. 37–38. This letter was intercepted by the police and used as evidence against Serno. See TsGAOR, III *otdel.,* I *eksped., delo* 230, *chast'* 110 (1862), *list* 2.

58. Lemke, *Ocherki,* p. 33.

59. Ibid., p. 37. On Vasilii Kel'siev's brother, Ivan, and his criticism of Ogarev and Herzen, see Linkov, pp. 411–15.
60. M. P. Dragomanov, ed., *Pis'ma Bakunina A. I. Gertsenu i N. P. Ogarevu*, pp. 90–91.
61. Rudnitskaia, *Ogarev*, p. 319.
62. Ibid., p. 332.
63. Klevenskii, p. 259.
64. Kel'siev's wife worked for A. A. Kraevskii, the editor of *Otechestvennye zapiski* and *Golos*, earning 2,000 rubles a year, until Kel'siev, obviously threatened by her abilities and success, forced her to stop. See A. V. Nikitenko, *Dnevnik*, 3 vols. (Moscow: Gosizdat, 1956), 3:215.
65. Ibid., p. 105. Although the "Confession" was rejected for publication, Kel'siev did publish a memoir, *Perezhitoe i peredumannoe* (St. Petersburg: Golovin, 1868), in which he included much of the same material.
66. Nikitenko, p. 133.
67. Ibid., p. 148.
68. Klevenskii, p. 258. See also the bibliography of Kel'siev's works, pp. 262–64.
69. A. P. Chebyshev-Dmitriev, quoted by Klevenskii, p. 216. On Mikhailovskii's critique of Kel'siev, see James Billington, *Mikhailovsky and Russian Populism* (Oxford: Oxford University Press, 1958), p. 49. For a more extensive discussion of Kel'siev's last years, see Paul Call, *Vasily Kelsiev: An Encounter between the Russian Revolutionaries and the Old Believers* (Belmont, Mass.: Nordland Publishing Co., 1979), pp. 181–204.
70. P. G. Ryndziunskii, "I. I. Kelsiev–Gertsenu i Ogarevu," *Literaturnoe nasledstvo* 62 (1955): 220.
71. See Kel'siev's 1862 letter to Countess E. V. Salias, in I. Zverev, "K biografii I. I. Kel'sieva," *Literaturnoe nasledstvo* 41–42 (1941): 105–10.
72. Linkov, p. 411.
73. See Kel'siev's letters in Ryndziunskii, pp. 219–58.
74. Linkov, pp. 411–12.
75. Ibid., p. 413.
76. Ryndziunskii, p. 232.
77. Zverev, p. 109.
78. Ryndziunskii, pp. 227–28.

8. A. A. Serno-Solov'evich: Beyond Herzen

1. Lemke, "K biografii A. A. Serno-Solov'evich," *Ocherki*, p. 260.
2. Ibid., p. 237.

3. M. V. Korochkin, *Russkie korrespondenty K. Marksa* (Moscow: Mysl', 1965), p. 9.
4. Lemke, "A. A. Serno-Solov'evich," p. 258.
5. Ibid., p. 264.
6. Shelgunov, *Vospominaniia*, p. 158.
7. Serno reflected on these feverish days and nights of rebellious activity in a letter to Natalia Tuchkova-Ogareva (1865). See Koz'min, "Aleksandr Serno-Solov'evich: Materialy dlia biografii," p. 739.
8. Korochkin, p. 39.
9. Lemke, "A. A. Serno-Solov'evich," p. 269; B. P. Koz'min, "A. A. Serno-Solov'evich v I Internatsionale i v Zhenevskom rabochem dvizhenii," pp. 79–80; Venturi, *Roots of Revolution*, p. 277.
10. A. A. Serno-Solov'evich, "Piatnadtsat' neopublikovannykh pisem," *Zven'ia* 5 (1935): 396.
11. Serno to Ogarev, quoted in B. P. Koz'min, "A. A. Serno-Solov'evich–Ogarevu," *Literaturnoe nasledstvo* 62 (1955): 548–51. See also Serno to Tuchkova-Ogareva (1865), in Koz'min, "Aleksandr Serno-Solov'evich," p. 739.
12. Korochkin, pp. 47–49.
13. Koz'min, "Aleksandr Serno-Solov'evich," p. 700.
14. TsGALI, *fond* 1065, *opis'* 4, *ed. khran.* 72.
15. N. P. Ogarev, "Po povodu prodazhi imenii v Zapadnom krae," *Kolokol*, no. 224 (1 November 1866).
16. A. A. Serno-Solov'evich, *Question polonaise* (Geneva: Pfeffer, [1867]). Copy in TsGALI, *fond* 1065, *opis'* 4, *ed. khran.* 72. For two versions of the text in Russian, see F. Freidenfel'd, "Listovka A. A. Serno-Solov'evich protiv N. P. Ogareva," *Literaturnoe nasledstvo* 41–42 (1941): 113–15, and Koz'min, "Aleksandr Serno-Solov'evich," pp. 709–12.
17. Koz'min, "Aleksandr Serno-Solov'evich," p. 710.
18. Ibid., p. 712.
19. (Vevey, 1867).
20. The article appeared in three parts in *Kolokol:* no 230 (1 December 1866), no. 231–32 (1 January 1867), and no. 233–34 (1 February 1867).
21. Ibid.
22. All quotations in this section are from portions of Serno's essay as reproduced in Lemke, "A. A. Serno-Solov'evich," p. 270.
23. Ibid. p. 271.
24. Koz'min, "Aleksandr Serno-Solov'evich," p. 702. Not all émigrés were in agreement with Serno's critique (Gulevich, Merchinskii, and Mechnikov, among others), but they were in a dwindling minority. See Koz'min, *Iz istorii*, pp. 548–49.
25. *Sovremennost'* was edited by Nikoladze and L. I. Mechnikov.

26. Koz'min, "Aleksandr Serno-Solov'evich," p. 704.
27. A. A. Serno-Solov'evich, *Mikolka-Publitist* (Geneva, 1868). This brochure is an extremely rare item. The copy used here was found in the Lenin Library in Moscow.
28. Ibid., pp. 4–5.
29. Ibid., p. 9.
30. Ibid., p. 11.
31. Ibid., pp. 12–13.
32. Ibid., p. 14.
33. Ibid., p. 8.
34. Koz'min, "Aleksandr Serno-Solov'evich," pp. 728–29.
35. Serno-Solov'evich, "Piatnadtsat' neopublikovannykh pisem," p. 391; see also p. 395.
36. Koz'min has attempted to identify at least one of these articles as Serno's after conducting a textual and stylistic comparative analysis with Serno's other published writings. See Koz'min, "A. A. Serno-Solov'evich i I Internatsionale," pp. 96–98.
37. According to one historian, Serno here was struggling to combine aspects of Russian populist socialism with European conceptions of economic materialism. See Venturi, *Roots of Revolution*, p. 280.
38. Ibid., p. 281.
39. Koz'min "A. A. Serno-Solov'evich i I Internatsionale," p. 111.
40. Serno-Solov'evich, "Piatnadtsat' neopublikovannykh pisem," p. 396.
41. *K. Marks, F. Engel's i revoliutsionnaia Rossia*, p. 162. The letter is dated 20 November 1868.
42. Ibid., p. 164.
43. Ibid., p. 165.
44. See Koz'min, "A. A. Serno-Solov'evich i I Internatsionale," pp. 114–17.
45. Ibid., p. 120.
46. M. Sleptsova, "Shturmany griadushchei buri (iz vospominanii)," *Zven'ia* 2 (1933): 414.
47. Koz'min, "Aleksandr Serno-Solov'evich," p. 701. In letters to Natalia Tuchkova-Ogareva (August 1865, ibid., p. 736), and M. V. Ivashova-Trubnikova (December 1868, "Piatnadtsat' neo-publikovannykh pisem," p. 397), Serno continually asked about his son, whom Shelgunova had taken with her when she returned to Russia. He told Tuchkova-Ogareva that he "cries every day" over his lost, loved son, who was born in 1864. See Koz'min, "Aleksandr Serno-Solov'evich," p. 737.
48. On Cherkesov, see the biographical material in Koz'min, "Aleksandr Serno-Solov'evich," p. 731, and Cherkesov's letter to Herzen on Serno's hospitalization, ibid., pp. 732–33.
49. Ibid., pp. 701, 703–4.
50. Korochkin, p. 80.

51. Koz'min, "Aleksandr Serno-Solov'evich," p. 738.
52. Ibid., p. 726.
53. Serno-Solov'evich, "Piatnadtsat' neopublikovannykh pisem," p. 391.
54. Koz'min, "Aleksandr Serno-Solov'evich," p. 707.

9. On the Eve: Toward the Development of Ideology

1. For a good discussion of Nechaev's impact on Russian youth at this time, see B. P. Koz'min, *Nechaev i nechaevtsy* (Moscow-Leningrad: Gosizdat, 1931). For recent studies of Nechaev and his later impact on the Russian emigration, see Stephen T. Cochrane, *The Collaboration of Nechaev, Ogarev, and Bakunin in 1869* (Giessen: W. Schmitz Verlag, 1977); and Philip Pomper, *Sergei Nechaev* (New Brunswick, N.J.: Rutgers University Press, 1979), esp. pp. 69–98, 133–66.

2. The best existing studies on Sokolov are the following: the long chapter in Feliks Kuznetsov, *Publitsisty 1860-kh godov* (Moscow: Molodaia gvardiia, 1969), pp. 243–326; V. P. Leikina-Svirskaia, "Utopicheskii sotsialist 60-kh godov N. V. Sokolov," in *Revoliutsionnaia situatsiia v Rossii v 1859–1861 gg.*, (Moscow: Nauka, 1970), pp. 139–54; A. Efimov, "Publitsist 60-kh godov N. V. Sokolov," *Katorga i ssylka*, no. 11–12 (1931): 63–104; B. P. Koz'min. "N. V. Sokolov," *Literatura i istoriia* (Moscow: Khudozh. lit., 1969), pp. 373–443; and the very brief section in Venturi, *Roots of Revolution*, pp. 328–29, which, although inadequate, remains the only discussion of Sokolov in English.

3. Although Sokolov recorded his birth as 1832 in his "Avtobiografiia" (*Svoboda* [Paris], no. 1 [1889]), the archives show his date of birth to be 1835. See Leikina-Svirskaia, p. 140.

4. Kuznetsov suggests that Sokolov was influenced by the progressive administrative policies of Count N. N. Murav'ev-Amurskii during Sokolov's visit to Eastern Siberia as part of the trip to China. Kuznetsov compares this to Peter Kropotkin's experience there (pp. 254–56).

5. This discussion is based on the portion of Sokolov's autobiography which is included in Kuznetsov, pp. 250–59. This portion was not part of the previously published section of Sokolov's memoir, "Avtobiografiia."

6. See L. F. Panteleev, *Vospominaniia* (Moscow: Izdat. khudozh. lit., 1958), esp. p. 255; and Leikina-Svirskaia, p. 140.

7. Some of Sokolov's best pieces in *Russkoe slovo* were published in his *Ekonomicheskie voprosy i zhurnal'noe delo* (St. Petersburg: Golovin, 1866). See also the discussion in Kuznetsov, pp. 259–70.

8. N. S. Rusanov, *V emigratsii* (Moscow: Politkatorzhan, 1929), p. 30.

9. N. V. Sokolov, *Die Soziale Revolution* (Bern: Buchdruckerei von Rudolf Jenni, 1868).

10. Leikina-Svirskaia, 146.
11. Quoted in Kuznetsov, p. 276.
12. Ibid., p. 274.
13. Ibid.
14. Ibid., p. 277.
15. Leikina-Svirskaia, p. 146. These terms were first discussed in this context by O. V. Aptekman in his memoir-history, *Obshchestvo "Zemilia i Volia" 70-kh godov*, 2nd ed. (Moscow-Petrograd: Gosizdat, 1924), pp. 90–91. The book was originally written in 1882.
16. Kuznetsov, p. 282; Leikina-Svirskaia, p. 146.
17. St. Petersburg: Golovin, 1866.
18. The connection of this book to *Les Refractaires* (Paris, 1866), by Jules Valles, and the question of Sokolov's joint authorship with Zaitsev, are discussed in Leikina-Svirskaia, p. 151, and in Kuznetsov, pp. 287–89.
19. Readers interested in this very rare book, a copy of which is in the Lenin Library, will find an extended discussion of it and its influence in Kuznetsov, pp. 289–303, and in Koz'min, "N. V. Sokolov," pp. 374–76.
20. See Rudnitskaia, *Nikolai Nozhin*, pp. 124–26, 163–66. On Nozhin, see the discussion in chapter 7 of the present volume.
21. See Sokolov's pain-filled letters cited in Kuznetsov, p. 322. On Sokolov's activities in the Russian émigré communities in Paris and Geneva during his last years, see Koz'min, "N. V. Sokolov," pp. 412–21.
22. In addition to the materials cited below, upon which this discussion is based, there are some scattered Mechnikov materials listed in the text and notes in A. K. Lishina, "Russkii garibal'diets L. I. Mechnikov," in *Rossiia i Italiia*, ed. S. D. Skazkin (Moscow: Nauka, 1968), pp. 167–73. Lenin seems not to have ever noticed Mechnikov's activities, even though Plekhanov praised him. In the absence of any biography or bibliography by either Soviet or Western scholars, Mechnikov's place in Russian revolutionary history has yet to be established.
23. B. P. Koz'min, "L. I. Mechnikov–Gertsenu i Ogarevu," *Literaturnoe nasledstvo* 62 (1955):388.
24. Lishina, pp. 174–75.
25. For a more detailed discussion of Mechnikov's Italian campaign, see ibid., pp. 177–85.
26. These included *Sovremennaia letopis'*, *Russkii vestnik*, *Sovremennik*, *Russkoe slovo*, and *Delo*. See Koz'min, "L. I. Mechnikov," pp. 388–90.
27. Koz'min, "Gertsen, Ogarev i 'molodaia emigratsiia,'" p. 521.
28. According to Koz'min (ibid., p. 525), the congress included P. I. Iakobi, A. A. Serno-Solov'evich, N. I. Zhukovskii, M. S. Gulevich, N. I. Utin, V. I. Kasatkin, S. A Usov, V. F. Luginin. V. O.

Kovalevskii, L. P. Shelgunova, A. A. Cherkesov, V. I. Bakst, and A. F. Stuart, each of whom recorded a position for or against Herzen's policy on *Kolokol*'s editorial orientation. See also B. P. Koz'min, "Predstaviteliam 'molodoi emigratsii,' " *Literaturnoe nasledstvo* 61 (1953): 271–78.

29. For these, see Koz'min, "L. I. Mechnikov," p. 390; and M. Klevenskii, "Gertsen-izdatel' i ego sotrudniki," *Literaturnoe nasledstvo* 41–42 (1941): 599.

30. In one instance Herzen wrote of the émigrés that he had little respect for most of them in terms of their political and literary abilities, but he did admit that "Mechnikov knows how to write" (quoted in Koz'min, "L. I. Mechnikov," p. 390).

31. A. K. Lishina and O. V. Lishin, "Lev Mechnikov," *Literaturnoe nasledstvo* 87 (1977): 463. Mechnikov published several articles on his Spanish trip in *Otechestvennye zapiski*, nos. 2–5, 8, 11, and 12 (1869).

32. On this period of Mechnikov's career, see Lishina and Lishin, esp. pp. 471–507.

33. Published as *La Civilisation et les grands fleures historiques* (Paris, 1889).

34. The only published part of Mechnikov's memoirs was his "M. A. Bakunin v Italii v 1864 godu," *Istoricheskii vestnik* 67 (March 1897): 807–34.

35. See the archival documents published in Lishina and Lishin, pp. 478–96.

36. L. G. Deich, "Nikolai Ivanovich Zhukovskii," *Russkaia revoliutsionnaia emigratsiia 70-kh godov* (Petrograd: Gosizdat, 1920), p. 18.

37. On Peter Ballad's "pocket press," see Koz'min, *Iz istorii*, pp. 273, 276, 277; and Venturi, *Roots of Revolution*, pp. 251, 298.

38. The letter is in *Kolokol*, no. 144 (8 September 1862), p. 1196. See also Klevenskii, p. 591. For the police file on Zhukovskii's activities, see TsGAOR, *fond III otdel., I eksped., ed. khran.* 230, *chast'* 58 (1862), *listy* 3, 33.

39. The decision was reached on 16 October 1864. See B. P. Koz'min, ed., *Deiateli revoliutsionnogo dvizheniia v Rossii*, 4 vols. in 5 (Moscow: Vsesoiuznoe obshchestvo, 1927–34), vol. 1, pt. 2, p. 127.

40. E. L. Rudnitskaia, "N. I. Zhukovskii–Ogarevu," *Literaturnoe nasledstvo* 62 (1955): 136.

41. Ibid.

42. Ibid., pp. 137–38.

43. See Ogarev's articles in issues 237, 239, and 240 of *Kolokol* (March–May 1867).

44. Koz'min, *Iz istorii*, pp. 542–43.

45. The content of *Narodnoe delo* is discussed in chapter 11, in the section on the émigré press in the 1860s (see pp. 195–98).

46. Deich, p. 18. Much of the present discussion of Zhukovskii's personality is taken from Deich's chapter on him (pp. 17–23).
47. Feliks Kuznetsov, the only Soviet scholar to have written anything of substance on Zaitsev, introduced his subject by asking, "Who is V. A. Zaitsev?" and admitted that very few people actually knew anything about him. See Kuznetsov, p. 142. One collection of Zaitsev's many articles was published, but a promised second volume never appeared, and the volume that was published is a bibliographic rarity. See V. A. Zaitsev, *Izbrannye sochineniia* (Moscow: Politkatorzhan, 1934), with its introductory essay by B. P. Koz'min. The only other published accounts of Ziatev's life and activities are A. Khristoforov's obituary for Zaitsev in *Obshchee delo*, no. 47 (1882); and his wife's memoir, M. Z. [Mariia Zaitseva], "V. A. Zaitsev za granitsei," *Minuvshie gody*, 1908, no. 11:81–110.
48. Zaitsev's early years are treated by Khristoforov, and by Kuznetsov, pp. 147–48.
49. This linkage has been suggested and documented with evidence by Kuznetsov, pp. 148–60.
50. Shelgunov, *Vospominaniia*, p. 191. For a good discussion of Zaitsev's articles in *Russkoe slovo*, see Kuznetsov, pp. 163–97. Thirty-one of these articles are collected in Zaitsev, *Izbrannye sochineniia*, pp. 51–461.
51. Blagosvetlov later became an important figure in the emigration. See Kuznetsov's extensive chapter on his career (pp. 8–141).
52. See Kuznetsov, pp. 198 *et seq.*
53. B. P. Koz'min, "Iz istorii intelligentsii 60-kh godov," *Krasnyi arkhiv* 52 (1932): 285. The police file on this aspect of Zaitsev's career, prior to his emigration, is in TsGAOR, III *otdel.*, I *eksped., delo* 100, *chast'* 14 (1866–69).
54. M. Z., "Zaitsev," p. 84.
55. Ibid., pp. 85–86.
56. For a bibliography of these articles, see Kuznetsov, p. 220.
57. M.Z., "Zaitsev," p. 84.
58. Ibid., p. 85.
59. Ibid.
60. Ibid.
61. Nekrasov rejected this article when he saw it and scolded Zaitsev for maligning "such struggling servants of freedom, the republic, and the people as Jules Favre, Jules Simon, and Ernest Pickard" (ibid., pp. 85–86).
62. The full title of Zaitsev and Iakobi's article is "O polozhenii rabochikh v zapadnoi evrope s obshchestvenno-gigienicheskoi tochki zreniia." It was published in the September 1870 volume of the *Arkhiv sudebnoi meditsiny i obshchestvennoi gigieny*, bk. 3, pp. 160–216. See the discussion of this project, which resulted in a

NOTES TO PAGES 162–165

strong censorship act by the authorities, in V. V. Trifonov, "Odna iz pervykh popytok poznakomit' russkogo chitatelia s *Kapitalom*," *Voprosy istorii*, no. 4 (1976): 211–15.

63. Very little is known about Zaitsev's role in forming the Italian section of the International, though mention of it appears in the relevant studies. See, e.g., S. D. Skazkin, ed., *Rossiia i Italiia* (Moscow: Nauka, 1968), pp. 218–19; and McClellan, *Revolutionary Exiles*, p. 198.

64. M.Z., "Zaitsev," p. 89. Kuznetsov, following the interpretation of the leading historian of anarchism, Max Nettlau, argues that Zaitsev never was an anarchist revolutionary, in spite of his closeness to Bakunin at this time. See Kuznetsov, p. 221.

65. For a discussion of some of these articles, see Kuznetsov, pp. 227–37. On the journal and its editors, see B. P. Koz'min, "Iz istorii russkoi nelegal'noi pressy. Gazeta *Obshchee delo* (1877–1890)," *Istoricheskii sbornik* 3 (1934): 163–218. There is also an anonymous article on Herzen which one scholar has attributed to Zaitsev, but this is still undocumented. See. B. P. Koz'min, "Anonimnaia broshiura o Gertsene 1870 g.," *Literaturnoe nasledstvo* 41–42 (1941): 164–72.

66. *Obshchee delo*, no. 47 (1882).

10. N. I. Utin: Emigré Internationalism

1. From "Intrigi gospodina Utina," in *Materialy dlia biografii M. Bakunina*, ed. V. Polonskii, 3 vols. (Moscow: Gosizdat, 1922–23), 3:412; quoted in Venturi, *Roots of Revolution*, p. 442.

2. McClellan, *Revolutionary Exiles*, p. 14. The same author states that Bakunin "considered [Utin] a mere annoyance easy to eliminate when the occasion demanded" (p. 248) and, also echoing Bakunin, calls Utin "an insignificant little man" (p. 85).

3. Ibid., p. 84.

4. TsGAOR, "O byvshem studente Nikolae Utine"; quoted in McClellan, pp. 187–88.

5. F. M. Dostoevsky, *Pis'ma*, ed. A. S. Dolinin, 4 vols. (Moscow-Leningrad: Gosizdat, 1928–59), 2:31; quoted in B. P. Koz'min, "N. I. Utin–Gertsenu i Ogarevu," *Literaturnoe nasledstvo* 62 (1955): 607.

6. L. F. Panteleev (*Iz vospominanii proshlogo* [Moscow: Academia, 1934], p. 281) mentions that Utin was twenty-one years old in the winter of 1861–62. The year 1845 is given as Utin's date of birth by Klevenskii ("Gertsen-izdatel' i ego sotrudniki," *Literaturnoe nasledstvo* 41–42 [1941–42]: 612) and also by Koz'min (*Deiateli revoliutsionnogo dvizheniia v Rossii*, vol. 1, pt. 2, p. 240), but clearly this is erroneous; we know that Utin was enrolled at St. Petersburg

University in 1858, and he would have been only thirteen at that time according to this calculation.

7. Koz'min, "N. I. Utin–Gertsenu i Ogarevu," p. 607.

8. Boris Utin was a liberal publicist on the board of *Vestnik Evropy;* Evgenii Utin became a well-known lawyer and also contributed to *Vestnik Evropy;* Iakov Utin worked in the Ministry of Justice and published specialized papers on judicial affairs; even Utin's sister followed this path by marrying the historian and publicist M. M. Stasiulevich, who edited *Vestnik Evropy.*

9. See D. I. Pisarev, "Nasha universitetskaia nauka," in *Sochineniia v chetyrekh tomakh,* 4 vols. (Moscow: Gosizdat, 1955–56), 2:127–227.

10. See Utin's somewhat romanticized account of this plunge into the world of student *tovarishchestvo* in *Narodnoe delo* (Geneva), nos. 2–3 (1868): 29. The facts of Utin's participation in these student organizations have been corroborated in Panteleev, *Vospominaniia,* p. 180.

11. Panteleev, *Iz vospominanii proshlogo,* p. 74. The commission, chaired by K. D. Kavelin, was abolished by the government in the spring of 1861 before it could accomplish its purpose.

12. Ibid., pp. 102–3.

13. This period of Utin's activities has been studied in a number of works. See especially N. N. Novikova, "N. I. Utin i *Velikoruss,*" in *Revoliutsionnaia situatsiia v Rossii v 1859–1861 gg.,* ed. M. V. Nechkina (Moscow: Nauka, 1970), pp. 124–38; E. L. Rudnitskaia, *N. P. Ogarev v russkom revoliutsionnom dvizhenii* (Moscow: Nauka, 1969), pp. 345–63; and Vilenskaia, *Revoliutsionnoe podpol'e v Rossii,* pp. 134–35, 153–56, 169–74, 372–74.

14. M. K. Lemke, *Politicheskie protsessy v Rossii 1860-kh gg.* (Moscow-Petrograd: Gosizdat, 1923), pp. 178–79.

15. Koz'min, "N. I. Utin–Gertsenu i Ogarevu," pp. 612–17.

16. Ibid., p. 617. See also V. M. Korochkin, *Russkie korrespondenty K. Marksa* (Moscow: Mysl', 1965), p. 38.

17. Koz'min, "N. I. Utin–Gertsenu i Ogarevu," p. 617. See also M. K. Lemke, *M. M. Stasiulevich i ego sovremenniki v ikh perepiskakh,* 3 vols. (St. Petersburg: Stasiulevich, 1911–12), 1:406–8.

18. Koz'min, "N. I. Utin–Gertsenu i Ogarevu," p. 618.

19. No. 169 (15 August 1863).

20. See Utin's letter to Ogarev, dated 23 November 1863, in Koz'min, "N. I. Utin–Gertsenu i Ogarevu," p. 628.

21. Utin to Ogarev, 22 June 1864, ibid., p. 657. Herzen had rejected an article by Utin for publication in *Kolokol* in November 1863, which stung Utin's pride, but this was certainly not the major cause of his break with Herzen. In fact, Herzen had already published an article by Utin on Chernyshevskii in *Kolokol,* no. 189 (15 September

1864), and was discussing the possibility of future contributions with him. See Klevenskii, "Gertsen-izdatel'," pp. 612–13, for Utin's other writings in *Kolokol*.

22. Utin to Ogarev, 9 July 1864, in Koz'min, "N. I. Utin–Gertsenu i Ogarevu," pp. 660–65.
23. Korochkin, p. 53.
24. Ibid., p. 58.
25. Utin wrote for *Vestnik Evropy* during the years 1867–71 under various pseudonyms. It will be recalled that his brother-in-law, Stasiulevich, was the editor at this time (see note 8 above).
26. Utin to Ogarev, 14 February 1867, in Koz'min "N. I. Utin–Gertsenu i Ogarevu," pp. 679–85.
27. See Utin's letter to A. Trusov (May–June 1869), ibid., pp. 687–90.
28. See Venturi, *Roots of Revolution*, p. 431.
29. This claim is made by Korochkin, p. 62, although the published correspondence between Utin and Marx does not begin until the spring of 1871.
30. B. S. Itenberg, *Pervyi Internatsional i revoliutsionnaia Rossiia* (Moscow: Mysl', 1964), p. 37.
31. For a discussion of Utin's ideas in *Narodnoe delo* during these years (1868–70), see Korochkin, pp. 107–27, on which the present discussion is based.
32. See I . S. Knizhnik-Vetrov, *Russkie deiatel'nitsy Pervogo Internatsionala i parizhskoi kommuny* (Moscow: Nauka, 1964), pp. 229–30; Itenberg, *Pervyi Internatsional*, pp. 35–68; R. P. Koniushaia, *Karl Marks i revoliutsionnaia Rossiia* (Moscow: Polit. lit., 1975), pp. 411–27; McClellan, *passim;* Korochkin, pp. 130–51.
33. *K. Marks, F. Engel's i revoliutsionnaia Rossiia*, pp. 168–70. One may legitimately wonder why a Russian émigré in Geneva was asking permission from a German émigré in London to be the representative of the Russian working class in an organization that few of these workers had as yet even heard of.
34. The letters are dated 24 July and 9 December 1870. See ibid., pp. 172–80, 181–84.
35. This letter is dated 17 April 1871. See ibid., p. 188.
36. Marx to Utin, 27 July 1871, ibid., pp. 201–3.
37. Koniushaia, p. 417.
38. Utin to Marx, 28 October 1871, in *K. Marks*, pp. 219–24.
39. On these activities, see Koniushaia, pp. 418–26; and the Utin-Marx correspondence in *K. Marks*, pp. 234–43, 249–56, 264–72.
40. Quoted in McClellan, p. 240.
41. Ibid.
42. Quoted from the minutes of the London conference by Venturi, *Roots of Revolution*, p. 785, n. 45.
43. P. L. Lavrov, *Narodniki-propagandisty* (St. Petersburg: Anderson,

1907), p. 28. Perhaps he recalled the examples of Kel'siev before and of Tikhomirov later.

11. The Russian Emigré Press: In the Shadows of Kolokol

1. On the literally hundreds of periodicals that appeared in Paris during 1848, see George Duveau, *1848: The Making of a Revolution* (New York: Random House, 1967), and Priscilla Robertson, *Revolutions of 1848* (Princeton: Princeton University Press, 1967).
2. B. C. Sciacchitano, "The Exile World of Alexander Herzen" (Ph.D. diss., University of Illinois, 1979), p. 68.
3. Ibid., p. 130. According to James Billington's recent study of revolutionary movements in Western Europe, Herzen was actively involved for a short time in October 1849 with Proudhon's *La Voix du peuple,* an involvement that was mediated by Sazonov, who knew both Herzen and Proudhon. "And Herzen, baptized in revolutionary journalism on Proudhon's publications of the revolutionary era [i.e., 1848–49], transferred this tradition to Russia, founding in 1857 in London the first illegal revolutionary periodical in Russian history: *Kolokol*" (Billington, *Fire in the Minds of Men,* pp. 320–21).
4. M. Klevenskii, "Gertsen-izdatel' i ego sotrudniki," *Literaturnoe nasledstvo* 41–42 (1941): 572. It is not certain who his "friends" were, but Herzen corresponded with M. K. Reikhel about these matters during the early 1850s, as Klevenskii points out.
5. Ibid.
6. Ibid., p. 574.
7. *Poliarnaia zvezda,* no. 1 (1955): 11–14.
8. For a detailed analysis of the impact of *Poliarnaia zvezda* as well as a listing of the large number of anonymous contributors and their publications in Herzen's journal, see N. Ia. Eidel'man, *Tainye korrespondenty "Poliarnoi zvezdy"* (Moscow: Mysl', 1966).
9. For an illuminating discussion of these negotiations, see V. A. Chernykh, "Iz istorii vol'noi russkoi pechati: A. I. Gertsen i N. Trubner. Pervyi period sotrudnichestva," in *Epokha Chernyshevskogo,* ed. M. V. Nechkina (Moscow: Nauka, 1978), pp. 61–77.
10. *Kolokol,* no. 1 (1 July 1857), p. 3.
11. Venturi, *Roots of Revolution,* p. 104.
12. For an alphabetical listing of most of these contributors, see Klevenskii, "Gertsen-izdatel'," pp. 581–617. See also N. Ia. Eidel'man, "Nachalo izdaniia *Kolokola,* i ego pervye korrespondenty," in *Revoliutsionnaia situatsiia v Rossii v 1859–1861 gg.,* ed. M. V. Nechkina (Moscow: Nauka, 1970), pp. 173–95. At the height of its popularity, Herzen's newspaper was printed in editions of between 2,000 and 3,000 copies. However, because the issues were

passed around from hand to hand, many thousands more people must be counted among the paper's readership. See Gleason, *Young Russia*, pp. 83–98, for a recent discussion of the influence of Herzen's paper in Russia.

13. *Blagonamerennyi*, no. 1 (1859): 1–76.

14. Ibid., no. 2 (1859): 68–80. Because it is signed "L," it is possible that Golovin did not write it, but he certainly would not have published it in his journal if he had not agreed with it.

15. Ibid., no. 6 (1860) and no. 7 (1860). To my knowledge, this essay is the first serious, detailed study of the French Revolution between 1789 and 1799 by a Russian émigré.

16. See especially "English Shadows," ibid., no. 2 (1859): 1–68; "History of Ferdinand VII of Spain," ibid., no. 4 (1860): 1–103; and "Germany and the Germans," ibid., no. 9 (1860): 1–53.

17. Ibid., no. 10 (1861): i–viii.

18. Ibid., no. 12 (1861).

19. After twenty-five issues with this title in 1861, Dolgorukov changed the journal's name first to *Pravdivyi* (*Le Véridique*) and then to *Listok*, which lasted for twenty-two issues through 1864.

20. This discussion is based on the material in *Budushchnost'*, no. 1 (15 September 1860): 1–3. Some of Dolgorukov's journal articles are reprinted in Dolgorukov, *Peterburgskie ocherki*.

21. *Budushchnost'*, no. 1 (15 September 1860): 3.

22. Ibid., nos. 10–11 (12 April 1861): 87–88.

23. Eight issues of *Svobodnoe slovo* appeared in 1862, published in Berlin by Ferdinand Schneider. The pagination is consecutive from issue to issue, with a total of 589 pages in the entire volume for 1862.

24. *Svobodnoe slovo*, 1862, pp. 1–2.

25. Ibid., p. 62.

26. Ibid., pp. 62–63.

27. Ibid., p. 64.

28. "Russko-pol'skii vopros," ibid., pp. 5–20.

29. "Zametka na stat'iu N. P. Ogareva," ibid., pp. 36–43. Ogarev's article appeared in *Kolokol*, nos. 119 and 120.

30. "Russkiia knigi za granitseiu," *Svobodnoe slovo*, 1862, pp. 50–56.

31. "Ustavnaia gramota russkogo gosudarstva," ibid., pp. 83–96. Bliummer mentions Herzen, Ogarev, Dolgorukov, A. I. Turgenev, M. L. Mikhailov, and A. I. Koshelev as contemporaries who also contributed to the resolution of the constitutional problem in Russia.

32. Ibid., pp. 170–78.

33. Ibid., pp. 179–91, 212–14.

34. "Sovremennoe polozhenie russkogo pravitel'stva," ibid., pp. 231–50. On another occasion, discussing the 1830 Polish uprising, Bliummer

admitted that revolutionary upheaval was justified. When the regime prevents all other avenues of peaceful change, bloodshed by the people in the name of freedom must be supported; such was the case in Poland, he concludes. See "Pol'skaia revoliutsiia, 1830–31 gg.," ibid., pp. 389–411.

35. "Kto narod i kto nenarod? Otnoshenie politicheskikh partii k nashemu krest'ianstvu," ibid., pp. 449–75. The reference to Kavelin was to his book *Dvorianstvo i osvobozhdenie krest'ian* (Moscow, 1862). For Dolgorukov, Bliummer cited his *Des reformes en Russie* (1862). The socialist works Bliummer mentioned in his article included the works of Herzen and Ogarev, and the pamphlet *Molodaia Rossiia* by Zaichnevskii (1861).

36. "Otvet na predidushchee pis'mo," *Svobodnoe slovo*, 1862, pp. 283–89.

37. Dolgorukov to I. S. Gagarin, 31 (19) October 1862, TsGALI, *fond* 1245, *opis'* 1, *ed. khran.* 3.

38. See, e.g., the police reports on Vladimirov and Konstantinov in TsGAOR, *fond* 109, I *eksped.*, *delo* 222 (1866), *listy* 174 and 280.

39. TsGAOR, *fond* 112, *opis'* 1, *ed. khran.* 70, 71. In one of the few discussions of Bliummer's political ideas, a Soviet historian has quoted evidence to indicate that Bliummer cooperated with the Third Section against the émigrés. The same historian testifies to the popularity of Bliummer's liberalism among Russians. See N. G. Sladkevich, *Ocherki istorii obshchestvennoi mysli Rossii v kontse 50-kh nachale 60-kh gg. XIX v* (Leningrad: Izdat. universiteta, 1962), pp. 118–21.

40. *Letuchie listki*, no. 1 (Heidelberg: Bangel and Schmitt, 1862), includes, in addition to the three *Velikoruss* documents, two responses reprinted from *Kolokol*, and Mikhailov's "K molodomu pokoleniiu,"

41. On these activities, see Vilenskaia, *Revoliutsionnoe podpol'e v Rossii*, pp. 369–80.

42. Elpidin, it should be noted, neglects to point out that peasants standing near Karakozov were responsible for wrestling him to the ground and holding him until the police arrived. "Fools," Karakozov was quoted as shouting at the peasants, "I did this for you." See Venturi, *Roots of Revolution*, p. 347.

43. The first issues of *Polnol'noe slovo*, no. 1 (July 1866, 48 pp.) and no. 2 (August 1866, 40 pp.), were published in Geneva by Elpidin. Elpidin remained active in émigré politics for decades, and according to some accounts of later émigrés, was believed to have been employed as an agent of the Okhrana.

44. Herzen to Ogarev, 26 February 1867, quoted in Klevenskii, "Gertsen-izdatel'," p. 567. See also Herzen's letters to G. N.

Vyrubov, where he both laments and tries to comprehend the declining interest in *Kolokol* ("Pisma A. I. Gertsena G. N. Vyrubovu, 1866–1869," *Vestnik Evropy,* 1913, no. 1: 80–97).

45. "Very Dangerous!" *Kolokol,* no. 44 (1 June 1859): 363–64.

46. "Lishnie liudi i zhelcheviki," *Kolokol,* no. 83 (15 October 1860): 689.

47. *Kolokol,* no. 110 (1 November 1861): 917.

48. Herzen, *My Past and Thoughts,* p. 1319. On Katkov's critique of Herzen and its impact, see Martin Katz, *Mikhail N. Katkov* (The Hague: Mouton, 1966), pp. 72–77. On the "White Terror," see Venturi, *Roots of Revolution,* p. 347.

49. Klevenskii, "Gertsen-izdatel'," p. 577. Herzen tried a French-language version of *Kolokol* in 1868 as well as several other related publications, but none succeeded. On the publication history of Herzen's final years, see ibid., pp. 577–80.

50. Acton, *Alexander Herzen and the Role of the Intellectual Revolutionary,* pp. 159–60, 177.

51. *Sovremennost',* 1868, no. 7, cited in Koz'min, "L. I. Mechnikov–Gertsenu i Ogarevu," p. 389.

52. See the discussion in Lishina and Lishin, "Lev Mechnikov," p. 464.

53. *Sovremennost',* 1868, no. 7:102–3.

54. See the discussion of Serno's *Mikolka-Publitsist,* pages 142–43 above.

55. See the articles "Russkaia emigratsiia" and "Dva pokoleniia" *Sovremennost',* 1868, no. 6. See also Lishina and Lishin, pp. 464, 465.

56. *Sovremennost',* 1868, no. 7:103–5.

57. Ibid., 1868, no. 2:26.

58. See the discussion in Lishina and Lishin, p. 464. In this article, the authors strain to place Mechnikov's philosophically materialistic writings in *Sovremennost'* not only in a Chernyshevskian framework, which is quite plausible, but also in a Marxist one, which is less so. See especially pp. 466–67.

59. *Narodnoe delo,* 1868, no. 1:1–2.

60. Ibid., pp. 4–5.

61. "Nasha programma," ibid., p. 7.

62. See the discussion of Utin, pages 170–73 above.

63. *Narodnoe delo,* 1870, no. 1: 1.

64. Ibid., p. 2.

65. Ibid., pp. 3–4. It should be noted that in addition to the change in ideology, there was a severe reduction in the size of the journal. In its Bakuninist phase, the average issue had between 25 and 60 pages; in its Marxist period, the issues contained only 4 pages, with the exception of the last, which had 8 pages. The format also

changed from journal-size pages to larger, newspaper-size pages
during 1870 under Utin.

66. Specifically, *Vpered!*, *Rabotnik*, *Obshchina*, and *Vestnik narodnoi
voli* reflect the characteristics that first appeared in *Narodnoe delo*
and *Sovremennost'*. This became even more true for the Marxist
organs of the late 1890s and after. On the Russian radical press, see
G. A. Kuklin, *Itogi revoliutsionnogo dvizheniia v Rossii* (Geneva:
Kuklin, 1903).

67. See especially *Obshchee delo*, edited by N. A. Belogolovyi during
the 1880s. This journal, which reflects the currents that predomi-
nated during the earlier period of émigré journalistic individualism,
had the distinction of surviving longer (1877–90) than any other
nineteenth-century Russian émigré organ, including Herzen's
Kolokol. This same minority tendency can also be seen in the pages
of *Krasnoe znamia*, edited by Alexander Amfiteatrov at the time of
the 1905 revolution, a lone voice of individualism in an age of
editorial collectivism and revolutionary ideology in the émigré press.

12. The Emigration and Revolution

1. On the immediate response to Herzen's death by the European
press as well as his closest friends and associates, see L. R. Lanskii,
"Otkliki na smert' Gertsena," *Literaturnoe nasledstvo* 63 (1956):
523–40. For Natalie Herzen's account of her father's death, see
Antsiferov, "Starshaia doch' Gertsena (Tata)," ibid., pp. 480–84.
Dostoevsky's comment shortly after Herzen's death was that Herzen
never actually emigrated; "He was already born an emigrant." See
Dostoevsky's *Diary of a Writer* (New York: George Braziller, 1954),
p. 5.

2. Kozmin, "Anonimnaia broshiura o Gertsene," pp. 176–77. Kozmin
believes the author of this brochure was Zaitsev.

3. Michael Confino, ed., *Daughter of a Revolutionary: Natalie Herzen
and the Bakunin-Nechaev Circle* (La Salle, Ill.: Library Press,
1973), p. 120.

4. Ibid., p. 12. Prior to his emigration, Herzen was arrested by the
authorities in Moscow in 1834 and was sentenced to "administrative
exile" in the Ural town of Viatka. He was not permitted to return to
Moscow until 1842.

5. See, e.g., the account by E. V. Evropeus in B. P. Koz'min, "K istorii
emigratsii 1860-kh godov," *Krasnyi arkhiv* 6, no. 49 (1931): 151. To
another friend, Herzen confessed at this time that if he had a choice
between emigration and exile, he would choose the latter. He also
said that anyone in Russia contemplating emigrating should be
warned how "terrible a thing it is for a Russian . . . it is neither his

life nor death but something worse than death. . . . I know of nothing on earth more miserable, more aimless, than the situation of the Russian émigré." See N. A. Belogolovyi, *Vospominaniia* (Moscow: Aleksandrov Press, 1898), p. 541.

6. G. N. Vyrubov, "Revoliutsionnyia vospominaniia (Gertsen, Bakunin, Lavrov)," *Vestnik Evropy*, 1913, no. 1:56.

7. P. L. Lavrov, *German Aleksandrovich Lopatin* (Petrograd: Kolos, 1919). Lavrov was describing conditions abroad in 1870, the year of Herzen's death.

8. Vasilii Kel'siev, *Perezhitoe i peredumannoe. Vospominaniia* (St. Petersburg: Golovin, 1868), pp. 319, 392, 394. Melancholy, depression, and nostalgia for Russia are frequent themes in émigré memoirs. See also the account of Evgenii Gizhitskii abroad in N. N. Modestov, "Kak on stal emigrantom (iz epokhu 60-kh godov)," *Trudy Orenburgskoi uchenoi arkhivnoi komissii*, vol. 35 (1917): 123–38. Gizhitskii used the emotion-laden word *toska* to describe his feelings of loneliness and isolation abroad.

9. K. A. ——v, "Shutovstvo russkoi emigratsii," *Golos*, no. 154 (6 [18] June 1870): 1.

10. Lavrov, *G. Lopatin*, p. 31.

11. On the plan to free Chernyshevskii, see Venturi, *Roots of Revolution*, p. 182.

12. On this linkage, see Martin A. Miller, "Ideological Conflicts in Russian Populism: The Revolutionary Manifestoes of the Chaikovskii Circle, 1869–1874," *Slavic Review* 29, no. 1 (1970): 1–21. The best study of the Zurich colony remains J. Meijer, *Knowledge and Revolution: The Russian Colony in Zurich, 1870–1873* (Assen: Van Gorcum, 1955). See also Philip Pomper, *Peter Lavrov and the Russian Revolutionary Movement* (Chicago: University of Chicago Press, 1972), and Boris Sapir, ed., *Lavrov: Gody emigratsii*, 2 vols. (Dordrecht: D. Reidel, 1974). Documents on Bakunin's involvement in the Zurich colony can be found in Arthur Lehning, ed., *Michel Bakounine et ses relations slaves, 1870–1875* (Leiden: Brill, 1974).

13. For the detailed reports on connections between the revolutionary activity of the early 1870s in Russia and the émigré centers in Europe that were compiled for the tsarist government, see *Istoriia sotsial'no-revoliutsionnogo dvizheniia, 1861–1887* (St. Petersburg: Tipografiia Ministerstva vnutrennykh del, 1887), particularly chap. 10, "Russkaia emigratsiia v Shveitsarii, 1870–74 gg."

14. K. A. ——v, "Shutovstvo russkoi emigratsii," p. 4. It should be noted that this article contained extensive quotations from Bakunin's censored writings, and thereby provided many Russians with the opportunity of becoming directly acquainted with his ideas for the first time.

15. "Russkie emigranty," *Moskovskie vedomosti,* no. 14 (18 January 1873): 4. Given the very large circulation of this paper at the time, it can reasonably be assumed that this article had a wide readership, particularly in view of the increased interest in the émigrés in Europe as a result of the Nechaev affair, the recalling of the students in Switzerland back to Russia, and news of the Russian émigrés' participation in the First International.

16. M. B. Millard, "Russian Revolutionary Emigration, Terrorism, and the Political Struggle," (Ph.D. diss., University of Rochester, 1972), p. 31. According to Vera Figner, "The significance of the Russian emigration diminished for revolutionary Russia" in the late 1870s. From that moment, the Russian movement "became independent [of the emigration], adopting its own forms and orientations" (see Vera Figner, *Zapechatlennyi trud* [Moscow: Mysl', 1964], 1:245).

17. For a discussion of the Russian political émigré community in Germany at this time, see Williams, *Culture in Exile,* pp. 28–33.

18. Lenin's retrospective tributes to the Russian emigration for its "indispensable contribution to the revolutionary struggle" are discussed in Kiperman, *Raznochinskaia revoliutsionnaia emigratsiia,* pp. 145–46. The impact of Lenin's émigré existence on the formulation of his ideas and on his behavior as a party leader has yet to be examined in any systematic manner, though there are indications in some recent work that this interrelationship is being taken seriously in the Soviet Union. See, in particular, E. Ia. Zazerskii and A. V. Liubarskii, *Lenin: Emigratsiia i Rossiia* (Moscow: Izdatel'stvo politicheskoi literatury, 1975).

A related problem is the role of the emigration in the formation of the main opposition political parties in Russia. In particular, the Kadets under Miliukov and Struve, the Socialist Revolutionaries under Chernov, the anarchists under Kropotkin, and the Social Democrats (Menshevik and Bolshevik factions), to name the most prominent, all coalesced abroad, where they published their writings and developed many of their major strategies and tactics in emigration. Among the many studies which either explicitly or implicitly tie together the émigré press and the rise of Russian radical political parties abroad, see the following: S. Galia, "Early Russian Constitutionalism, *Vol'noe slovo,* and the 'Zemstvo Union'," *Jahrbücher für Geschichte Osteuropas* 22, no. 1 (1974): 35–55; V. Zasulich, "*Vol'noe slovo* i emigratsiia," *Vospominaniia* (Moscow: Politkatorzhan, 1931), pp. 99–112; James Duran, Jr., "L. A. Tikhomirov and the End of the Age of Populism in Russia" (Ph.D. diss., University of Illinois, 1957); Donald Senese, "S. M. Kravchinskii and the National Front against Autocracy," *Slavic Review* 34, no. 3 (1975), esp. pp. 518–20; and Gary Hamburg,

"The London Emigration and the Russian Liberation Movement: The Problem of Unity," *Jahrbücher für Geschichte Osteuropas* 25, no. 3 (1977): 321–39.

Among the many biographical studies of the major émigré Russian revolutionaries, see the following: Abraham Ascher, *Pavel Axelrod and the Development of Menshevism* (Cambridge: Harvard University Press, 1972); Samuel H. Baron, *Plekhanov* (Stanford: Stanford University Press, 1963); Isaac Deutscher, *The Prophet Armed: Trotsky, 1879–1921* (New York: Random House, Vintage Books, 1965); Martin A. Miller, *Kropotkin* (Chicago: University of Chicago Press, 1976); Richard Pipes, *Struve: Liberal on the Left* (Cambridge: Harvard University Press, 1970); Oliver Radkey, *The Agrarian Foes of Bolshevism* (New York: Columbia University Press, 1958); and Rolf H. W. Theen, *Lenin: Genesis and Development of a Revolutionary* (Princeton: Princeton University Press, 1973).

19. D. Rikhter, "Emigratsiia," *Entsiklopedicheskii slovar'* (St. Petersburg: Brockhaus-Efron, 1904), 40:732–59. The earliest estimates on Russian emigration provided here are for 1876.

20. Archives nationales (Paris), F7.12339, no. 416 (1840). These files include reports from the Prefet de Police to the Ministry of the Interior on the surveillance of the activities of certain Russians in France.

21. See, e.g., TsGAOR, "Otchet o deistviiakh III otedeleniia sobstvennoi ego imperatorskogo Velichestva kantseliarii i korpusa zhandarmov za 1855 g.," *listy* 4–27.

22. A summary example of these tables is as follows: For the year 1856, of the 6,036 Russians who went abroad, 2,390 were gentry, 2,936 were "men of commerce and industry," 326 were scholars and artists, and 384 were servants (TsGAOR, "Otchet za 1856," *list* 142). In 1857 the number or Russians who went abroad was 15,102, in 1858 it was 17,243, and in 1863 it was 28,048. Each year the total number rises, the proportion of gentry to the general total declines, and the absolute number of students, *meshchanin*, and peasants increases. For later figures, see Rikhter, "Emigratsiia"; and Gustave Chandèze, *De l'Intervention des pouvoirs publics dans l'emigration et l'immigration au XIXe siecle* (Paris: Imp. Paul Dupont, 1898), pp. 185–94.

23. Iu. N. Yemelianov, "Spisok lits vyezzhavshikh za granitsu v 1857–1861 gg.," in *Revoliutsonniaia situatsiia v Rossii v 1859–1861 gg.*, ed. M. V. Nechkina (Moscow: Nauka, 1970), pp. 354–75.

24. A. Ia. Kiperman, "Glavnye tsentry russkoi revoliutsionnoi emigratsii 70–80-kh godov XIX v.," *Istoricheskie zapiski*, no. 88 (1971): 271–72.

25. See E. A. Grigor'eva, "Revoliutsionno-narodnicheskaia emigratsiia kontsa XIX veka" (Kandidat. diss., University of Moscow, 1970), pp. 70–72.

26. See *Khronika sotsialisticheskogo dvizheniia v Rossii, 1878–1887* gg. (Moscow: Sablin, 1907), pp. 137–38.

27. *Istoriia sotsial 'no-revoliutsionnogo dvizheniia, 1861–1887*, chap. 10.

28. Kiperman, "Glavnye tsentry," pp. 294–95.

29. See pp. 29–30 of the present volume.

30. These quotations are from Venturi, *Studies in Free Russia*, pp. 148, 175, and 180.

31. The phrase is Akhmatova's and is quoted most recently in Ronald Hingley, *Nightingale Fever: Russian Poets in Revolution* (New York: Knopf, 1981), p. xiii.

32. The constitutionalism of these émigrés differs considerably from the more state-oriented constitutionalism of Russians like Kavelin, Chicherin, and their followers inside Russia. See Sladkevich, *Ocherki*, pp. 112–18; and V. A. Kitaev, *Ot frondy k okhranitel'stvu. Iz istorii russkoi liberal'noi mysli 50–60-kh godov XIX veka* (Moscow: Mysl', 1972).

33. Two other categories, early death of parents and the influence of older siblings, turn up in a number of cases among the émigrés, but not enough to determine a clear trend.

34. See the discussion in Cadot, pp. 73–80. One émigré in the early 1870s reported on the existence of what he called *poluemigranty*, literally "half-émigrés," but better translated as either "temporary" or "partial" émigrés. The term referred to Russian visitors to Europe, the dabblers in politics abroad, those who could return to their homeland without fear of reprisal after a brief sojourn in the émigré milieu. Marx once expressed amazement at these "half-émigrés" from Russia "who lived abroad, call themselves émigrés, speak only furtively to one another, are fearful at every step of compromising themselves, and then return home to Russia and live there, as they did before, in a most comfortable manner." See "Russkie emigranty," *Moskovskiia vedomosti*, 16 January 1873, p. 5. The author of this unsigned article is believed to have been E. K. Gizhitskii. On this problem, see Koz'min, "Gertsen, Ogarev i 'molodaia emigratsiia,'" p. 484, n. 1.

35. Nicholas Hayes, "The Intelligentsia in Exile: 'Sovremennye Zapiski' and the History of Russian Emigré Thought, 1920–1940" (Ph.D. diss., University of Chicago, 1976), pp. 38–44. The term was used earlier in a broader context by Franz L. Neumann, "The Social Sciences," in *The Cultural Migration: The European Scholar in America*, ed W. Rex Crawford (Philadelphia: University of Pennsylvania Press, 1935), pp. 4–25.

36. V. Komkov, "Sovremennaia politicheskaia emigratsia," *Obrazovanie*, 1908, no. 12:69.

37. W. H. Auden, "September 1, 1939," *New York Times Book Review*, 12 August 1979, p. 7.

38. Ibid.

Bibliography

For the reader's convenience, the sources used in this study are arranged somewhat unconventionally. Rather than list them all alphabetically under various categories of scholarship, as is usually done, I have chosen a design which parallels the thematic arrangement of the book. Archival collections, general reference works, and unclassified books and articles are listed first. Then, books and articles either by or about a specific individual (or group, as in the case of the Heidelberg colony) are listed together under the individual's name. The names of the émigrés are arranged chronologically, following the sequence of the chapters in the text. The works of each émigré are arranged chronologically by date of publication. Unpublished sources such as dissertations are listed along with published materials in each category. Archival citations are given in full in the endnotes and need not be repeated here. The two main Soviet repositories for documents from the early emigration are the Central State Archive of the October Revolution (TsGAOR) and the Central State Archive for Literature and Art (TsGALI), both of which are located in Moscow.

ARCHIVAL COLLECTIONS

U.S.S.R.
Moscow
Tsentral'nyi Gosudarstvennyi Arkhiv Oktiabr'skoi Revoliutsii (TsGAOR)
The files of the Third Section and the collections of the Ministry of the Interior and the State Senate which contain materials on the activities of the émigrés (*fundy* 109, 112)
Tsentral'nyi Gosudarstvennyi Arkhiv Literatury i Iskusstva (TsGALI)
Private collections of letters to and from the Russian emigrés

FRANCE
Paris
Archives Nationales
Reports by the French police on the Russian émigrés in Paris
during the nineteenth century (F7 collection)
Nanterre
Bibliothèque Documentation Internationale Contemporaine,
University of Paris, Nanterre
A rich collection of nineteenth-century Russian émigré newspapers
and journals
UNITED KINGDOM
London
British Library (formerly the British Museum Library), Colindale
Annex
A fine collection of Russian pre-revolutionary émigré newspapers
U.S.
New York, N.Y.
Butler Library, Columbia University
Stanford, Calif.
Hoover Institution
The Nicolaevskii Collection, which includes police reports on
Russian émigrés in Western Europe, collections of newspaper
articles on émigré revolutionaries, and some private collections of
émigré correspondence

GENERAL REFERENCE WORKS

Elpidin, M. *Bibliograficheskii katalog*. Geneva: Libraire-Editeur, 1906.
Itenberg, B. S. *Svodnyi katalog russkoi nelegal'noi i zapreshchennoi
pechati XIX veka*. 9 vols. Moscow: Biblioteka im. Lenina, 1971.
Kluge, E. E. *Die Russische Revolutionäre Presse in der zweiten Hälfte
des Neunzehnten Jahrhunderts, 1855–1905*. Zurich: Artemis-Ver-
lag, 1948.
Lesure, M. *Les Sources de l'histoire de Russie aux Archives nationales*.
Paris: Mouton, 1970.
Mez'er, A. V. *Slovarnyi ukazatel' na knigovedeniiu*. 3 vols. Moscow-
Leningrad: Sots-ek. izdat., 1931–34.
Ossorguine-Bakounine, T. *L'Emigration russe en Europe*. Vol. 1, *1855–
1940*. Paris: Institut d'Etudes Slaves, 1976.
Rubakin, N. A. *Sredi knig*. 3 vols. Moscow: Knigoizdatel'stvo nauka,
1911–15.
Valk, S. N., and B. N. Koz'min, eds. *Russkaia podpol'naia i
zarubezhnaia pechat'. Bibliograficheskii ukazatel'. Donarodovol'-
cheskii period, 1831–1879*. Moscow: Politkatorzhan, 1935.

Zaleski, E. *Mouvements, ouvriers et socialistes. La Russie.* 2 vols. Paris: Les Editions ouvrieres, 1956.

MATERIALS ON THE WORLD OF EMIGRATION AND THE RUSSIAN EMIGRATION

Annenkov, P. V. *Extraordinary Decade.* Ann Arbor: University of Michigan Press, 1968.

Annenkov i ego druz'ia. St. Petersburg, 1892.

Aptekman, O. V. *Obshchestvo "Zemlia i Volia" 70-kh godov.* 2nd ed. Moscow-Petrograd: Gosizdat, 1924.

Billington, James. *Fire in the Minds of Men.* New York: Basic Books, 1980.

Boborykin, P. D. "Ot Gertsena do Tolstogo," *Vospominaniia,* 2:507–40. Moscow: Khudozh.lit., 1965.

Brock, Peter. "Polish Democrats and English Radicals, 1836–1862," *Journal of Modern History* 25 (1953): 139–56.

———. "The Polish Revolutionary Commune," *Slavonic and East European Review* 35, no. 84 (1956): 116–28.

———. "The Socialists of the Polish 'Great Emigration.'" In *Essays in Labour History,* edited by A. Briggs and J. Saville, pp. 140–73. London: Macmillan, 1960.

Cadot, M. *La Russie dans la vie intellectuelle française.* Paris: Feyard, 1967.

Carr, E. H. *The Romantic Exiles.* Boston: Beacon Press, 1961.

Chandèze, Gustave. *De l'Intervention des pouvoirs publics dans l'emigration et l'immigration au XIXe siècle.* Paris: Imp. P. Dupont, 1898.

Deich, L. G. *Russkaia revoliutsionnaia emigratsiia 70-kh godov.* Petrograd: Gosizdat, 1920.

Dragomanov, M. P., ed. *Pis'ma M. A. Bakunina k A. I. Gertsenu i N. P. Ogarevu.* Geneva, 1896.

Emelianov, Iu. N. "Spisok lits vyezzhavshikh za granitsu v 1857–1861 gg." In *Revoliutsionnaia situatsiia v Rossii v 1859–1861 gg.,* edited by M. V. Nechkina, pp. 354–75.

Field, D. "Kavelin and Russian Liberalism," *Slavic Review* 32, no. 1 (1973): 59–78.

Gleason, Abbot. *Young Russia: The Genesis of Russian Radicalism in the 1860s.* New York: Viking Press, 1980.

Golovacheva-Panaeva, A. Ia. *Vospominaniia.* St. Petersburg, 1890.

Grigor'eva, E. A. "Revoliutsionno-narodnicheskaia emigratsiia kontsa XIX veka." Kandidat. diss., University of Moscow, 1970.

Haupt, George. "Rôle de l'exil dans la diffusion de l'image de l'intelligentsia revolutionnaire," *Cahiers du monde russe et soviétique* 19, no. 3 (1978): 235–49.

Hayes, Nicholas. "The Intelligentsia in Exile: 'Sovremennye Zapiski' and the History of Russian Emigré Thought, 1920–1940." Ph.D. diss., University of Chicago, 1976.

Howes, R. C., and L. D. Orton, eds. *The Confession of Mikhail Bakunin.* Ithaca, N.Y.: Cornell University Press, 1977.

Istoriia sotsial 'no-revoliutsionnogo dvizheniia, 1861–1887. St. Petersburg: Ministry of Internal Affairs, 1887.

Itenberg, B. S. *Pervyi Internatsional i revoliutsonnaia Rossiia.* Moscow: Mysl', 1964.

———. "Nekotorye voprosy izucheniia revoliutsionno-demokraticheskogo dvizheniia poreformennoi Rossii," *Istoriia SSSR,* no. 1 (1978): 168–79.

Khronika sotsialisticheskogo dvizheniia v Rossi 1878–1887 gg. Moscow: Sablin, 1907.

Kiperman, A. Ia. "Glavnye tsentry russkoi revoliutsionnoi emigratsii 70–80-kh godov XIX v." *Istoricheskie zapiski,* no. 88 (1971): 257–95.

———. *Raznochinskaia revoliutsionnaia emigratsiia (1861–1895).* Tambov: Tambovskii Gosudarstvennyi Pedagogicheskii Institut, 1980.

Kitaev, V. A. *Ot frondy k okhranitel'stvu. Iz istorii russkoi liberal'noi mysli 50–60-kh godov XIX veka.* Moscow: Mysl', 1972.

Knizhnik-Vetrov, I. S. *Russkie deiatel'nitsy Pervogo Internatsionala i parizhskoi kommuny.* Moscow: Nauka, 1964. Includes biographies of E. L. Dmitrieva, A. V. Zhaklar, and E. G. Barteneva.

Komkov, V. "Sovremennaia politicheskaia emigratsiia," *Obrazovanie,* 1908, no. 12:67–90.

Koz'min, B. P. "K istorii emigratsii 1860-kh godov." *Krasnyi arkhiv* 6, no. 49 (1931): 283–86.

———. *Nechaev i nechaevtsy.* Moscow-Leningrad: Gosizdat, 1931.

———. "Iz istorii russkoi nelegal'noi pressy, Gazeta *Obshchee delo* (1877–1890)." *Istoricheskii sbornik* 3 (1934): 163–218.

———. "Predstaviteliam 'molodoi emigratsii.'" *Literaturnoe nasledstvo* 61 (1953): 271–78.

———. *Russkaia sektsiia Pervogo Internatsionala.* Moscow: Akademiia nauk, 1957.

———. "Gertsen, Ogarev i 'molodaia emigratsiia,'" *Iz istorii revoliutsionnoi mysli v Rossii,* pp. 483–577. Moscow: Akademiia nauk, 1961. This essay originally appeared in *Literaturnoe nasledstvo* 41–42 (1941): 1–48.

———. "Raskol v nigilistakh." *Iz istorii revoliutsionnoi mysli v Rossii,* pp. 20–67. Moscow: Akademiia nauk, 1961.

———, ed. *Deiateli revoliutsionnogo dvizheniia v Rossii.* 4 vols. in 5. Moscow: Vsesoiuznoe obshchestvo politicheskikh katorzhan i ssyl'no-poselentsev, 1927–33.

Kuklin, G. A. *Itogi revoliutsionnogo dvizheniia v Rossii.* Geneva: Kuklin, 1903.

————. *Materialy k izucheniiu istorii revoliutsionnogo dvizheniia v Rossii*. Geneva: Kuklin, 1905

Kuznetsov, F. *Publitsisty 1860-kh godov*. Moscow: Molodaia gvardiia, 1969.

Lavrov, P. L. *Narodniki-propagandisty*. St. Petersburg: Anderson, 1907.

————. *German Aleksandrovich Lopatin*. Petrograd: Kolos, 1919.

Lehning, A. Muller. "The International Association, 1855–1859," *International Review of Social History* 3 (1938): 185–286.

Lemke, M. K. *Ocherki osvoboditel'nogo dvizheniia "shestidesiatykh godov."* St. Petersburg: Popov, 1908.

————. *Politicheskie protsessy v Rossii 1860-kh gg*. Moscow-Petrograd: Gosizdat, 1923.

————, ed. *M. M. Stasiulevich i ego sovremenniki v ikh perepiskakh*. 3 vols. St. Petersburg: Stasiulevich, 1911–12.

Linkov, Ia. I. *Revoliutsionnaia bor'ba A. I. Gertsena i N. P. Ogareva i tainoe obshchestvo "Zemlia i Volia" 1860-kh godov*. Moscow: Nauka, 1964.

McClellan, Woodford. *Revolutionary Exiles: The Russians in the First International and the Paris Commune*. London: F. Cass, 1979.

Mechnikov, I. "A. O. Kovalevskii: Ocherk iz istorii nauk v Rossii," *Vestnik Evropy*, 1902, no. 12: 773–75.

————. *Etiudy optimizma*. Moscow, 1907.

Millard, M. B. "Russian Revolutionary Emigration, Terrorism, and the 'Political Struggle.'" Ph.D. diss., University of Rochester, 1972.

Modestov, N. N. "Kak on stal emigrantom (iz epokhu 60-kh godov)," *Trudy Orenburgskoi uchenoi arkhivnoi komissii* 35 (1917): 123–38.

Modestov, V. I. "Zagranichnyia vospominaniia," *Istoricheskii vestnik* 11 (1883), no. 2: 383–406, no. 3: 575–600, and no. 4: 103–24.

Nikitenko, A. V. *Dnevnik*. 3 vols. Moscow: Gosizdat, 1956.

Neuman, Franz, "Intelligentsia in Exile." In *Critical Sociology*, edited by Paul Connerton, pp. 423–41. Middlesex, Eng.: Penguin, 1976.

Novikova, N. N. *Revoliutsionery 1861 goda*. Moscow: Nauka, 1968.

Orlik, O. V. *Rossiia i Frantsuzskaia revoliutsiia 1830 goda*. Moscow: Mysl', 1968.

————. *Peredovaia Rossiia i revoliutsionnaia Frantsiia*. Moscow: Nauka, 1973.

Panteleev, L. F. *Iz vospominanii proshlogo*. 2 vols. Moscow: Academia, 1934.

————. *Vospominaniia*. Moscow: Gosizdat, 1958.

Payne, Howard C., and Henry Grosshans, "The Exiled Revolutionaries and the French Political Police in the 1850s." *American Historical Review* 68 (1963): 954–73.

Pisarev, D. I. "Nasha universitetskaia nauka." In *Sochineniia v chetyrekh tomakh*. 4 vols. Moscow: Gosizdat, 1894.

Rikhter, D. "Emigratsiia." *Entsiklopedicheskii slovar'*, 40:732–59. St. Petersburg: Brockhaus-Efron, 1904.

Rosental', V. N. "Narastanie 'krizisa verkhov' v seredine 50-kh godov XIX veka." In *Revoliutsionnaia situatsiia v Rossii v 1859–1861 gg.*, edited by M. V. Nechkina. Moscow: Nauka, 1962.

Rudnitskaia, E. L. *N. P. Ogarev v russkom revoliutsionnom dvizhenii.* Moscow: Nauka, 1969.

Rusanov, N. S. *V emigratsii.* Moscow: Politkatorzhan, 1929.

"Russkie emigranty v Shveitsarii." *Istoriia sotsial'no-revoliutsionnogo dvizheniia v Rossii, 1861–1881 gg.*, pp. 73–179. St. Petersburg: Ministry of Internal Affairs, 1887.

Shelgunov, N. V. *Vospominaniia.* 2 vols. Moscow: Khudozh. lit., 1967.

Sladkevich, N. G. *Ocherki istorii obshchestvennoi mysli Rossii v kontse 50-kh nachale 60-kh gg. XIX v.* Leningrad: Izdat. universiteta, 1962.

Sleptsova, M. "Shturmany griadushchei buri (iz vospominanii)." *Zven'ia* 2 (1933): 386–464.

Sliwowska, W. *W kregu poprzedników Hercena.* Warsaw: Instytut Historii Polskiej Akademii nauk, 1971.

Speier, Hans. "The Social Conditions of the Intellectual Exile." *Social Order and the Risk of War*, pp. 86–94. New York: MIT Press, 1952.

Starr, S. F. *Decentralization and Self-government in Russia, 1830–70.* Princeton: Princeton University Press, 1972.

Tabori, Paul. *The Anatomy of Exile.* London: Harrap, 1972.

Turgenev, I. S. *Fathers and Sons,* translated and edited by R. E. Matlaw. New York: Norton, 1966.

Veilleumier, M., ed. *Revolutionnaires et exiles du XIXe siecle: Autour d'Alexandre Herzen.* Geneva: Droz, 1973.

Venturi, Franco. *Roots of Revolution.* New York: Knopf, 1960.

———. *Studies in Free Russia.* Chicago: University of Chicago Press, 1982.

Vilenskaia, E. S. *Revoliutsionnoe podpol'e v Rossii.* Moscow: Nauka, 1965.

Vyrubov, G. N. "Revoliutsionnyia vospominaniia (Gertsen, Bakunin, Lavrov)." *Vestnik Evropy,* 1913, no. 1: 53–79 and no. 2:45–70.

Wicks, M. *The Italian Exiles in London, 1816–1848.* Manchester: Manchester University Press, 1937.

Williams, Robert C. "European Political Emigrations: A Lost Subject." *Comparative Studies in Society and History* 12 (1970): 140–148.

WORKS ON OR BY THE RUSSIAN REVOLUTIONARY EMIGRES

A. I. Herzen

Acton, Edward. *Alexander Herzen and the Role of the Intellectual Revolutionary.* Cambridge: Cambridge University Press, 1979.

Antsiferov, N. P. "Starshaia doch' Gertsena (Tata): Pis'ma, Avtobiograficheskie nabroski, Vospominaniia," *Literaturnoe nasledstvo* 63 (1956): 443–504.

Berlin, Isaiah. "Alexander Herzen," *Russian Thinkers*, pp. 186–209. New York: Viking Press, 1978.

———. "Herzen and His Memoirs," *Against the Current*, pp. 188–212. New York: Viking Press, 1980.

Chernykh, V. A. "Iz istorii vol'noi russkoi pechati: A. I. Gertsen i N. Trubner. Pervyi period sotrudnichestva." In *Epokha Chernyshevskogo*, edited by M. V. Nechkina, pp. 61–77. Moscow: Nauka, 1978.

Confino, Michael, ed. *Daughter of a Revolutionary: Natalie Herzen and the Bakunin-Nechaev Circle.* La Salle, Ill.: Library Press, 1973.

Eidel'man, N. Ia. *Tainye korrespondenty "Poliarnoi zvezdy"* (Moscow: Mysl', 1966).

———. "Nachalo izdaniia *Kolokola* i ego pervye korrespondenty." In *Revoliutsionnaia situatsiia v Rossii v 1859–1861 gg.*, edited by M. V. Nechkina. Moscow: Nauka, 1970.

Egorov, B. F., et al., eds. *Letopis' zhizni i tvorchestva A. I. Gertsena, 1812–1870.* 3 vols. Moscow: Nauka, 1974–83.

Gershenzon, M. "Gertsen i Zapad." *Obrazy proshlago*, pp. 175–282. Moscow: Levenson, 1912.

Herzen, A. I. *Du développement des idées révolutionnaires en Russie.* Paris, 1851.

———. *Sobranie sochinenii.* 30 vols. Moscow: Akademiia nauk, 1954–65.

———. *My Past and Thoughts*, translated by Constance Garnett. 4 vols. New York: Knopf, 1968.

Klevenskii, M. "Gertsen-izdatel' i ego sotrudniki." *Literaturnoe nasledstvo* 41–42 (1941): 572–620.

Koz'min, B. P. "Anonimnaia broshiura o Gertsene 1870 g." *Literaturnoe nasledstvo* 41–42 (1941): 164–77.

Lanskii, L. R. "Otkliki na smert' Gertsena," *Literaturnoe nasledstvo* 63 (1956): 523–40.

Lemke, M. K. "Ocherk zhizni i deiatel'nosti Gertsena, Ogareva i ikh druzei," *Sovremennyi mir*, January 1906, pp. 67–69.

Literaturnoe nasledstvo (Moscow), 39–40 (1941), 41–42 (1941), 61 (1953), 62 (1955), 63 (1956).

Malia, Martin. *Alexander Herzen and the Birth of Russian Socialism.* Cambridge: Harvard University Press, 1961.

Melgunov, S. "Gertsen, Rossiia i Emigratsiia." *Golos minuvshego*, 1926, no. 3 (16):257–91.

Partridge, M. "Alexander Herzen and the English Press." *Slavonic and East European Review* 36, no. 8 (1958): 453–70.

———. "Aleksandr Gertsen i ego angliiskie sviazi." In *Problemy izucheniia Gertsena,* edited by V. P. Volgin and Iu. G. Oksman, pp. 348–69. Moscow: Akademiia nauk, 1963.

Plekhanov, G. V. "Gertsen-emigrant." *Sochineniia,* 23:414–45. Moscow-Leningrad: Gosizdat, 1926.

Sciacchitano, B. C. "The Exile World of Alexander Herzen." Ph.D. diss., University of Illinois, 1979.

N. I. Turgenev

Fetisov, I. "Iz perepiski N. I. Turgeneva v 40-60-ye gg." *Pamiati dekabristov,* 3:87–103. Leningrad: Akademiia nauk, 1926.

Hollingsworth, B. "N. I. Turgenev and *Kolokol.*" *Slavonic and East European Review* 41, no. 96. (1962): 89–100.

Istoriia russkoi ekonomicheskoi mysli, vol. 1, pt. 2, pp. 165–92. Moscow: Akademiia nauk, 1955.

Miliukov, P. "N. I. Turgenev v Londone." *Vremennik obshchestva druzei russkoi knig* (Paris) 3 (1932): 61–78.

Nechkina, M. V. *Dvizhenie dekabristov.* 2 vols. Moscow: Akademiia nauk, 1955.

Oksman, Iu. G. "Pis'ma N. I. Turgeneva k Gertsenu." *Literaturnoe nasledstvo* 62 (1955): 583–90.

Semevskii, V. "Nikolai Ivanovich Turgenev." *Entsiklopedicheskii slovar',* 67: 106–13. St. Petersburg: Brockhaus-Efron, 1890–1904.

Shchegolev, P. E. "Pomilovanie N. I. Turgeneva." *Byloe,* 1907, no. 9:33–36.

Shebunin, A. N. *Nikolai Ivanovich Turgenev.* Moscow: Gosizdat, 1925.

Tarasova, V. M. "Dekabrist N. I. Turgenev: Sotrudnik *Kolokola.*" In *Problemy izucheniia Gertsena,* edited by V. P. Volgin and Iu. G. Oksman, pp. 239–50. Moscow: Akademiia nauk, 1963.

———. "O vremeni znakomstva Ivana Turgeneva s N. I. Turgenevym." In *Turgenevskii sbornik,* edited by M. P. Alekseev, 1:276–78. Moscow-Leningrad: Nauka, 1964.

———. "*Rossiia i Russkie:* N. I. Turgenev o Rossii 30–50-kh godov XIX v." *Uchenye zapiski Mariiskogo gos. ped. instituta im. N. K. Krupskoi, Kafedra istorii* (Ioshkar-Ola) 27 (1965).

———. "Dekabrist N. I. Turgenev i ego mesto v istorii obshchestvennogo dvizheniia Rossii 20–60-kh godov XIX v." Kandidat. diss., University of Leningrad, 1966.

———. "Iz istorii polemiki vokrug knigi N. I. Turgeneva *Rossiia i Russkie.*" In *Pushkin i ego vremia,* vol. 2, edited by M. M. Kalaushin. Leningrad: Izdatel'stvo gosudarstvennogo Ermitazh 1966.

———. "N. I. Turgenev v zapadnoi Evrope v 30–50-kh godov XIX veka i ego obshchestvenno-politicheskie sviazi." *Uchenye zapiski*

Mariiskogo ĝos. ped. instituta im. N. K. Krupskoi, Kafedra istorii (Ioshkar-Ola) 28 (1966): 85–136.

———. "Iz istorii izdaniia knigi N. I. Turgeneva *Rossiia i Russkie.*" In *Problemy istorii obshchestvennogo dvizheniia i istoriografii*, edited by N. M. Druzhinin et al., pp. 93–101. Moscow: Nauka, 1971.

———. "N. I. Turgenev v 1861 g." In *Revoliutsionnaia situatsiia v Rossii, 1859–1861 ĝĝ.*, edited by M. V. Nechkina, pp. 426–44. Moscow: Nauka, 1973.

———. "Rol' N. I. Turgeneva v obshchestvennom dvizhenii Rossii 20–70-kh godov XIX v." In *Istoriia i istoriki*, edited by M. V. Nechkina, pp. 107–25. Moscow: Nauka, 1973.

———. "K voprosu ob obshchestvenno-politicheskikh sviaziakh N. I. Turgeneva v gody revoliutsionnoi situatsii." *Revoliutsionnaia situatsiia v Rossii, 1859–1861 ĝĝ.*, edited by M. V. Nechkina, pp. 278–94. Moscow: Nauka, 1974.

Turgenev, I. S. "Nikolai Ivanovich Turgenev." *Polnoe sobranie sochinenii i pisem*, vol. 14, pp. 214–23, 518–25. Moscow: Nauka, 1967.

Turgenev, N. I. *La Russie et les Russes.* 3 vols. Paris, 1847.

———. "Economic Results of the Emancipation of Serfs in Russia." *Journal of Social Science*, 1869, no. 1:147–49.

———. *Opyt teorii nalogov* (1818). 3rd ed. Moscow: Gosizdat, 1937.

Vishnitser, M. L. "Baron Shtein i N. I. Turgenev." *Minuvshie ĝody*, July 1908, pp. 232–72, and Oct. 1908, pp. 234–78.

I. G. Golovin

Bakalov, G. "Pervaia revoliutsionnaia broshiura russkoi emigratsii: *Katekhizis russkogo naroda* I. G. Golovina, 1849 goda." *Zven'ia* (1932): 195–217.

Golovin, I. G. *L'Esprit de l'économie politique.* Paris, 1842.

———. *Des Economistes et des socialistes.* Paris, 1845.

———. *Russia under the Autocrat, Nicholas I.* 2 vols. London: Henry Colburn, 1846.

———. *Types et caractères russes.* Paris, 1847.

———. *A Russian Sketch-Book.* 2 vols. London: T. C. Newby, 1848.

———. *Quelques vérités à la France à propos de mon expulsion.* London, 1850.

———. *The Nations of Russia and Turkey.* London: Trubner, 1854.

———. *Stars and Stripes.* London and New York, 1856.

———. *Zapiski Ivana Golovina.* Leipzig: Gerhardt, 1859.

———. *Der Russische Nihilismus. Meine Beziehungen zu Herzen und zu Bakunin.* Leipzig: L. Senf, 1880.

Lemke, M. K. "Emigrant Ivan Golovin." *Byloe*, 1907, no. 5(17):24–52 and no. 6(18):261–85.

Sliwowska, W. "Un émigré russe en France: Ivan Golovine, 1816–1890."
Cahiers du monde russe et soviétique 11, no. 2 (1970): 221–43.

N. I. Sazonov

Koz'min, B. P. "Iz literaturnogo nasledstva N. I. Sazonova." Literaturnoe
nasledstvo 41–42 (1941): 178–252.
Modzalevskii, B. "N. I. Sazonov." Russkii biograficheskii slovar', 18:56–
58. St. Petersburg: Demakov, 1904.
Nikolaevskii, B. "Pis'mo N. I. Sazonova k Gervegu." Letopisi Marksizma
6 (1928): 76–81.
"Pis'mo N. I. Sazonova–N. P. Ogarevu," Zven'ia 6 (1936): 345–53.
Riazanov, D. I. [pseud. for D. I. Gol'dendakh]. Karl Marks i russkie liudi
sorokovykh godov. Petrograd: Izdanie Petrogradskogo Soveta, 1918.
Sazonov, N. I. "Ob istoricheskihk trudakh Mullera." Uchenye zapiski
Moskovskogo universiteta 60 (1833).
———. Rodnoi golos na chuzhbine. Russkim plennym vo Frantsii.
London: Free Russian Press, 1855.
———. "Alexander Herzen." Gazette du Nord, no. 13 (26 May 1860).
———. "La Vérité sur l'empereur Nicholas." Literaturnoe nasledstvo,
41–42 (1941): 202–48.
Zastenker, N. E. "N. I. Sazonov–Gertsenu." Literaturnoe nasledstvo 62
(1955): 522–45.

P. V. Dolgorukov

Alekseev, M. P. "Viktor Giugo i ego russkie znakomstva." Literaturnoe
nasledstvo 31–32 (1937): 837–38.
Bakhrushin, S. B. "Respublikanets-kniaz' Petr Vladimirovich Dol-
gorukov." In P. V. Dolgorukov, Peterburskie ocherki, pp. 5–102.
Moscow: Academia, 1934.
Barsukov, M. I. "P. V. Dolgorukov o tsarskoi Rossii i o duele A. S.
Pushkina s Dantesom." Zven'ia 1 (1932): 77–85.
Dolgorukov, P. V. Rossiiskii rodoslovnyi sbornik. 4 vols. St. Petersburg:
E. Prats, 1840–41.
———. Notice sur les principales familles de la Russie. Paris: Didot
Frères, 1843.
———. Dictionnaire historique de la noblesse russe. Brussels, 1858.
———. La Vérité sur la Russie. Paris, 1860.
———. Des reformes en Russie. Paris, 1862.
———. O Peremene obraza pravleniia v Rossii. Paris, 1862.
———. La France sous le régime Bonapartiste. 2 vols. Brussels, 1864.
———. Memoires du Prince Dolgorukow. Geneva, 1867.
———. Peterburgskie ocherki. Moscow: Academia, 1934.

Field, D. "P. V. Dolgorukov's Emigration from Russia." *Slavonic and East European Review* 48 (April 1970): 261–65.

Hollingsworth, B. "The 'Republican Prince': The Reform Projects of Prince P. V. Dolgorukov." *Slavonic and East European Review* 47 (1969): 447–68.

Kitaev, V. A. *Ot frondy k okhranitel'stvu. Iz istorii russkoi liberal'noi mysli 50–60-kh godov XIX veka*. Moscow: Mysl', 1972.

Koz'min, B. P. "Dolgorukov i Elpidin." *Krasnyi arkhiv* 3, no. 34 (1929): 231–32.

Lemke, M. K. "Kniaz' P. V. Dolgorukov v Rossii." *Byloe*, 1907, no. 2 (14): 144–67.

———. "Kniaz' P. V. Dolgorukov—emigrant." *Byloe*, 1907, no. 3 (15): 153–99.

The Heidelberg Colony

Cherniak, Ia. Z. "Ogarev–V. I. Bakstu i drugim organizatoram Geidel'bergskoi chital'ni." *Literaturnoe nasledstvo* 63 (1956): 107–25.

Rudnitskaia, E. L. *Shestidesiatnik Nikolai Nozhin*. Moscow: Nauka, 1975.

Svatikov, S. "Russkie studenty v Geidel'berge." *Novyi zhurnal dlia vsekh*, 1912, no. 12:70–82.

———. "Turgenev i russkaia molodezh' v Geidel'berge." *Novaia zhizn'*, 1912, no. 12: 148–85.

I. A. Khudiakov

Vilenskaia, E. S. *Khudiakov*. Moscow: Molodaia gvardiia, 1969.

I. I. Kel'siev

Ryndziunskii, P. G. "I. I. Kel'siev–Gertsenu i Ogarevu." *Literaturnoe nasledstvo* 62 (1955): 219–58.

Zverev, I. "K biografii, I. I. Kel'sieva." *Literaturnoe nasledstvo* 41–42 (1941): 105–10.

V. I. Kel'siev

Call, Paul. *Vasily Kelsiev: An Encounter between the Russian Revolutionaries and the Old Believers*. Belmont, Mass.: Norland Publishing Co., 1979.

Kel'siev, V. I. *Perezhitoe i peredumannoe. Vospominaniia*. St. Petersburg: Golovin, 1868.

———. "Iz razskazov ob emigrantakh." *Zaria* (St. Petersburg), 1869, no. 3:76–99.

Klevenskii, M. *"Ispoved'* V. I. Kel'sieva." *Literaturnoe nasledstvo* 41–42 (1941): 253–470.

Ryndziunskii, P. G. "I. I. Kel'siev–Gertsenu i Ogarevu." *Literaturnoe nasledstvo* 62 (1955): 219–58.

A. A. Serno-Solov'evich

Freidenfel'd, F. "Listovka A. A. Serno–Solov'evicha protiv N. P. Ogareva." *Literaturnoe nasledstvo* 41–42 (1941): 111–15.

Koz'min, B. P. "A. A. Serno-Solov'evich v I Internatsionale i v Zhenevskom rabochem dvizhenii." *Istoricheskii sbornik* 5 (1936): 77–123.

———. "A. A. Serno-Solov'evich–Ogarevu." *Literaturnoe nasledstvo* 62 (1955): 548–51.

———. "Aleksandr Serno-Solov'evich: Materialy dlia biografii." *Literaturnoe nasledstvo* 67 (1959): 698–744.

Lemke, M. K. "K biografii A. A. Serno-Solov'evicha," *Ocherki osvoboditel'nogo dvizheniia "shestidesiatykh godov,"* pp. 231–276. St. Petersburg: Popova, 1908.

Serno-Solov'evich, A. A. *Nashi domashnie dela.* Vevey, 1867.

———. *Question polonaise.* Geneva: Pfeffer, [1867].

———. *Mikolka-Publitsist.* Geneva, 1868.

———. "Piatnadtsat' neopublikovannykh pisem." *Zven'ia* 5 (1935): 375–414.

Smirnov, A. F. "Dva pis'ma Gertsena k A. A. Cherkesovu i A. A. Serno-Solov'evichu," *Literaturnoe nasledstvo* 67 (1959): 741–44.

N. V. Sokolov

Efimov, A. "Publitsist 60-kh godov N. V. Sokolov." *Katorga i ssylka,* 1931, no. 11–12: 63–104.

Koz'min, B. P. "N. V. Sokolov: Ego zhizn' i literaturnaia deiatel'nost'." *Literatura i istoriia. Sbornik statei,* pp. 373–443. Moscow: Khudozh. lit., 1969.

Kuznetsov, Feliks. "Nikolai Sokolov." *Publitsisty 1860-kh godov,* pp. 243–326. Moscow: Molodaia gvardiia, 1969.

Leikina-Svirskaia, V. P. "Utopicheskii sotsialist 60-kh godov N. V. Sokolov." In *Revoliutsionnaia situatsiia v Rossii v 1859–1861 gg.,* edited by M. V. Nechkina, pp. 139–54. Moscow: Nauka, 1970.

Sokolov, N. V. *Ekonomicheskie voprosy i zhurnal'noe delo.* St. Petersburg: Golovin, 1866.

———. *Otshchepentsy.* St. Petersburg: Golovin, 1866.

———. *Die Soziale Revolution.* Bern: Buchdruckerei von Rudolf Jenni, 1868.

———. "Avtobiografiia." *Svoboda* (Paris), no. 1 (1889): 21–23.

L. I. Mechnikov

Koz'min, B. P. "L. I. Mechnikov–Gertsenu i Ogarevu." *Literaturnoe nasledstvo* 62 (1955): 388–94.

Lishina, A. K. "Russkii garibal'diets L. I. Mechnikov." In *Rossiia i Italiia*, edited by S. D. Skazkin, pp. 167–73. Moscow: Nauka, 1968.

Lishina, A. K., and O. V. Lishin. "Lev Mechnikov: revoliutsionnyi publitsist i uchenyi." *Literaturnoe nasledstvo* 87 (1977): 461–507.

Mechnikov, L. I. *La Civilisation et les grands fleures historiques.* Paris, 1889.

———. "M. A. Bakunin v Italii v 1864 godu." *Istoricheskii vestnik* 67 (March 1897): 807–34.

White, James D. "Despotism and Anarchy: The Sociological Thought of L. I. Mechnikov." *Slavonic and East European Review* 54, no. 3 (1976): 395–411.

N. I. Zhukovskii

Deich, L. G. "Nikolai Ivanovich Zhukovskii." *Russkaia revoliutsionnaia emigratsiia 70-kh godov*, pp. 17–23. Petrograd: Gosizdat., 1920.

Rudnitskaia, E. L. "N. I. Zhukovskii–Ogarevu." *Literaturnoe nasledstvo* 62 (1955): 133–39.

V. A. Zaitsev

Khristoforov, A. Kh. "V. A. Zaitsev." *Obshchee delo*, no. 47 (1882).

Koz'min, B. P. "Iz istorii intelligentsii 60-kh godov." *Krasnyi arkhiv* 52 (1932): 283–86.

———. "Anonimnaia broshiura o Gertsene 1870 g." *Literaturnoe nasledstvo* 41–42 (1941): 164–77.

Kuznetsov, F. "Varfolomei Zaitsev." *Publitsisty 1860-kh godov*, pp. 142–242. Moscow: Molodaia gvardiia, 1969.

Trifonov, V. V. "Odna iz pervykh popytok poznakomit' russkogo chitatelia s *Kapitalom.*" *Voprosy istorii*, no. 4 (1976): 211–15.

Zaitsev, V. A. *Izbrannye sochineniia.* Moscow: Politkatorzhan, 1934. Introductory essay by B. P. Koz'min.

[Zaitsev, V. A., and P. I. Iakobi]. "O polozhenii rabochikh v Zapadnoi Evrope s obshchestvenno-gigienicheskoi tochki zreniia." *Arkhiv sudebnoi meditsiny i obshchestvennoi gigieny*, September 1870, b. 3, pp. 160–216.

Z[aitseva], M[ariia]. "V. A. Zaitsev za granitsei." *Minuvshie gody*, 1908, no. 11: 81–110.

N. I. Utin

Koz'min, B. P. "N. I. Utin–Gertsenu i Ogarevu." *Literaturnoe nasledstvo* 62 (1955): 607–90.

Novikova, N. N. "N. I. Utin i *Velikoruss*." In *Revoliutsionnaia situatsiia v Rossii v 1859–1861 gg.*, edited by M. V. Nechkina, pp. 124–38. Moscow: Nauka, 1970.

Utin, N. I. "Propaganda i organizatsiia. Delo proshloe i delo nyneshnee." *Narodnoe delo*, 1868, no. 2–3: 29–41.

MARX, ENGELS, AND THE RUSSIAN EMIGRATION

Eaton, Henry. "Marx and the Russians." *Journal of the History of Ideas* 41, no. 1 (1980): 89–112.

K. Marks, F. Engel's i revoliutsionnaia Rossiia. Moscow: Izdatel'stvo politicheskoi literatury, 1967.

Koniushaia, R. P. *Karl Marks i revoliutsionnaia Rossiia.* Moscow: Izdatel'stvo politicheskoi literatury, 1975.

Korochkin, V. M. *Russkie korrespondenty K. Marksa.* Moscow: Mysl', 1965.

Riazanov, D. I. [pseud. for D. I. Gol'dendakh]. *Karl Marks i russkie liudi sorokovykh godov.* Petrograd: Izdanie Petrogradskogo Soveta, 1918.

Index

Aksakov, Konstantin, 66, 67
Aksel'rod, Pavel, 155, 204
Alexander I (tsar of Russia), 36
Alexander II (tsar of Russia): promises peasant emancipation, 22, 82; and Turgenev, 37, 47–48, 61; and Golovin, 61–62; and Sazonov, 85; and Dolgorukov, 92, 100–101; and V. Kel'siev, 129; émigrés call on, for reforms, 179, 182, 183, 188, 192; assassination of, 191, 208
Alliance for Socialist Democracy, 145, 158, 172
Anarchism, 4, 150–52, 194, 195
Annenkov, Pavel, 23–27, 29, 211

Babst, I. K., 75
Bakst, Vladimir, 114, 190, 210
Bakunin, Mikhail Aleksandrovich: and anarchism, 4, 114, 194; and revolutionary populism, 4, 148–49, 203; and Herzen, 18, 30, 98, 220–21; and Annenkov, 24, 26–27; and Polish question, 26, 63–64, 71; and Turgenev, 33–34, 48; and Golovin, 63–64; and Sazonov, 66; and Marx and Marxism, 68, 162, 164, 172, 202; and Heidelberg Russian colony, 98; and Dolgorukov, 98, 99, 220; and Left Hegelianism, 106; and Pan-Slavism, 106; Russian government's sentence against, 106; and Khudiakov, 121; returns to Russia, 122, 131; and V. Kel'siev, 129; and A. Serno-Solov'evich, 145–46; and International, 145–46, 162, 164, 172, 202; and Sokolov, 150, 152; and Mechnikov, 153, 170, 194, 210; and Zhukovskii, 156, 158, 170, 195, 196; and Zaitsev, 162, 210; and Nikoladze, 194; and *Narodnoe slovo*, 195, 196; and Nechaev, 202; and Lavrov, 202–3; and League of Peace and Freedom, 219, 220–21
Barni, Jules, 219
Bartenev, Ekaternia, 171
Bartenev, Viktor, 171
Bauer, Heinrich, 15
Belinskii, Vissarion, 84, 107, 180, 183
Belogolovyi, N., 162–63
Blagonamerennyi, 62–63, 181–83
Blagosvetlov, G. E., 155, 160
Blanc, Louis, 18, 42, 74
Bliummer, Leonid, 98, 184–90, 209, 210
Budushchnost', 96, 97, 183–84, 185

Carr, E. H., 23, 64
Catalan, Adolf, 144
Cherkesov, A. A., 136, 137, 146